CW01095845

CLASSIC
GOLF HOLE
DESIGN

CLASSIC GOLF HOLE DESIGN

USING THE GREATEST HOLES AS INSPIRATION FOR MODERN COURSES

Robert Muir Graves

Geoffrey Cornish

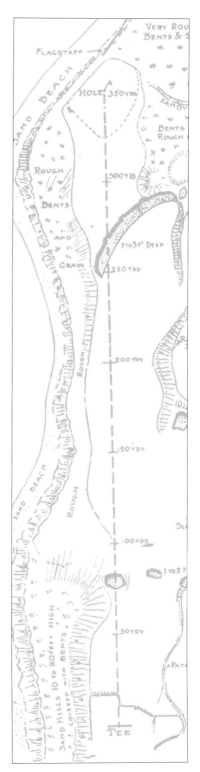

John Wiley & Sons, Inc.

Graphics marked "Copyright © DuCam Marketing (UK) Ltd." were selected by the authors from the Strokesaver® Edition for that individual golf course and are used in this publication courtesy of Strokesaver.

This book is printed on acid-free paper. ∞

Copyright © 2002 by John Wiley & Sons, Inc. All rights reserved

Published by John Wiley & Sons, Inc., Hoboken, New Jersey
Published simultaneously in Canada

No part of this publication may be reproduced, stored in a retrieval system, or transmitted in any form or by any means, electronic, mechanical, photocopying, recording, scanning, or otherwise, except as permitted under Section 107 or 108 of the 1976 United States Copyright Act, without either the prior written permission of the Publisher, or authorization through payment of the appropriate per-copy fee to the Copyright Clearance Center, Inc., 222 Rosewood Drive, Danvers, MA 01923, (978) 750-8400, fax (978) 750-4470, or on the web at www.copyright.com. Requests to the Publisher for permission should be addressed to the Permissions Department, John Wiley & Sons, Inc., 111 River Street, Hoboken, NJ 07030, (201) 748-6011, fax (201) 748-6008, e-mail: permcoordinator@wiley.com.

Limit of Liability/Disclaimer of Warranty: While the publisher and author have used their best efforts in preparing this book, they make no representations or warranties with respect to the accuracy or completeness of the contents of this book and specifically disclaim any implied warranties of merchantability or fitness for a particular purpose. No warranty may be created or extended by sales representatives or written sales materials. The advice and strategies contained herein may not be suitable for your situation. You should consult with a professional where appropriate. Neither the publisher nor author shall be liable for any loss of profit or any other commercial damages, including but not limited to special, incidental, consequential, or other damages.

For general information on our other products and services or for technical support, please contact our Customer Care Department within the United States at (800) 762-2974, outside the United States at (317) 572-3993 or fax (317) 572-4002.

Wiley also publishes its books in a variety of electronic formats. Some content that appears in print may not be available in electronic books.

Library of Congress Cataloging-in-Publication Data:

Graves, Robert Muir.
   Classic golf hole design : using the greatest holes as inspiration for modern courses / Robert Muir Graves, Geoffrey Cornish
      p. cm.
   Includes bibliographical references (p.   ) and index.
   ISBN 0-471-41372-0 (alk. paper)
   1. Golf courses—Design and construction. I. Cornish, Geoffrey S. II. Title.
   GV975 .G584 2002
   796.352'06'8—dc21

                                2002003825

Printed in the United States of America
10 9 8 7 6 5 4 3 2 1

CONTENTS

FOREWORD

There are few subjects debated more hotly by golfers than the merits of their favorite golf course. Each of us is firm in our convictions that several holes on our favorite track possess characteristics that make it great. We will argue with our friends, playing partners, and even strangers about these special golf holes.

The reality among golf course architects is that we've all copied, or been heavily influenced in some fashion by, the work of our predecessors. Something we've seen or played strikes a chord in us and inspires us to incorporate it into one of our new projects. What makes this process interesting is how the golf course architect adapts the characteristics of the original golf hole within the context of the new project site. How faithful is the copy to the original? What personal touches has the new architect added? Is the new hole even distinguishable as one influenced by a famous hole? Perhaps there is even a more basic question: Are there great holes on the earliest golf courses that cannot be translated into the modern world of golf?

A colleague of mine has said that there are no new design ideas, only variations of a theme. So that raises an interesting question: Are there certain golf holes that have such strong character or contain strategic elements so fundamental to the enjoyment of the game that they have been copied all over the world? Is there a group of holes that can be considered classics? The *Redan*, the *Cape*, the *Island Green* are a few of the golf holes that have been adapted to courses all over the world. What are the true features of these holes that have challenged generations of golfers and inspired so many golf course architects? These famous holes, along with many others, are covered inside this book.

The task of identifying golf holes that could be considered classic is a daunting one. The fact that Geoff Cornish and Robert Muir Graves took on this job doesn't surprise me. Bob and Geoff are two of the grand old men of the design fraternity. Both are past presidents of the American Society of Golf Course Architects and have been speaking and teaching together for years. They first began team teaching at a five-day seminar on golf course design sponsored by the Northern California Golf Association and the Golf Course Superintendents Association of California. This was followed by a series of nationwide seminars on golf course design for the Golf Course Superintendents Association of America and the Professional Golfers Association. Later, the Harvard Graduate School of Design asked them to join the faculty of its summer program.

On several occasions, I have watched from the back row of the classroom at Harvard as Bob and Geoff have patiently delved into the fundamentals of golf course architecture. Their students—who range from young to old—come from a variety of backgrounds. Some are seasoned land planners or landscape architects; others have a background in the golf business. Cornish, the elder of the duo, is more the historian. With a faint resemblance to Alistair Cooke and his dignified New England manner, he recounts the origins of the profession to the class.

Graves is a great counterpoint to Cornish. Relaxed, with a down-home attitude that reflects his midwestern roots, he takes the students through the technical aspects of golf course design. Neither man assumes an attitude of superiority, or comes with the large ego that one might expect of a respected designer. The students find them to be very approachable, and Bob and Geoff are genuinely excited to share their knowledge of the art and science of golf course architecture.

The two have never been reticent about sharing their collective knowledge with anyone, and that brings us back to this book. After several years of research and the evaluation of thousands of golf holes, they have put before us their findings. It is my belief that their purpose was not to write the absolute, definitive book on classic holes, but to instigate interest, debate, and discussion among even casual golfers. After reading this book, we'll all wonder if our favorite holes fit one of the classic models. For many, reading this book will be the beginning of a wonderful journey of discovery.

Enjoy the trip.

Damian Pascuzzo
Past President, American Society of Golf Course Architects
El Dorado Hills, California

PREFACE

Golf was not forged by a single incident; a long process over generations, centuries and revolutions was needed. When civilization was on the march, golf was too; it only required a certain space. After several abortive efforts it found that space in Scotland.

—F. W. HAWTREE
British Golf Course Architect and Writer

The wildly undulating, sparsely vegetated, sandy fields of Scotland, between high tide and higher land, are known as the links or as linksland. Here a game involving a club, a ball, and a distant hole developed. The unpredictable, undulating terrain added excitement, while the dramatic surroundings awed players and probably contributed to their sense of well-being. Together, terrain and surroundings helped shape the magical game of golf, the game that mirrors life itself.

Much has been written documenting the history of golf. Likewise, many books describe the evolution of golf equipment, rules, attire, tournaments, and even golf courses. The final category—golf courses—has drawn increasing attention over recent years, as writers, architects, and others have charted the history of the game's playing fields. Surprisingly, very little research has been devoted to the development of individual golf holes. Often, the design and evolution of specific holes have been overshadowed by discussions of courses in general. Important as that is, the parts that make up the whole must not be overlooked.

In graphic form and text, this book will examine golf holes, the literal building blocks of golf, and introduce how they are linked together to form a course. The first were created by nature and discovered by golfers. Whether sand or water, hazard or heroic carry, hill or depression, the natural topography of the Scottish links held all the components of a golf hole. As generation after generation played game after game, the most exciting routes for the hole eventually became established.

Though the mystical linksland is plentiful in Scotland—it also encircles Great Britain and Ireland—golf spread to many distant shores, each with its own characteristics. Golfers in these new lands also looked for striking sites, and if none was found, they created their own impressive golfing grounds. In doing so, the early pioneers of course design heightened the drama of the game by enhancing the charm of its playing fields. In this way, hole by hole, golf architecture was born. At the same time, the architects also adapted "classic" holes from the hallowed links, and even holes with no obvious connections to the "classics" include principles adapted from them. It has been said that, despite the infinite variety of holes on the world's golf courses, each hole is truly a new version of an ancient hole adapted to new terrain and environment by creative minds.

The playing fields of golf have evolved into magnificent and sophisticated landscapes often supplemented by elaborate structures for social events. Today, golf courses truly rank among the most beautiful landscapes created by our species. A handful of golf courses, hundreds of golf holes, and countless features found on the links have, in fact, withstood the test of time and continue to serve as models of lasting significance and value. They are an intrinsic part of the game and its traditions.

Our book describes these classics, near classics, and adaptations. In doing so, we never forget that golf holes are magic, but they are basic compositions for a game that mirrors life itself, a game forged over centuries, first on the wild links of Scotland and then on countless landforms around the globe.

Your attention is directed to the end of this book, where you will discover an accurate and beautiful aerial photo of the St. Andrews golf complex in Scotland. The collective wisdom of the golf industry acknowledges that there, on the Old Course, resides the origin of golf as we know it. It can be said that every golf hole in existence had its origin there. As you follow the spread of golf's prima donnas throughout the world, that one photo will continually stimulate your interest and help you trace the flow of ideas as our golf courses evolved.

Robert Muir Graves
Geoffrey S. Cornish

ACKNOWLEDGMENTS

No one could ask for more than what our associates, colleagues, and friends have provided us in preparing this work. Their aid includes, but is by no means limited to, encouragement, concepts, text and illustrations.

Yet we credit two young people of this new and dynamic generation, namely Susan Richardson of Amherst, Massachusetts, who took time from an immensely busy schedule to assist in producing our work, and Patrick White of Notown Communications in Montpelier, Vermont, an eloquent writer who added many touches to our mundane passages.

We thank Patrick White's employer, the acclaimed golf editor and writer Bob Labbance, for his encouragement and also our editor at John Wiley & Sons, Margaret Cummins, who never lost her enthusiasm for the project during periods of high hopes and heavy-heartedness that are common in the preparation of works such as this. Margaret took time to meet us in distant outposts such as at an annual meeting of the ASGCA in Columbus, Ohio, and in a crowded diner one Sunday afternoon in Stamford, Connecticut. Later, with one of the authors recovering from an injury, Margaret gave up a beautiful sunny weekend, traveled to California, and put in two and a half solid days of work on illustrations.

Many of our colleagues in golf course architecture assisted us with suggestions and criticism and provided examples of the golf holes we sought. Ever helpful Paul Fullmer, executive secretary of the association, gave us assistance whenever required, as did his assistant, Chad Ritterbusch.

Our own business associates were very helpful. These included Brian Silva and Mark Mungeam, partners of Cornish, together with two of their brilliant assistants, namely Timothy Gerrish and Brian

Johnson. Indeed, the latter, following a playing and photographic tour of the homeland of golf, made his slides available to us.

Similarly, the firm of Graves and Pascuzzo was involved throughout the whole laborious process. Anna and Damian Pascuzzo, Tracy Lewis, Andy Staples, John Bush, and Randy De Valle all helped tremendously in locating and developing illustrations and historical data. Damian encouraged the crew to help us out at the expense of time for their regular chores and project development.

In addition to our fellow golf course designers, we were helped tremendously by many golf course superintendents, golf professionals, club and course owners, and staff. Where we were able to use material, we have strived to give appropriate credit. However, the material reflects only a small portion of the excellent drawings and photos that were so graciously submitted.

During our extensive research, we contacted many companies that produce the popular golf course play/yardage booklets. Among them, there were several companies that were particularly helpful. Alistair Mackinnon and David Duckering at Strokesaver in Paisley, Scotland, Don Gamer at Holeview in Bloomfield, Connecticut, and Joe Nemeth of Course Manager International in Fair Oaks, California, were most prominent among them. They not only provided access to dozens of their excellent diagrams, but helped in the research effort as well. We are deeply grateful to Strokesaver, Holeview, and Course Manager International for their gracious assistance.

Last and most important, we acknowledge our wives and families. In addition to the usual encouragement, they worked as hard as or harder than we did to accomplish our goals.

1

ARCHITECTURE AND ART
THE NATURE OF GOLF COURSE DESIGN

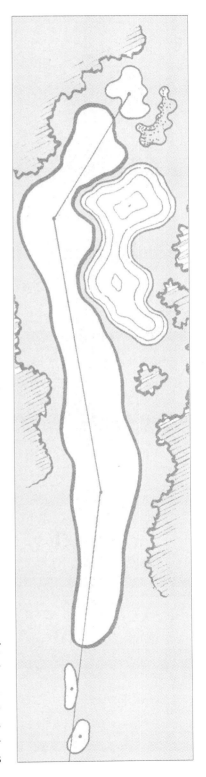

"Architecture is life, or at least it is life itself taking form and therefore it is the truest record of life as it was lived in the world yesterday, as it is lived today or ever will be lived," declared Frank Lloyd Wright, among the most renowned of all 20th-century architects. Wright, in his 1932 autobiography, described his residential design work as "organic architecture," explaining that his style "proceeds, persists, and creates, according to the nature of man and his circumstances as they both change."

The Case for Architecture

It requires only a small leap to translate Wright's views on architecture to the profession of golf course design. Viewing its history over the years, we see a record of life as it was and as how it and the circumstances surrounding golf (such as the move from Scottish linksland to North American terrain) have changed. Finally, we get a glimpse of life as it may be, most notably by guarding against the ever-greater impact of technology on the game.

Wright designed more than 1000 structures during his career, though only about 400 were ever built. His ideas were controversial, often meeting with resistance and skepticism, but there was no questioning his status as an architect. Those who design the playing fields of golf are not as easily granted that title; in fact, there is controversy about how to classify the profession. Eminent course designer Robert Trent Jones, perhaps golf's answer to Frank Lloyd Wright, once decreed that his profession "provides the cornerstone of the game." Despite the undisputed importance of the profession, it is not universally accepted that course design necessarily and neatly fits the technical definition of architecture.

Webster's defines *architecture* as "the art, profession or science of designing and constructing buildings," including any framework, system, and so forth. Perhaps more applicable is the definition of *landscape architecture* as "the art or profession of planning or changing the natural scenery of a place for a desired effect, for human use and enjoyment." From these definitions, one can conclude that golf course design is an art form *and* a branch of landscape architecture. Further, it must rank among the purest forms of landscape architecture because it involves both modifying the existing terrain and vegetating it.

The American Society of Golf Course Architects (ASGCA) doesn't hesitate to define its members as architects: "by virtue of their knowledge of the game, training, experience, vision and inherent ability, they are in all ways qualified to design and prepare specifications for a golf course of functional and aesthetic excellence and to oversee their implementation on the ground to create an enjoyable layout that challenges golfers of all abilities."

Mead and Ackerman state, somewhat controversially, that architecture is the application of art to engineering construction, but it is no less a branch of engineering. To those who design the playing fields of golf, Frank Lloyd Wright's somewhat more romantic vision of architecture may seem more appropriate to their profession. "No house should ever be on a hill or *on* anything. It should be of the hill. Belonging to it. Hill and house should live together each the happier for the other," concluded Wright. And surely the same spirit applies to course design.

Semantics aside, this book is not intended to be a broad text exploring the field of golf architecture. Two recent books by course architects (one by Dr. Michael Hurdzan and the other by Robert Muir Graves and Geoffrey S. Cornish) have covered that subject. We emphasize that the design of a golf course involves three basic considerations: *aesthetics, maintainability,* and *the game itself.* Supporting these factors is the environment, with that word used in its broadest meaning to include natural surroundings and the socioeconomics of the community in which the course is located. These three basic considerations, and the environment in which they are developed, are depicted as an equilateral triangle, with each consideration providing one side and the environment occupying the interior (Figure 1-1).

Landscape architect Kenneth L. Helphand concludes that "The evolution of the golf course is the prototypical example of a set of universal processes in the history of design. Distinctive forms evolve in the history of design. Distinctive forms evolve in particular circumstances. In this case a landscape from the Scottish linksland serves as a model or prototype which then goes through a process of formal evolution as it is brought to other environments."

It was this type of evolution that propelled Frank Lloyd Wright's vision. He designed houses that served many of the same warmth and shelter functions performed by traditional structures, but gone were the colonial ties to symmetry, the Roman columns, the Palladian windows—any sense of tradition. In their place were modern lines and a greater sense of harmony with the surrounding environment. Wright built his houses not on flat parcels of open land, but on rocky, heavily treed, severely sloping sites which before would have been thought unfit for residential construction. Still, these sites fit his style of architecture and vice versa. Similarly, as the game of golf moved from traditional linksland sites in Scotland, course architects evolved their designs to fit less traditional American sites, while always using the first courses as prototypes.

The renowned landscape architect Hideo Sasaki once said that "The thing basic to solving all the problems is the critical thought process." Course designers have certainly lived out these words as they sought to bring a Scottish game to alien shores. Along with "the critical thought process," they have, in fact, demonstrated creativity and vision in executing the basic considerations of course design on sites unlike any the game had ever previously seen.

That is not to say course designers ignored the elements of classic golf course design. In fact, they often labored to adapt them in North America. Charles Blair Macdonald, the father of American golf course architecture and the person who coined the title of the profession, believed strongly in "revering anything in life which has the testimony of the ages of being unexcelled, whether it be literature, painting, poetry, tombs—even a golf hole." To reinforce his statement, he cited a quote from landscape architect "Prince Puckler," who held that "Time is not able to bring forth new truths, but only an unfolding of timely truths."

FIGURE 1-1

The objective of this book is to demonstrate how design concepts have been carried forward through time. Here is the triangle of basic considerations, with the interior occupied by the environment. The three Ps were suggested as a way to remember the considerations. Although research failed to discover an earlier version of this triangle, it is probable that the same considerations were basic to course design from its inception.

In 1901, Macdonald set out to build a truly great American golf course—one comparable to the best in the United Kingdom as an incentive for improving the game here in this country. Called the National Golf Links of America, the course opened in 1911 and impressed golfers and writers alike, even to this day. Cornish and Whitten say, "It was a course without peer. Its excellence would cause the rebuilding of many an American course." The National was truly the classic golf course in America (see Figure 4-7).

Although golf architects Walter Travis and Devereux Emmet had dabbled in adapting classic British holes to America, and Scottish professionals, including the Dunns ("Old" Willie, Tom, "Young" Willie, John Duncan, and Seymour), had been influenced by the classics—and on occasion had tried to emulate them on American landscapes—it was Macdonald who successfully adapted and, some say, improved them. At the National, five of Macdonald's holes were inspired by the British classics, while the remaining holes were influenced by those Macdonald and his friend Emmet had studied in Britain. (Emmet purchased hunting dogs in the South in the spring, trained them on Long Island throughout the summer, and then sold them in Ireland in the autumn. He would then spend the winter golfing in Britain. One such winter he spent measuring and sketching British and Irish holes for Macdonald's use in planning the National Golf Links.) Their partnership and careful study helped bring classic golf design concepts to America—and with them a sense of legitimacy for the game in its new home.

The Principles of Art

The principles of art (arrangement) are embodied in golf course design and increasingly so as more landscape architects enter the profession. Though wildly undulating linksland does not lend itself to artistic arrangement, these principles are truly part of inland design. Indeed, by employing the principles of art, contemporary golf architects work to create the most impressive layouts since golf spread around the world from Scotland.

The principles of art include harmony, proportion, balance, rhythm, and emphasis. Each of these is described exceedingly well in Harriet and Vetta Goldstein's *Art in Everyday Life*. Nowhere in that wonderful work do the Goldsteins discuss golf courses, but their explorations of the principles of art are both eminently understandable by, and applicable to, golf course designers. Following is a brief look at these principles.

Harmony, according to the Goldsteins, is "the art principle which produces an impression of unity through the selection and arrangement of content." The Goldsteins maintain that harmony has five aspects (Figure 1-2):

- Line and shape
- Size
- Texture
- Idea
- Color

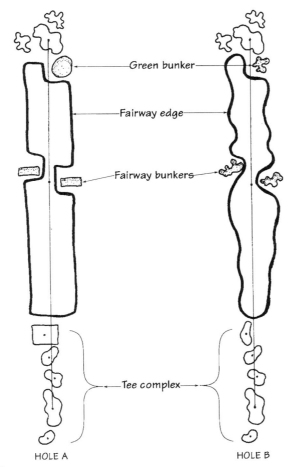

HOLE A   HOLE B

FIGURE 1-2
Harmony is achieved by texture (grass, trees, sand) and color (usually natural). However, line, shape, and size can vary and augment or destroy harmony among golf course elements. The mix of geometric and natural shapes in hole A is anything but harmonious, while hole B uses similarity in shapes or their style to blend the elements into a harmonious picture.

ARCHITECTURE AND ART

Proportion is referred to by the Goldsteins as the "law of relationship." It involves (Figure 1-3):

- Arrangements that hold interest
- Sizes and shapes (scale)
- The grouping of sizes (scale)

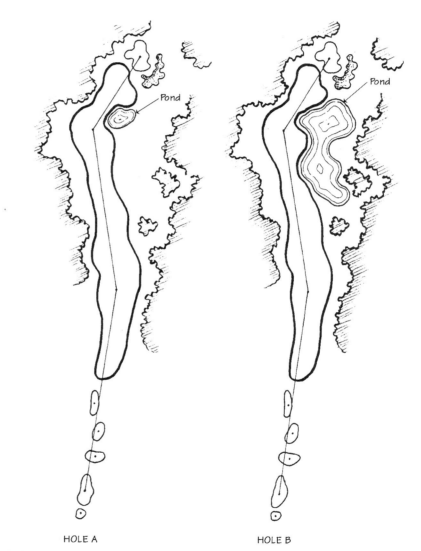

HOLE A   HOLE B

FIGURE 1-3

Elements of a golf hole can vary in size and shape, making grouping and space relationships all-important. The overriding scale of the arrangement—or proportion— is what the golfer sees or senses. The small pond in hole A is out of scale and not in proportion to the mass of the golf hole and its surroundings. Hole B with a larger pond keeps all elements in comfortable scale with one another.

CLASSIC GOLF HOLE DESIGN

Balance, the Goldsteins explain in terms of "balance in rest or repose." They add that "The restful effect is obtained by grouping shapes and colors around a center to achieve equal attraction on each side of the center." Balance is *formal* if the objects on each side of the center are identical, whereas balance is *informal* if it is not achieved by identical objects but by two sides attracting equal attention (Figure 1-4).

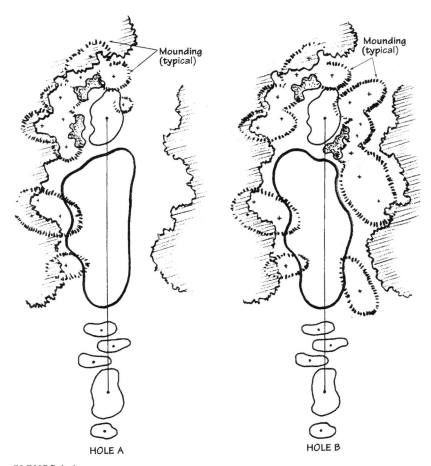

HOLE A   HOLE B

FIGURE 1-4

With the exception of strong winds, the elements of a golf hole are in a state of repose. They don't move. Therefore, their size or mass must be balanced, often around the centerline. That may be bisymmetrical, that is, even-sided or formal; asymmetrical with varied sizes or masses but at appropriately varying distances from the centerline; or informal. In hole A, the interesting features are overloaded on the left side, leaving the right side without interest. Hole B balances the topography and bunkers asymmetrically for a pleasing scene.

ARCHITECTURE AND ART

Rhythm is "related to movement" and can be achieved by repetition of shapes, progression of sizes, and continuous line movement. The Goldsteins introduce the concept of radiation in relation to rhythm, describing it as a method to attain organized movement because movement grows out of a central point or axis (Figure 1-5).

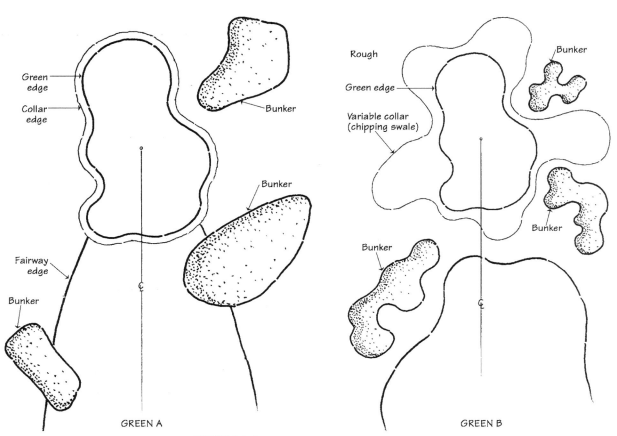

GREEN A

GREEN B

FIGURE 1-5

Rhythm is related to movement and limited to the connected path the golfer's eye ideally follows. This rhythmic relationship may be self-contained or part of the experience of leading the eye to the main focal point of the golf hole: usually the green. We also use a general repetition of shapes or shape styles along with progressions of sizes. Mowing patterns incorporating various turf heights create a pleasing continuous line movement that leads to a comfortable rhythm and a sense of contentment.

In green A, lack of similarity in shapes or progression in size of the bunkers negates any rhythm in this green setting. In green B, the shapes are used to create a compatible juxtaposition of curving forms. The combination of green, collar, and rough turf in mildly contrasting heights sets up a pattern that flows in and around the green area in a rhythmic manner.

Emphasis, according to the Goldsteins, is the principle of art in which the eye is first carried to the most important aspect of the composition (Figure 1-6).

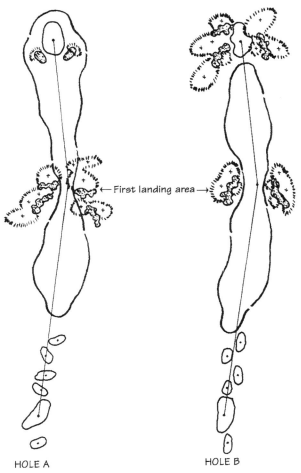

← First landing area →

HOLE A   HOLE B

FIGURE 1-6

Simplicity is the "most important factor in emphasis." The placement or groupings of typical golf hole elements are used to create the desired emphasis, focused on the green, which is the most important feature in the composition. Too simple a background for a green causes it to melt into the landscape, while an appropriate grouping of shapes and sizes can create subtle but effective directions to tell the eye the path to follow. Tree color and texture often help to emphasize the green area, making it the most important element in a hole.

In hole A, the emphasis is directed to the first landing area. This is an acceptable start. However, emphasis is not reestablished by the green area. That is left undeveloped or treated as an afterthought. In hole B, emphasis is easily transferred from the first landing area to the green.

THE BIOLOGICAL APPEAL OF GOLF LANDSCAPES

Applying the principles of art to golf course design obviously contributes a sense of well-being to those golfers who are playing with the objectives of relaxing and enjoying themselves. On the other hand, touring professionals out to win concentrate on getting the ball into the tiny hole and may be forced to ignore beautiful surroundings. Yet one suspects that the beauty of a course provides even them with relaxation during periods of extreme stress. This sense of well-being may be somewhat similar to the feeling of security that arises in people from having mowed lawns surrounding their dwellings. Perhaps that feeling harks back to a need to see one's prey or enemy at a distance through a focal point past trees and over short grass.

An evolutionary biologist has told the authors that most golfers play the game in order to relax and enjoy themselves, and there may be biological reasons that the landscape design of golf courses contributes to these feelings. The human species spent most of its evolutionary history as hunter-gatherers in habitats like those of golf courses, only much larger—specifically, open savannas, grasslands with scattered trees and bushes that supply nutritious food (browsing and grazing animals, berries, seeds, buried roots), shade from the sun, refuges where we can stalk prey and hide from predators, and frequent changes in elevation that enable us to orient in space and thus find our way to remembered places that provide important resources, such as food, water, and shelter. Evolutionary biologists and psychologists, such as Orians and Heerwargen, have found a preference for such savanna-like landscapes across human cultures, and they suggest that it reflects an evolved learning bias that allowed us to psychologically adapt to living in this habitat. We could invent challenging golflike games in which balls are hit through habitats that are much less expensive to maintain, such as dense woods, open land that is flat and barren, or a desert, which would be one continuous sand trap! But we don't, and part of the reason for not doing so is that such landscapes are just not appealing to the majority of our species and do not provide that sense of well-being that golf architects strive to create.

Indeed, the landscape of a golf hole presents a savanna in miniature. It's also noteworthy that artists over the centuries have recognized the appeal of such landscapes. Leonardo da Vinci, for one, painted a partially open landscape as the background for his Mona Lisa.

It is worth repeating that the principles of art have little or no connection to the original links of Scotland, although the latter resemble savannas whose wildly undulating terrain represents the opposite of arrangement. In fact, the first classic holes did not arise naturally from the land—but came about when greenkeepers and professionals modified it. Through logical thinking and good taste, these pioneering designers employed principles of art they had probably never heard of.

The Arrangement of Holes

Among the venerable links of Scotland, Bruntsfield had 6 holes; North Berwick, 7; Gullane, 13 and later 15; Musselburgh, 5 then 6 and then 7; Montrose, 25; and the Old Course at St. Andrews, 24. There was no standard. After the first four holes were converted to two in 1764, the routing at St. Andrews resulted in a nine-holes-out, nine-holes-home format. Shortly thereafter, this method of routing became standard practice, as did designing courses to consist of 18 holes. This was probably due to the preeminence of St. Andrews, though more romantic explanations exist. (The most common is that a bottle of whisky equaled 18 jiggers, and drinking a jigger was mandatory on each hole.)

Late in the 19th century, Old Tom Morris, who was then ranked as the top course designer, and others decided that two separate nine-hole circuits, each returning to the clubhouse, was the most convenient routing for golfers. In reaching that decision, they may have heard that the Royal Calcutta in India already had this arrangement (Figure 1-7). With many exceptions, this became—and still is—the standard routing. Still, many renowned architects, including Donald Ross and Stanley Thompson, continued the nine-holes-out, nine-holes-home arrangement on many of their masterpieces well into and after the Golden Age of Golf Course Design of the Roaring Twenties.

By the time of Robert Trent Jones, whose fame did not peak until after World War II, it was apparent that a par of 72, divided 36–36 between the two nines, was the preferred arrangement for contemporary golf. This arrangement included two par-3s, two par-5s, and five par-4s of varying length on each nine. For variety, each grouping of holes is typically designed to vary according to length, challenge, and orientation to the wind. Other aspects of hole arrangement, with numerous exceptions, include:

1. No par-3 before the third hole.

2. The three finishing holes include a par-3, par-4, and par-5, but the par-3 seldom serves as the 18th.

3. It is uncommon for two par-3s or two par-5s to be placed back to back, although the renowned Dr. Alister Mackenzie did not hesitate to do so at Cypress Point when existing terrain favored such a sequence.

4. It is desirable, but not often possible, to have the first four or five starting holes oriented into the wind in four different directions.

FIGURE 1-7

Perhaps to accommodate nine-hole-only play, the Royal Calcutta Golf Club, founded in 1829, was among the first to incorporate two returning nine-hole loops in its routing. Although tees and greens are not so closely clustered around the clubhouse as we normally see, the arrangement permitted a visit to the clubhouse between nines.

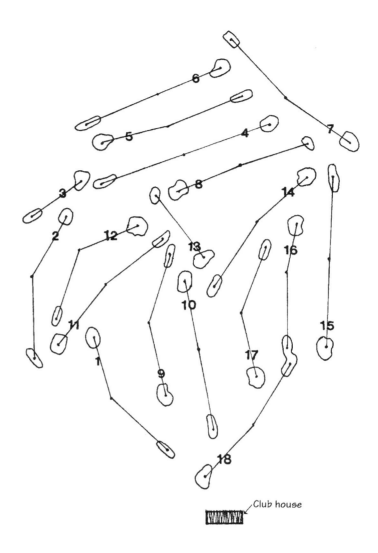

Club house

5. Routings with every sixth and even every third hole returning to the clubhouse have been attempted with modest success.

6. To enhance variety, architects have tried to arrange their routings so that similar pars, even 4s, do not follow each other, for example, 4–5–4–3–4–3–4–5–4. Almost inevitably, this seems artificial. Par rotation, dictated by terrain and other existing conditions, has created more exciting courses than has following rules of thumb. For example, architect Albert W. Tillinghast provided two par-5s for finishing holes at famed Baltusrol; Alister Mackenzie, at Cypress Point, had two par-5s (holes 10 and 11) and two par-3s (holes 15 and 16) (Figure 1-8), while Robert Foulis long ago provided three

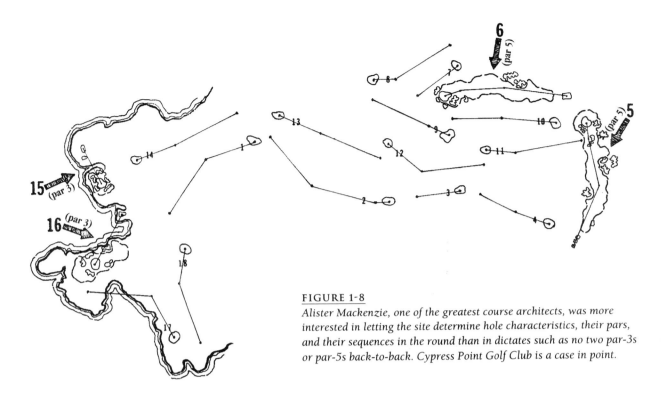

FIGURE 1-8

Alister Mackenzie, one of the greatest course architects, was more interested in letting the site determine hole characteristics, their pars, and their sequences in the round than in dictates such as no two par-3s or par-5s back-to-back. Cypress Point Golf Club is a case in point.

par-5s, namely holes 15, 16, and 17, back-to-back that have withstood the test of a century at the prestigious Town and Country Club in St. Paul, Minnesota.

7. Orientation of holes in relation to prevailing wind is of importance. Old Tom Morris advocated an arrangement where the player faced the wind in all four directions during the first few holes. All architects try to orient their holes into the wind in as many directions as possible.

8. Routing arrangements are legion. Indeed, writer Mark Leslie describes courses that include 19 holes, with the extra hole provided to settle bets or because there is a long distance between the 18th green and the clubhouse. It also provides a hole to use if a regular hole is out of play.

While the foregoing design practices are followed, they are never considered to be ironclad. They are guidelines at best, and golf architects rightly take immense liberties in the manner in which they choose to arrange and sequence holes depending on terrain, the players who will play the course, and other factors. Their objectives are the most exciting holes. As a sign of how critical these decisions are,

ARCHITECTURE AND ART

**COURSES WITH
19 HOLES**

Writer Mark Leslie lists eight
courses with 19 holes:

❖ Olde Farms GC, Bristol, Virginia, architect Bobby Weed

❖ Kinloch GC, Richmond,
Virginia, architect Lester
George

❖ Wykagyl GC, New Rochelle,
New York, architect Law-
rence Van Etten

❖ Knollwood GC, Elmsford,
New York, architect Law-
rence Van Etten, revised by
A. W. Tillinghast

❖ Double Eagle GC, Colum-
bus, Ohio, architects Jay
Morrish and Tom Weiskopf

❖ Loch Lomond GC, Scotland,
architects Jay Morrish and
Tom Weiskopf

❖ Stone Canyon GC, Tucson,
Arizona, architect Jay
Morrish

❖ Tradition GC, La Quinta,
California, architects Arnold
Palmer and Ed Seay

golf architect Forrest Richardson (ASGCA) has recently completed a book devoted entirely to routing a course.

Characteristics of a Successful Golf Course Architect

Golf is a game that has endured for a millennium or longer. Today, golfers enjoy more than a half million individual holes around the world. Each is a composition unique and beautiful, with some ranking among the most beautiful landscapes ever created and each a miniature savanna manifesting characteristics that contributed to the evolution of our species.

What personal characteristics have contributed most to a golf architect's ability to create (other than the opportunity to practice)? Formal education and experience have helped greatly when coupled with talent and organizing ability. Yet we feel that hard work and dedication are the factors that have contributed most to the creation of a half million magical compositions. And we think Mead and Ackerman's statement that "Architecture is the application of art to engineering" could be reversed; indeed, engineering makes architectural concepts feasible, including those that are mundane and those that are brilliant.

Writer and historian James W. Finegan listed, and eloquently so, the characteristics of a successful golf course architect when describing Perry Duke Maxwell as having "all the traits of a classic golf course architect; intelligence, a taste for the arts, an understanding of nature and an appreciation for thrift."

2

THE HISTORY OF GOLF COURSE ARCHITECTURE

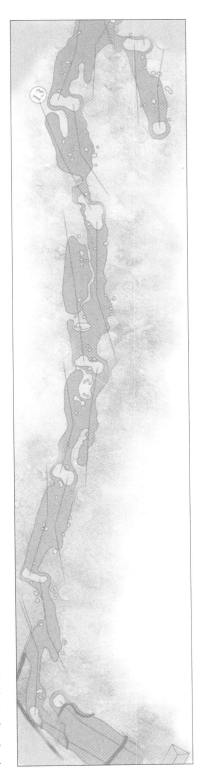

In the beginning, playing fields were needed for golf, and more space was required than for the somewhat similar games that had preceded it. Early sites took the form of city streets, frozen lakes, and then entrancing seashores. These were crafted by nature and by society, but they were *discovered* by golfers. As the popularity of golf grew, however, so too did people's desire to shape their playing fields.

In today's game, where professional architects carefully plot and plan every detail of a new layout, it's nearly impossible to comprehend the prospect of "discovering" a ready-made golf course. And today's golfers might not recognize the earliest natural playing fields as being in any way related to today's manicured courses. Nor did the games themselves always resemble golf. There were a variety of forebears to the game we know today. Some passed in and out of existence; others evolved; others migrated across international borders. Over hundreds of years, those games rattled around like balls in a lottery drawing until, from all of these, came golf.

Based on material from a number of different sources, Table 2-1 summarizes the rudimentary stick-and-ball games that influenced, in one way or another, the game of golf as we know it. Beginning with *paganica* in ancient Rome, golf has had many ancestors in many distant lands, all similar in one way or another to the game we know today. These now long-lost pastimes included *chole* (*soule* in Belgium), with similarities to both hockey and golf; *kolven* in the Nether-

A FEW EXCEPTIONS: READY-MADE GOLF COURSES

In the last decade, golf architects Coore and Crenshaw discovered a site that was almost a ready-made course near Mullens, Nebraska. It is now Sand Hills Golf Course. Likewise, golf architect David Kidd and later Tom Doak produced Bandon Dunes and Pacific Dunes, respectively, on the Oregon coast near Bandon on ready-made sites they and the owners had discovered. Preceding them, golf architect Bill Robinson had laid out Pacific Dunes on similar land nearby at Florence, where he followed contours nature had provided.

TABLE 2-1

Stick-and-Ball Games That Influenced Golf

Ancient Game	Other Names	Country of Origin	Ball Used	Club Used
Paganica	Cambuca	Ancient Rome; later played in England as cambuca	Leather stuffed with flock in Rome; a wooden ball in England	Not known
Pall-mall[a]	Jeu de mail; mail; pele mele	Italy, moving to France and then England		Eventually a club similar to an iron
Chole[b]	Soule	Flanders and northern France	Beechwood	Rigid shafts and iron heads
Kolven[c]	Kolf; Het Kolven	The Netherlands	Beechwood	Hazel shafts

[a]First played in a court with bounds and a prepared surface; the ball was lofted through a hoop. Later, it was moved to the countryside, where it was played along streets and roadways. Pall-mall preceded golf but was played long after golf became a game.

[b]One team hit a ball toward a target, sometimes miles away. After three shots, the opposing team had one turn to hit it in the opposite direction.

[c]Played in city streets and churchyards, sometimes on ice.

lands, sometimes played on ice and a game whose name may have evolved into the word "golf"; and *pall-mall* (also called *mail, pele mele, jeu de mail*), a game played first in the streets of Italy before spreading across Europe and finally arriving in Scotland. The impact of these games on the modern architecture of golf is remote, if it exists at all; yet they made golf possible.

An informative account of these pregolf games is presented by Robert Browning in his *History of Golf: The Royal and Ancient Game*. He states that "It was the Scots who devised the essential features of golf, the combination of hitting for distance with the final nicety of approach to an exiguous mark, and the independent progress of each player with his own ball free from interference by his adversary."

In compiling his history of the game, Browning made abundant use of Robert Clark's earlier work, *Golf: A Royal and Ancient Game*. The similarity in titles is unmistakable, with each paying homage to the honorable name given golf in its homeland. "The Royal and Ancient game of golf has ample justification for its historic title," wrote Browning. "During nearly 200 years from the peace of Glasgow in 1502 to the revolution of 1688, every reigning monarch of the Stuart Line—two kings and one queen of Scotland, four kings of the United Kingdom—was a golfer." Yet, in Scotland, golf remained a democratic game, played by individuals of all classes.

In their comprehensive work describing the origins of golf, Henderson and Stirk describe and explain the games that preceded golf. And golf course architect Fred W. Hawtree examines the origins of golf in great detail. Admitting he is not a historian and did not conduct original research, Hawtree provides a valuable service by examining the works of Browning and others from the viewpoint of a golf course architect. Hawtree concludes that "Golf was not forged by a single incident; a long process over generations, centuries and revolutions was needed. When civilization was on the march, golf was too; it required a certain space. After several abortive efforts it found that space in Scotland." That golf found a home in Scotland was not accidental but rather influenced by the space available and the natural landforms forming the links that were not unlike the savannas. This observation is key to understanding the evolution of the game and part of the evolution of our species and can best be explained by someone with intimate knowledge of the playing fields of golf, namely a course architect.

Hawtree says that, after 1500, the game of mail (pall-mall) that was formerly played in the streets evolved in two divergent directions. "On the continent it survived largely unchanged though increasingly refined. No palace could be without an indoor mail court. In Scotland it went to the outdoor uneven sandy links or gravelly heaths adjoining the town." It was these outdoor conditions, Hawtree surmises, that led to golf as we know it. To bolster his theory that golf evolved from mail, Hawtree provides informative sketches prepared with the insight of a course architect. His text and illustrations appear at the end of this chapter.

Early Golf and Golf Courses

Whatever the origins of golf, by the 16th century, the game was played widely in Scotland on informal layouts situated on the links and sometimes on other open spaces. There has been much speculation, and more than a little argument, regarding the earliest formal golf courses. Popular opinion says that the Old Course at St. Andrews, primitively in existence in the early 15th century, is the oldest. However, Ward Thomas et al., in their definitive work, *The World Atlas of Golf*, credit a six-hole layout at North Inch, near Perth, Scotland, as first. Devotees of Musselburgh, on the other hand, award the honor to the original (five, six, or seven) holes on that course. All must admit that the links of Leith, which no longer exist, ranks among the earliest courses. And there are records of golf on the links of Dornoch centuries before Old Tom Morris formally routed that venerable layout. Other sites in Scotland where the game was played prior to 1650 include Banff, Aberdeen, Montrose, Carnoustie, Leven, Edinburgh, and Bruntsfield. What's more, there was a seven-hole course in existence in Blackheath, England, by 1608.

The mystery surrounding golf's first formal course may never be solved, and, in reality, the outcome matters little, insofar as the spread of the game is concerned. It was not the development of golf courses that first sparked golf's explosion, but rather two other advancements. The arrival of the more durable and less costly gutta-percha ball in the middle of the 19th century stimulated golf and its architecture to spread around the world. In addition, the rapid expansion of the British railway system soon after the arrival of the gutty was a major force in popularizing the game, as it allowed golfers to reach the hallowed links of Scotland from as far away as London in a single day. Nevertheless, the handful of ancient links that existed before the arrival of the gutta-percha ball exerted a profound influence on the design of golf holes and the course designers that followed.

In the history of early course design, a few men and their accomplishments shine brightly through the haze of time. It is difficult to overstate the importance of Allan Robertson (1815–1859), who was considered the greatest player of his day and the world's first course designer, owing to the alterations he made to nature's work on the Old Course at St. Andrews. Other pioneers in the profession include Robertson's protégé, Old Tom Morris (1821–1908), as well as the twin Dunns, Old Willie (1821–1878) and his brother James, together with Willie's son Tom (1849–1902) (Figure 2-1).

Though we have listed a few ancient links above, we do not want to imply that golf was limited to them. On the contrary, it was played on countless informal links in and out of Scotland. Balls were also batted around and matches played on pastures, prairies, deserts, and other open areas where Scottish soldiers, sailors, and settlers found themselves as they extended the frontiers of the British Empire. These golfing grounds disappeared if the terrain did not provide sufficient interest, if the land was no longer available, or if those involved moved on.

FIGURE 2-1
Several of the Scottish "Old World Pioneers" in the early golf course design profession are shown at the Open Tournament in Leith in 1867. Left to right: A. Strath, Davie Park, Bob Kirk, Jamie Anderson, Jamie Dunn, Willie Dow, Willie Dunn, A. Greig, Tom Morris, Tom Morris, Jun., George Morris.

While these temporary golfing grounds helped spread the game, they had no direct influence on its architecture. On the other hand, those few established courses on the links of Scotland that endured provided the roots of course design. By the end of the 19th century, Scottish professional golfers and greenkeepers were carrying the principles of design, the lore of their links, and the game itself to the ends of the earth.

With the game growing and on the move, course design began to take on greater and greater importance. Students would do well to study the simple holes at Musselburgh drawn by George M. Colville. The first five, six, or seven holes on the course date back far into history, while the eighth was added in 1833 and the ninth a few years later. Regardless of when they originated, all the holes illustrate the relationship of golf to the totally natural links and indicate how the game evolved on these landforms. The holes at Musselburgh are significant in the history of course design not only for their age, but also because it was on these links that the first golfing members of the Dunn and Park families learned the game. Both families, influenced immeasurably by Musselburgh, later produced pioneer course designs on the other side of the Atlantic. Adding further to the fame of the course, Willie Campbell, the first professional at the Country Club in Brookline, Massachusetts, and the father of municipal courses in America, also hailed from Musselburgh. Campbell was one of the many Scots who laid out North America's original courses; all brought the lore and ancient traditions of the links with them, and all were influenced by the Musselburgh links and other landforms of

GOLF GIRDLES THE GLOBE:
THE EARLIEST CLUBS AND COURSES

Until the introduction of the less costly and more durable gutta-percha ball in 1848, the spread of golf from its homeland was slow. By 1857, there were only 17 golf clubs in Scotland.

Still, golf was played sporadically before that on informal layouts around the world wherever Scots found themselves as soldiers or business or professional people, and, by 1900, there were more golf courses in the United States than in the United Kingdom.

Argentina: Lomas Golf Course, 1892.

Australia: Royal Melbourne Golf Club, 1891.

Belgium: Royal Antwerp Golf Club, 1888.

Brazil: São Paulo Golf Course, 1900.

Canada: Montreal Golf Club (now Royal), 1873, was the first golf club in Canada, but golf was played along the banks of the St. Lawrence River soon after the War of 1812 and probably before that by Scottish fur traders as they roamed the continent.

China: Golf was played before 1900, but no courses existed between 1949 and the late 1970s, when several were restored as tourist attractions.

Denmark: A course was in existence before 1900, but golf did not flourish until after World War II.

Egypt: Alexandria Sporting Club, 1880, and Khedevial (now Gizaza) Sporting Club, 1882, were the earliest.

England: A seven-hole course was in existence at Blackheath by 1608. Golf was played at Molesey Hurst by 1758, and Old Manchester was opened around 1818 on Kersal Moor. Yet growth was slow. By 1888, there were only 58 courses.

Finland: Helsingfors Golf Course, 1932.

France: The Pau Golf Course, 1854.

Germany: Two nine-hole courses were opened at Bad Homburg and Baden-Baden in 1895.

Hong Kong: Hong Kong Golf Club (now Royal), 1889.

Iceland: Golfklubber Islands Golf Course, 1934.

India: Royal Calcutta Golf Club, 1829.
               Royal Bombay Golf Club, 1842.

Ireland: Golf was played as far south as Dublin by 1760. Yet, by 1888, there were only six golf courses. Royal Belfast (1881) and Royal Dublin (1885) were the first formal clubs.

Israel: Caesarea Golf and Country Club, 1960–1961.

Italy: Golf was first played by Scottish officers who followed Bonnie Prince Charlie into exile, but there were no formal courses until the last decades of the 19th century.

Jamaica:	Manchester Country Club, 1868.
Japan:	A nine-hole course at meeting Rokko near Kobe was in play by 1901. A club was opened at Yokohama in 1906. It is said that a Scot had laid out a four-hole course on a mountain by 1888.
Kenya:	A club was established in 1906 at Nairobi.
Korea:	Golf was first played around 1920. Seoul Country Club, established in 1932, was the first club.
Malaysia:	Perak Country Club, established at Taiping in 1888, and Royal Selangor, established at Kuala Lumpur a few years later, are the country's two oldest clubs.
Morocco:	Golf was introduced in the 1920s.
Netherlands:	Haagsche Golf Club, established at The Hague in 1893, is the oldest club. Yet, some claim that golf originated in the Netherlands as the game of *kolven*.
New Zealand:	The Otago Club (then the Dunedin) was established at Dunedin in 1871.
Norway:	Oslo Golfklubb, 1924.
Portugal:	A nine-hole course was in existence at Matozinhos as early as 1895.
Rhodesia (now Zimbabwe):	Bulawayo Country Club, 1895.
South Africa:	The first course was established near Capetown in 1882.
Spain:	Golf was introduced to the Canary Islands in 1891. The first course on the mainland was Madrid Polo and Golf Club established in 1904.
Sri Lanka:	Royal Colombo Club, 1882.
Sweden:	A privately owned course opened at Jönköping in 1888.
Thailand:	Royal Bangkok Club, 1890.
United States:	Golf was played sporadically from as early as 1728 when the Royal Governor of Massachusetts arrived in Boston with nine "goffe clubs." Formal golf clubs were in existence at Harleston Green, Charleston, South Carolina, and Savannah, Georgia, between 1779 and 1812. A four-hole course was opened in Burlington, Iowa, by 1881, and the nine-hole Oakhurst Golf Course in White Sulpher Springs, West Virginia, was in play in 1882. The first organized golf clubs were Dorset Field Club in Vermont, 1886; Foxburg Country Club in Pennsylvania, 1887; and St. Andrews Golf Club, Yonkers, New York, 1888. By 1900, there were more golf courses in the United States than in the United Kingdom. Between 1902 and 1912, C. B. Macdonald researched, planned, and built the National Golf Links on Long Island. Adapting classic holes from the home of golf and creating originals that were later adapted by others, the National revolutionized course design in North America and in several other countries.
Hawaii:	The first was Moanaluna Golf Course in 1898.
Wales:	By 1888, two courses were in play.

Scotland, despite the vastly different building sites they encountered in the New World.

Golf course architecture involves laying out the holes on totally natural land or, almost the opposite, sculpting the earth to create them. The creation of most great holes involves a combination of both. Such was not always the case in the early days of golf. Holes on the ancient links of Scotland, for example, were totally natural, while the holes created on the heathlands near London gave birth to the then (end of the 19th century) revolutionary concept of clearing trees, moving earth, and establishing turf to produce the composition.

Between the links and heathland eras, golf had already spread to England and Ireland. First played on their narrow bands of linksland, it was moved inland to take advantage of already cleared land. In so doing, it encountered heavy, poorly drained soils where the ball often became embedded in winter but rolled for long distances on rock-hard surfaces in summer. To compensate, bunkers were added across the fairways in a geometric manner determined by distances surveyed from tees. Straight lines and square features emerged.

Eighteen Stakes on a Sunday Afternoon and the Development of Golf Courses in America

Somewhat similarly, but in an even more primitive manner, early British designers in America laid out their courses by a method face-tiously known as "18 Stakes on a Sunday Afternoon." It involved siting the tee, and then with a general knowledge of where the green would be, the designer would pace off a set distance to where a bunker would be placed across the fairway. Rigidly straight rather than natural lines emerged, with even the greens square in shape. Nevertheless, there were designers with vision. Two of them were Scots Tom Bendelow and Donald Ross, although on occasion even they resorted to the primitive method, resulting in squarish putting surfaces.

Because lines were straight and shapes squarish, with hazard position determined by pacing, the 18-stakes way had much in common with the geometric method, although distances on the latter were determined with survey instruments and sited rigidly at set distances. Neither method, 18-stakes or geometric, is known to have produced a great course or hole. Yet each was a root, albeit a weak

FIGURE 2-2
In The Golden Age of Golf Design, *Geoff Shackelford shows an early 1900s example of geometric design at Annandale Golf Club in Pasadena, California. Perhaps as a breakaway from the square green design school, the rear of the green is rounded in contrast to the square front.*

one, in the tree of golf architecture that was to emerge in the coming years of the 20th century (Figure 2-2).

Willie Park, Jr., who had worked with his father and on his own laying out links courses in Scotland, was among the early heathland pioneers who were not afraid to sculpt the natural terrain to meet their needs. He was soon joined by Englishmen Harry Shapland Colt and Herbert Fowler. Later, all three architects crossed the Atlantic to mingle with the Scottish professionals who had preceded them to North America and already were planning courses there.

Owing in part to the functional design work of early Scottish emigrants, golf had planted its roots in America by 1900 and was here to stay. In fact, by the turn of the century, there were more courses in the United States (estimates vary from 750 to 1000) than in the United Kingdom. But with few exceptions these layouts emerged from the 18-stakes method of design. The Chicago Golf Club by C. B. Macdonald, Myopia near Boston by Herbert Leeds, the early Garden City Golf Club by Devereux Emmet, and Ekwanok in Manchester, Vermont, by Walter Travis, in collaboration with John Duncan Dunn, were among the few American layouts that stacked up to the great courses of the British Isles. Recognizing the general inferiority of their courses, American golfers demanded playing standards equal to those found on the links and heathlands of the United Kingdom.

In response to the demand, a supply of landmark American courses was produced. These included Merion (East) near Philadelphia, Oakmont near Pittsburgh, and the revised Garden City Golf Club on Long Island. This first wave of landmark courses led to the creation of ever-greater playing fields. Though World War I interrupted the development of golf in America, that dry spell was quickly followed by the Golden Age of Golf, which lasted until the Stock Market Crash of 1929, the Depression, and, finally, World War II. A flurry of course construction and reconstruction followed the end of World War II, but, by 1950, the Korean War was under way. It was not until 1953 that the expansion of golf again equaled the rate of the Roaring Twenties. Spanning the next quarter century or more, this prolific time is known as the Age of Robert Trent Jones. By the early 1970s, Pete and Alice Dye were practicing a links style of design with a North American flair. Their style became popular and, by the 1990s, was virtually universal.

Notwithstanding the magic of the game and its playing fields, course design is profoundly influenced by economics. In the magnificent book *Golf Course Designs*, celebrated course architect Tom Fazio, in collaboration with eminent golf writer Cal Brown, lists average development costs per hole over several decades as follows:

1960s	$ 10,000 to $ 20,000
1970s	$ 30,000 to $ 60,000
1980s	$ 70,000 to $200,000
1990s	$200,000 to $400,000

Though these astronomical increases in costs are due in part to inflation, they relate more to high contemporary standards and to near-perfect playing conditions on opening day in contrast to course openings 30 years ago. Then, perfection of the greensward was left to the superintendent to achieve over several years following the opening. In those days, many golfers were unable or unwilling to pay greens fees and membership fees large enough to support elaborate courses in perfect condition on opening day. In fact, profits were minimal on most courses, although many architects and the superintendents who collaborated with them achieved miracles with inadequate budgets. Still, most had to settle for work-in-progress courses whose layouts were opened before they were finished to bring in members and greens fees. The revenue generated was then used to complete them. The art of golf course design on most courses involved exceedingly careful management of the less-than-adequate funds that were available.

CLASSIC GOLF HOLE DESIGN

For the most part, architect-designed courses were considered finished when adequate instructions were left to complete the work. Yet achieving completion through "work-in-progress" courses had an impact on design, for better or for worse.

By 2000, with more adequate budgets and a thriving golf real estate market, a dynamic generation of architects and superintendents was producing the most impressive courses since golf spread from the links. These layouts provided the utmost perfection on opening day, and by the last years of the 20th century, many were returning handsome profits soon after opening. Assurance of immediate profitability has had an immense influence on design because it has stimulated imaginative people determined that the concepts of their talented minds will become realized.

While science and technology have had an impact on all aspects of society, the playing fields of the game have not been left out. Generous budgets and the power of formal education, together with chronicling and dissemination of research efforts and experience in this Information Age, have made it possible for designers, builders, and those who maintain and enhance golf courses to create works of art. These fascinate players and provide them and passersby with a sense of well-being. Perhaps, too, they help to satisfy "that thirst that from the soul doth rise," that we now hear arises from evolutionary history.

To outline the history of golf course architecture and allied professions, we provide five trees depicting the upward path of course design and turfgrass management, together with the history of clubs and balls (Figures 2-3 through 2-7). We also include a map of the world and a timeline of the spread of golf to many countries (Figures 2-8 through 2-13).

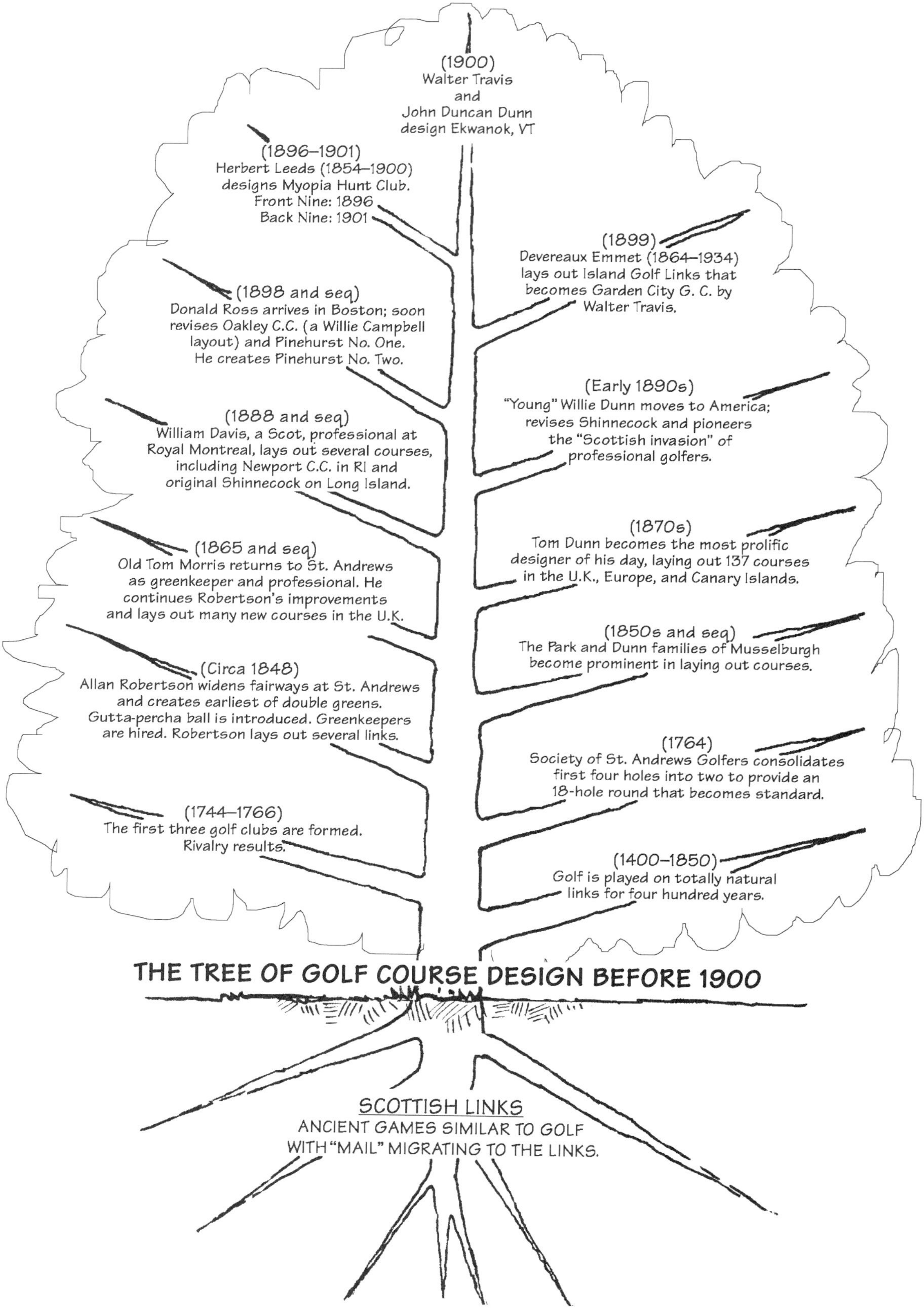

(1900)
Walter Travis
and
John Duncan Dunn
design Ekwanok, VT

(1896–1901)
Herbert Leeds (1854–1900)
designs Myopia Hunt Club.
Front Nine: 1896
Back Nine: 1901

(1899)
Devereaux Emmet (1864–1934)
lays out Island Golf Links that
becomes Garden City G. C. by
Walter Travis.

(1898 and seq)
Donald Ross arrives in Boston; soon
revises Oakley C.C. (a Willie Campbell
layout) and Pinehurst No. One.
He creates Pinehurst No. Two.

(Early 1890s)
"Young" Willie Dunn moves to America;
revises Shinnecock and pioneers
the "Scottish invasion" of
professional golfers.

(1888 and seq)
William Davis, a Scot, professional at
Royal Montreal, lays out several courses,
including Newport C.C. in RI and
original Shinnecock on Long Island.

(1870s)
Tom Dunn becomes the most prolific
designer of his day, laying out 137 courses
in the U.K., Europe, and Canary Islands.

(1865 and seq)
Old Tom Morris returns to St. Andrews
as greenkeeper and professional. He
continues Robertson's improvements
and lays out many new courses in the U.K.

(1850s and seq)
The Park and Dunn families of Musselburgh
become prominent in laying out courses.

(Circa 1848)
Allan Robertson widens fairways at St. Andrews
and creates earliest of double greens.
Gutta-percha ball is introduced. Greenkeepers
are hired. Robertson lays out several links.

(1764)
Society of St. Andrews Golfers consolidates
first four holes into two to provide an
18-hole round that becomes standard.

(1744–1766)
The first three golf clubs are formed.
Rivalry results.

(1400–1850)
Golf is played on totally natural
links for four hundred years.

THE TREE OF GOLF COURSE DESIGN BEFORE 1900

SCOTTISH LINKS
ANCIENT GAMES SIMILAR TO GOLF
WITH "MAIL" MIGRATING TO THE LINKS.

FIGURE 2-3. *Ancient games similar to golf that led to the Scottish links (see "Mail on the Links," page 34.)*

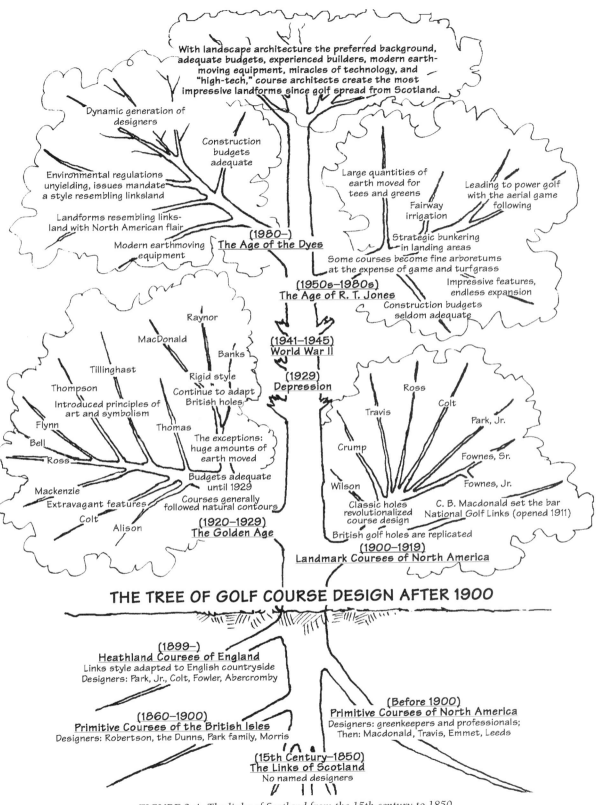

With landscape architecture the preferred background, adequate budgets, experienced builders, modern earth-moving equipment, miracles of technology, and "high-tech," course architects create the most impressive landforms since golf spread from Scotland.

Dynamic generation of designers

Construction budgets adequate

Environmental regulations unyielding, issues mandate a style resembling linksland

Landforms resembling linksland with North American flair

Modern earthmoving equipment

(1980–)
The Age of the Dyes

Large quantities of earth moved for tees and greens

Fairway irrigation

Leading to power golf with the aerial game following

Strategic bunkering in landing areas

Some courses become fine arboretums at the expense of game and turfgrass

Impressive features, endless expansion

(1950s–1980s)
The Age of R. T. Jones

Construction budgets seldom adequate

(1941–1945)
World War II

(1929)
Depression

Raynor

MacDonald

Banks

Tillinghast

Rigid style

Continue to adapt British holes

Ross

Colt

Thompson

Introduced principles of art and symbolism

Thomas

Travis

Park, Jr.

Flynn

The exceptions: huge amounts of earth moved

Crump

Fownes, Sr.

Bell

Ross

Fownes, Jr.

Mackenzie

Extravagant features

Budgets adequate until 1929

Wilson

Colt

Courses generally followed natural contours

Classic holes revolutionized course design

C. B. Macdonald set the bar National Golf Links (opened 1911)

Alison

(1920–1929)
The Golden Age

British golf holes are replicated

(1900–1919)
Landmark Courses of North America

THE TREE OF GOLF COURSE DESIGN AFTER 1900

(1899–)
Heathland Courses of England
Links style adapted to English countryside
Designers: Park, Jr., Colt, Fowler, Abercromby

(Before 1900)
Primitive Courses of North America
Designers: greenkeepers and professionals;
Then: Macdonald, Travis, Emmet, Leeds

(1860–1900)
Primitive Courses of the British Isles
Designers: Robertson, the Dunns, Park family, Morris

(15th Century–1850)
The Links of Scotland
No named designers

FIGURE 2-4. *The links of Scotland from the 15th century to 1850.*

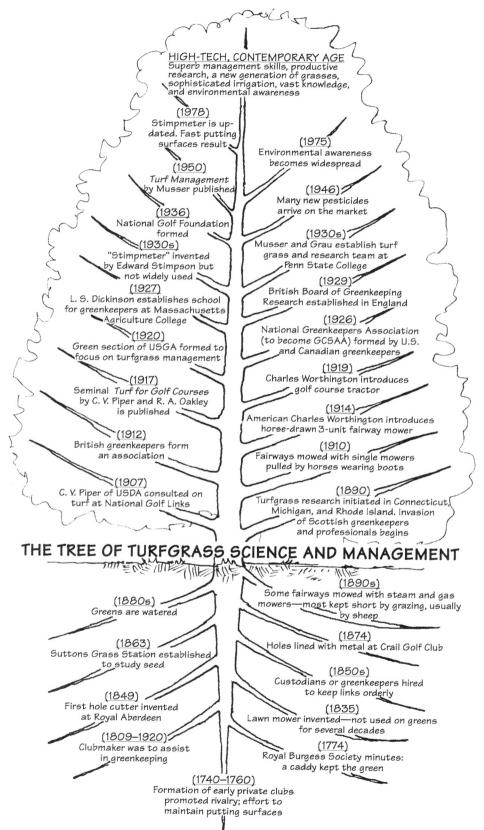

FIGURE 2-5. *Golf course design beginning at private clubs in Great Britain in 1740 up to today's high-tech era.*

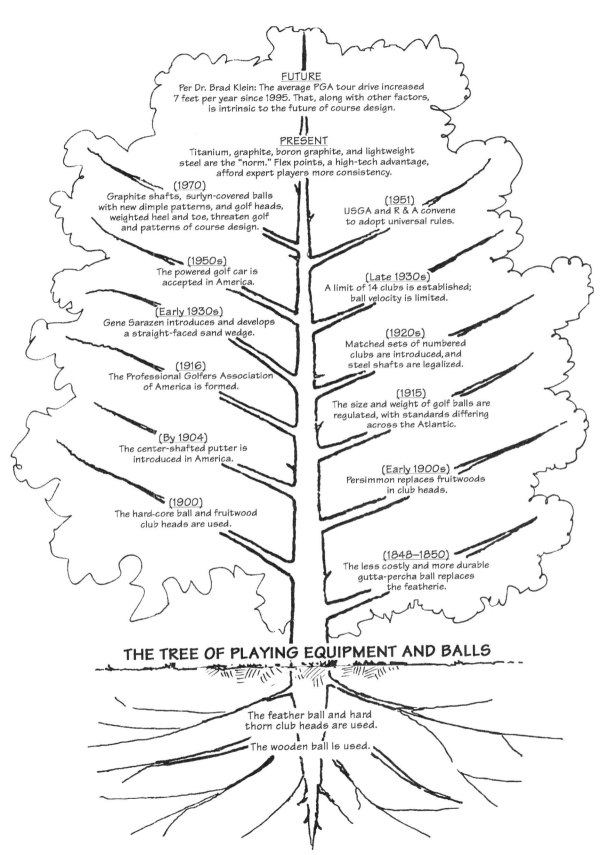

FIGURE 2-6. *The development of the ball, clubs, and rules that all affect golf course design.*

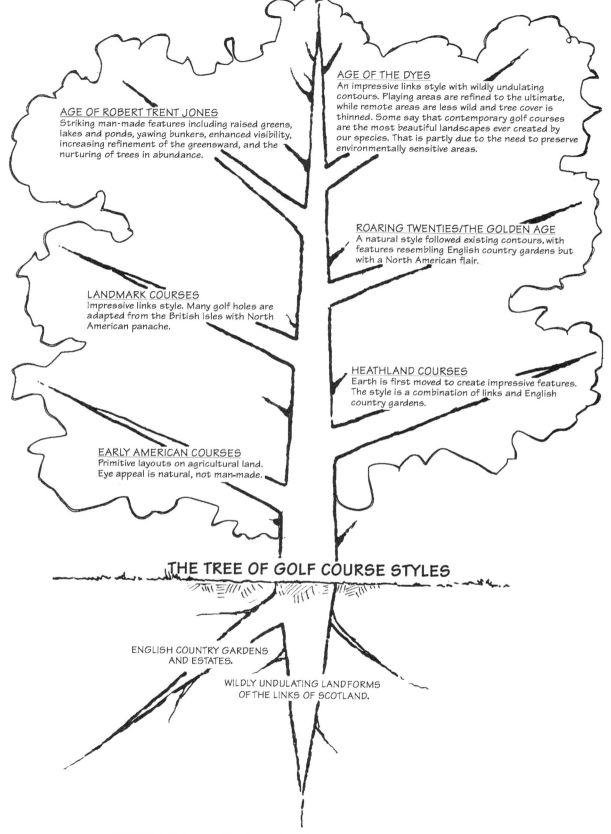

AGE OF ROBERT TRENT JONES
Striking man-made features including raised greens, lakes and ponds, yawing bunkers, enhanced visibility, increasing refinement of the greensward, and the nurturing of trees in abundance.

AGE OF THE DYES
An impressive links style with wildly undulating contours. Playing areas are refined to the ultimate, while remote areas are less wild and tree cover is thinned. Some say that contemporary golf courses are the most beautiful landscapes ever created by our species. That is partly due to the need to preserve environmentally sensitive areas.

ROARING TWENTIES/THE GOLDEN AGE
A natural style followed existing contours, with features resembling English country gardens but with a North American flair.

LANDMARK COURSES
Impressive links style. Many golf holes are adapted from the British Isles with North American panache.

HEATHLAND COURSES
Earth is first moved to create impressive features. The style is a combination of links and English country gardens.

EARLY AMERICAN COURSES
Primitive layouts on agricultural land. Eye appeal is natural, not man-made.

THE TREE OF GOLF COURSE STYLES

ENGLISH COUNTRY GARDENS AND ESTATES.

WILDLY UNDULATING LANDFORMS OF THE LINKS OF SCOTLAND.

FIGURE 2-7. *How golf has been adapted to varied landforms around the world.*

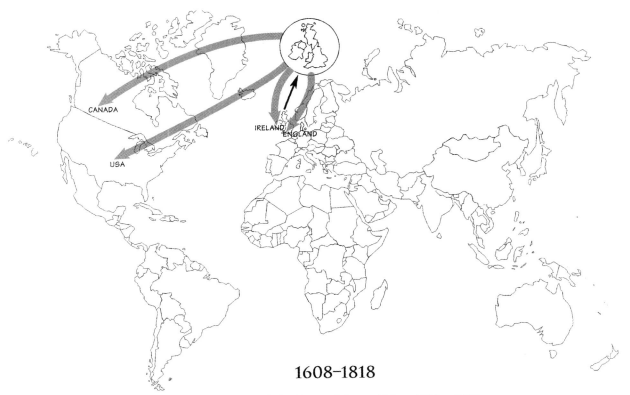

1608–1818

<u>FIGURE 2-8.</u> *The spread of golf around the world from 1608 to 1818.*

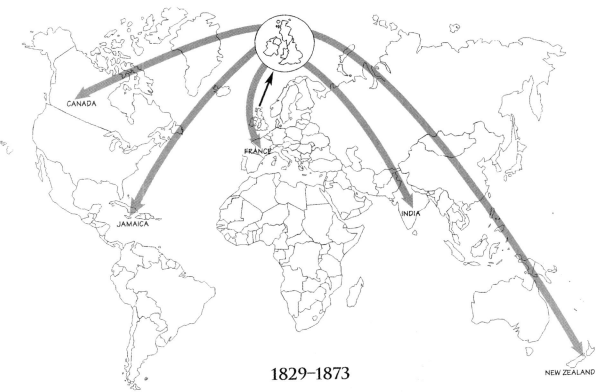

1829–1873

<u>FIGURE 2-9.</u> *The spread of golf around the world from 1829 to 1873.*

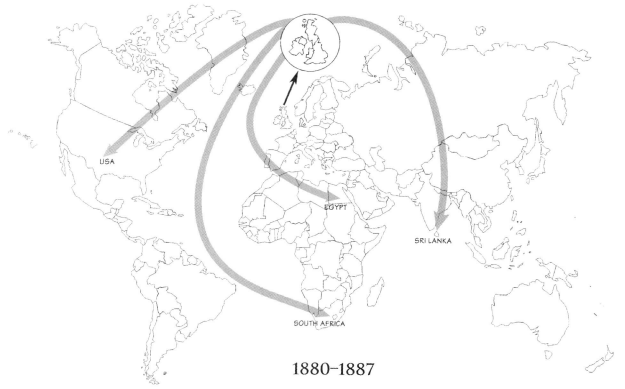

1880–1887

FIGURE 2-10. *The spread of golf around the world from 1880 to 1887.*

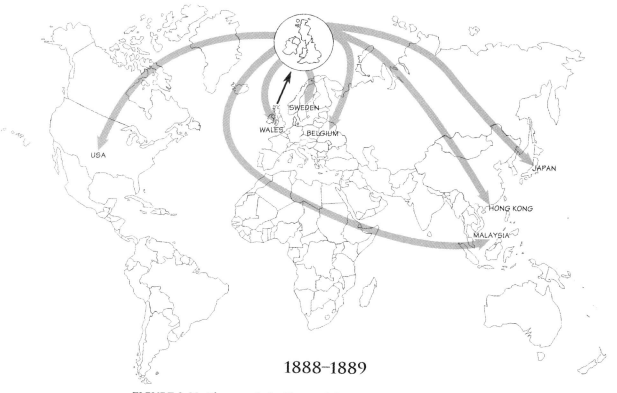

1888–1889

FIGURE 2-11. *The spread of golf around the world from 1888 to 1889.*

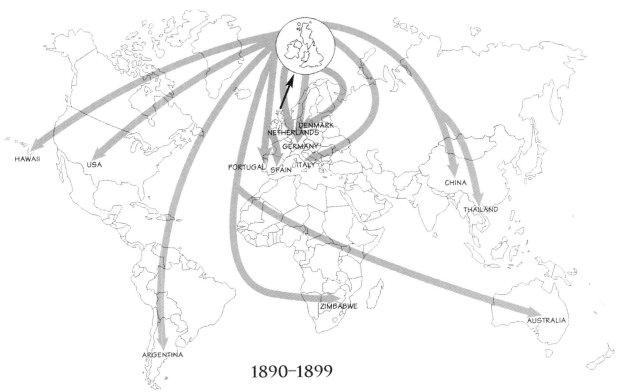

1890–1899

FIGURE 2-12. *The spread of golf around the world from 1890 to 1899.*

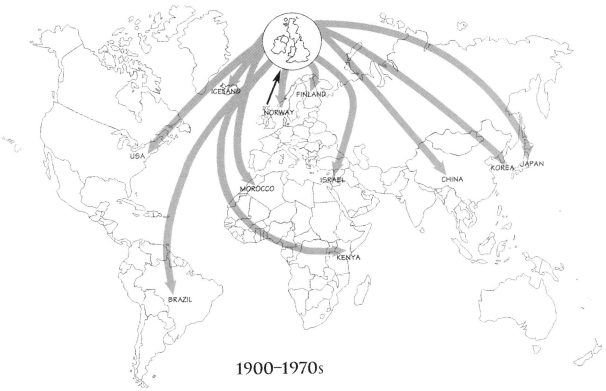

1900–1970s

FIGURE 2-13. *The spread of golf around the world from 1900 to 1970s.*

MAIL ON THE LINKS*

The following eleven pages contain an except from *Triple Baugé,* by golf course architect Fred W. Hawtree. The excerpt describes the games that were the forerunners of golf.

The Road Hole on the Old Course at Montpellier.

Jeu de Mail in the Hérault lasted longer than elsewhere and almost became golf. But it stayed on the roads for too long. When finally forced off by traffic, the players bought themselves a private field, but instead of laying out parcours de golf, *they laid out more roads. This huge mistake killed off* mail à la chicane *and golf had no further competitors.*

From Mail to Golf in Ten Easy Stages

1

The street game went in two new directions after 1500.

*"Mail on the Links," Chapter 9 of *Triple Baugé* by golf course architect Fred W. Hawtree. Reprinted by permission of his son, golf course architect Dr. Martin Hawtree. Courtesy Cambuc Archive.

a) In Europe, it survived largely unchanged though increasingly refined: no palace could be without one.

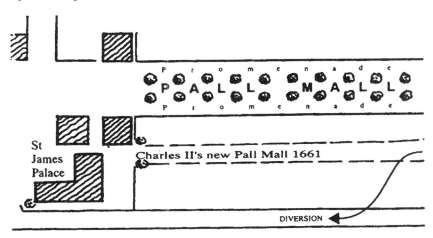

b) In Scotland, it went on to the uneven, sandy links or gravelly heaths adjoining the town. Under these conditions it could become golf.

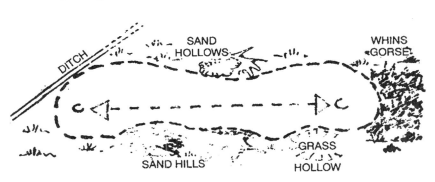

2 The earliest links malls used the flattest, smoothest areas. Apart from surface clearing (the extent of which, in play, had to be defined in the rules), there was no constructional work. These new "malls" (at Aberdeen they soon became "holes") were close to town. Gradually the passage of feet and striking the ball combined with the local environment to improve playing conditions and create further situations which have developed the clubs, the balls, and the Rules.

Although rabbits and sheep are generally credited with the initial grazing down of the grass to fairway length, grazing is only part of the story. Golf holes ran on the relatively level, lower-lying areas between the rough, elevated dunes with spiky, arid, indigestible herbage.

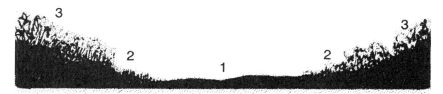

The flatter land (1) received most play and grazing. Its margins (2) had less wear and only occasional nibbles when lusher feed was thin. The outer rough (3) was seldom in play and too tough for grazing. A natural gradation—deep rough, semi-rough and fairway is correct historically.

Being close to the water table, the playing areas offered greener, more succulent grass preferred by herbivores. But these areas generally required quite elaborate ditch systems. In 1636 the Master of Aberdeen Grammar School wrote a Latin Grammar part of which described local golfing activities on the Links. He used the word *fovea* (a trap or hazard) translating it as "goat," the vernacular Scots term for a ditch. Early Rules always mention casual water.

3 The layout was still random and unstudied. If the Malls had distinguishing names, they referred to features (like *Thorntree* at Leith).

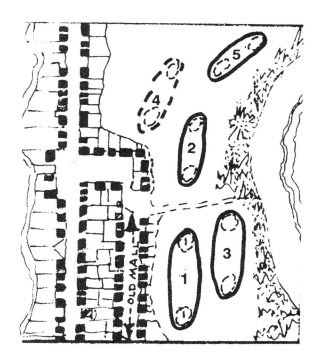

The numbers shown suggest an order of construction, not of play. Nos 1, 2, 3; No. 4 an attempt to stay close to the town; No. 5 moving on out into the country. But holes further from the sea, tended to be obliterated by the development of other activities or the expansion of the town even, in many later cases, by railways following the flattest route close to population. No. 4 would be at risk once the linear hole development (1 2 (5) etc.) became established in a later stage, moving away from town.

4 When it became necessary to walk some distance to find a vacant mall, there arose the idea that it would be still more agreeable to play the first mall, then another, then the new one and perhaps another new one before returning in reverse order to the start. Experiments on these lines were highly successful because the system produced varieties in length and character between each successive mall instead of the monotony of playing up and down a single mall. Coupled with changes in direction, the new system brought infinite variety in play.

Once the early malls were linked and played sequentially, new holes were simply added on at one end until halted by the limits of the land or of feasibility. Such extensions sometimes enabled an earlier

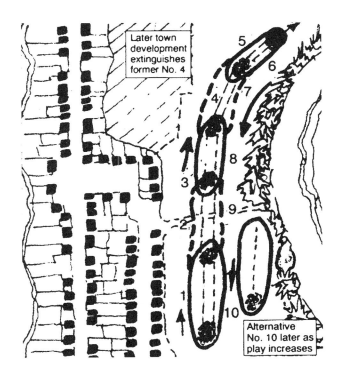

unpopular hole to be omitted by playing directly over its "green" to the next hole beyond.

5 Now further possibilities were opened up. Play was no longer concentrated near the starting point except latterly at Leith when space became more and more limited. At St. Andrews, new malls could only be made further and further from the town but players could now be golfing, not just walking, out to the extremity. The form of the layout could still only follow playable land. A happy conjunction of boundaries, climate, town development, tradition, law, history, social behaviour and topography has meant that the St. Andrews links has come down to the present time almost *intacta.*

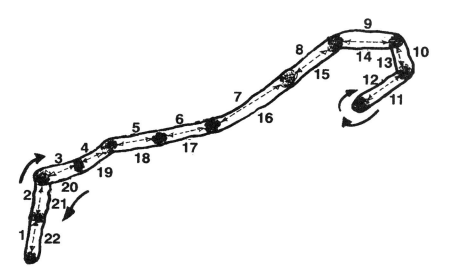

Above all, the acceptance of a standard series of connected malls permitted competition between several persons or teams at the same time instead of within one match alone. Players no longer chose which malls they would like to play. Playing them all produced variety in length and direction. The round could continue until bad ground forced an about-turn.

6 When finally the game became widely popular, pressure on the narrow malls brought essential widening beyond that so far achieved by the effects of play. At St. Andrews, the sole example of preserved mall development, greens and fairways were widened, so far as possible, and, to ease congestion, the committee decided to link four short malls remaining at the town end of the links (shown diagram-

matically). This reduced the number of holes from 22 to 18, a total eventually accepted generally as the perfect compromise.

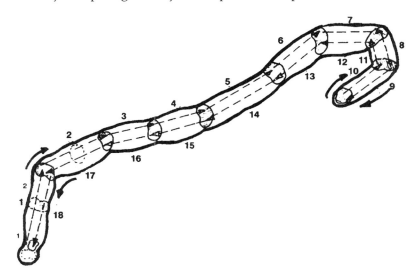

Once the layout had been established and players could enjoy competitions as well as singles and foursomes, it was time to form a club and adopt or build a club-house.

7 Finally the direction was reversed from clockwise to anti-clockwise; separate teeing grounds were provided; problems of railway sheds were overcome at No 17. The modern golf course had arrived.

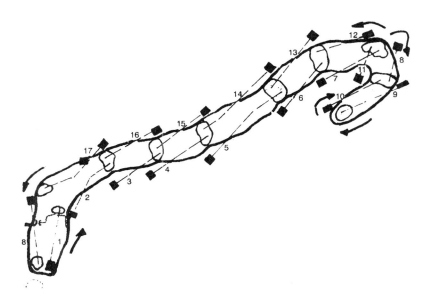

Its lessons could now be studied and academic notions of design developed. All were founded on the pure pragmatism of the previous five centuries. Elsewhere other forms of layout developed, each with its own plan and character stamped on it by the site. Some modern golf course designers ignore this virtue and impose artificial landscape of their own. It is becoming difficult to distinguish one golf course—and indeed one golf course architect—from another.

8 Leith Links

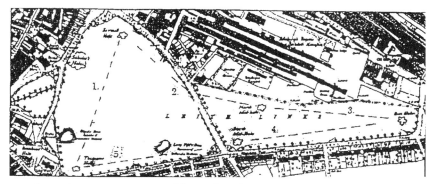

David Hamilton's reconstruction of the Leith Links in 1817

Once Leith's common grazing ground, the Scots fought over these links against the English and between themselves. French allies once encamped and fought there. Trenches to deter a Spanish invasion were once dug there; others, to bury the victims of the Plague, were even bigger. There are records of grazing in 1485, of golf in 1571 and of horse races and golf in Sir John Foulis' account books. All the time the town was encroaching, especially after the "Forty-five" when traditional overseas commerce was reinforced by home industries. Even the graves from the Plague are now under Wellington Place. The golf course was finally reduced to two triangles each with a base of some 500 yards. There were no Par 3's. Even the two at St. Andrews are coincidental. The fun of early golf resided in whacking the featherie as far as possible.

9 Aberdeen Links

Aberdeen burgh records of 1625 refer to the "part of the links betwixt the first hole and the Queenis hole." In 1696 they mention "the first holl of the links" and "the Footiseholl." Golf was played on the links in 1661. It was confined to the southern half—the Queen's links.

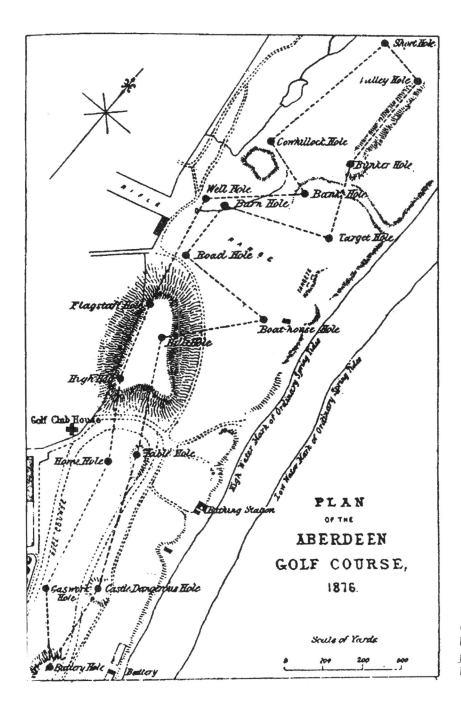

PLAN
OF THE
ABERDEEN
GOLF COURSE,
1876.

Scale of Yards

(The Queen's Links occupy the lower half of the plan). The original holes followed the traditional "out and home" pattern.

There were only seven holes, extending north as far as the Road Hole.

The first organized course was probably:

No. 1. Starting point to Castle Dangerous
　　2. Castle Dangerous to Table Hole
　　3. Table Hole to Hill Hole
　　4. Hill Hole to Road Hole
　　5. Road Hole back to Hill
　　6. Hill to Table
　　7. Table to Castle Dangerous

(There was also an odd starting hole at Leith.) The widening of the course later was able to provide new separate greens. There were many subsequent changes. The 14-hole course was the favorite until finally (1876), the extension to eighteen which also sorted out crossings and other danger points.

10 Montrose

Golf at Montrose was first recorded in 1627. This plan illustrates its development from the fifteenth to the nineteenth century. First (upper arrow) *The Mall,* with the promenade alongside for passers-by and spectators;

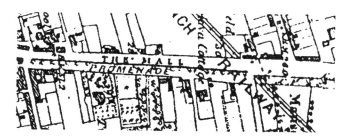

Secondly, (lower arrow) already rather nearer the sea, *Mid Links*—the golf. (Though still with a trace of pall-mall in the tree planting.)

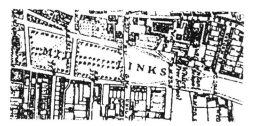

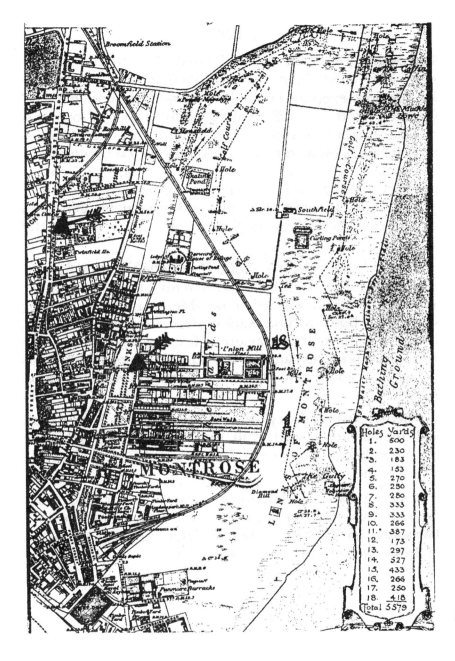

Holes	Yards
1.	500
2.	230
3.	183
4.	153
5.	270
6.	250
7.	280
8.	333
9.	333
10.	266
11.	387
12.	173
13.	297
14.	527
15.	433
16.	266
17.	250
18.	418
Total	5579

Montrose Links (1890)

Next, rope-making, flax mill, cottages and social services over-run golf and push it further from the town.

Finally, the arrival of the railway forms a *cordon sanitaire* and golf can work up to its final eighteen holes close to the sea without interference. Unfortunately, the town never became a fashionable resort like St. Andrews, but the golf was free.

THE HISTORY OF GOLF COURSE ARCHITECTURE

French towns also overran street games. *Rues de Mail* are frequently to be found but not the game.

The plan was drawn by John Sim, Captain of the Victoria Club, one of several using the links. In earlier days they met each other face to face playing up and down the same fairways. They adopted this "circular layout" to avoid danger and congestion. No doubt Mr. Sim devised it for them.

ENVOI

Regrettably, the links form of layout had to be adapted when, after 1850, the later Victorians found that the fashion for physical exercise could be followed comfortably and elegantly in the mainly healthful game of golf on land elsewhere than by the sea. They began to construct 9 or 18 artificial malls on inland sites. This process led eventually to the appearance of a new vocation—the "golf course architect." Drawn at first from the professionals, amateur golfers soon adopted this title and eventually golf club committees themselves improved on the work of the designers.

To avoid this disgrace, modern designers take refuge in eccentric designs, so elaborate and so full of inland seas, that future generations will never be able to afford to tamper with them. But environmental enthusiasts complain loudly at these misplaced extravaganzas. Current wisdom and due respect for posterity suggest the advisability of reverting to the original adaptation of natural formation without undue artifice.

Whether this tendency will take us all the way back to Pall Mall remains to be seen. If so, the old game will have to be played with new clubs until The Rules of Golf permit the return of the mallet.

It is not possible to indicate any historical texts supporting the gist of this chapter because they are not known to exist. Therefore as William Schevez, later Archbishop of St. Andrews, said in 1461 (or thereabouts)—

C'est tout!

3
GOLF HOLES ARE COMPOSITIONS

To create a composition, the painter uses brushes and paints. When composing a golf hole, the contemporary course architect first resorts to the drawing board and topographic base maps to make a plan. At one time, however, the land itself was the drawing board. Indeed, even today part of course planning is done on site, while heavy equipment and other mechanical marvels are the brushes used to bring concepts to reality. The paints are vegetation (grass and trees), water, sand, wind, natural features, and distant vistas, together with existing and created contours. But whether the artist works on an easel or on the earth, a composition is the end product, albeit one, in the case of a golf course, on a very broad canvas. And that broad canvas can be uphill, downhill, sidehill, flat, rolling, or a combination, as indicated in Figures 3-1 through 3-6.

Today, with an array of technology available, a golf hole is truly a composition and the creation of its architect. Before the advent of heavy earthmoving equipment, however, things were not always so easy to execute. Less than a century ago, the architect's brushes were horse- and mule-drawn equipment. Before that, they were men and wheelbarrows. And earlier still, it was nature alone that composed golf holes. Indeed, the earliest holes were probably determined as "golfers" selected the most exciting routes to the "greens" on Scottish linksland and later arranged the most pleasurable holes into sequences. Probably eye appeal played a role in the selection. Perhaps, too, the third side of the triangle (maintainability) was not ignored completely in that sites not prone to wind desiccation were sometimes selected for greens.

FIGURE 3-1
Port Ludlow Golf Course, Port Ludlow, Washington, was carved from a hilly and heavily wooded site. The Trail Nine site was difficult compared to the first 18, mostly because environmental restrictions had been severely tightened prior to the Trail Nine design and construction. A steep uphill ninth hole to bring the golfer back to the clubhouse resulted.

FIGURE 3-2A

Extremes in downhill shots are exemplified by this 1920s photo of the green at Lake Chabot Golf Club, Oakland, California. The ninth hole of 109 yards slopes steeply downhill as well. The steps reportedly have been removed.

FIGURE 3-2B

Hole 5 at Kooralbyn Valley Golf Club outside Beaudesert, Australia, is a 240-yard, steeply downhill hole designed by Desmond Muirhead. (Courtesy of Desmond Muirhead.)

FIGURE 3-3
The left half of the landing area on the 10th hole of Orinda Country Club, Orinda, California, slopes steeply downhill to the hole centerline. This 1920s photo shows the gully that complicates play on this short par-4.

FIGURE 3-4
This fifth hole at La Quinta Country Club, La Quinta, California, is essentially flat, as is most of the valley floor in the Palm Springs area.

FIGURE 3-5
Indian Pond Golf Club was created on a rolling and heavily wooded site in Kingston, Massachusetts. The terrain, a continuous combination of hills and valleys, ranged from three to one slopes to nearly flat, including every grade in between.

FIGURE 3-6

The Pebble Beach area contains a well-known combination of topographic conditions. Starting out relatively flat on holes 1 and 2, hole 3 slopes down to the green. The terrain is flat again until you reach (old) hole 5; then it's uphill to green 6, shown in this 1920s photo. The remaining holes are a continuation of gentle ups and downs or flat.

Early Golf Holes

These earliest of holes—"compositions" in a loose sense—were totally natural; nature was the architect, and nothing was done to modify existing contours, and little, if any, effort was made to refine the greensward that covered them. "Fairways" were grazed by cattle, and the turf surrounding the holes was grazed even closer by sheep and rabbits. The fairways were dotted by sandy scars, caused mainly by livestock trampling the turf. Owing partly to these hazards and more to the natural lay of the land, it took decades or even centuries of trial and error before the most interesting routings were established.

Over the decades, greens that had been established in the hollows and on the plateaus of Scottish linksland gradually changed as a result of repeated heavy topdressings with sand. In fact, it is accepted that some of the huge double greens at St. Andrews are several feet higher today than they were in the days of Allan Robertson and Tom Morris, in the mid- and late 19th century (Figure 3-7). (Since World War II, the introduction of aeration equipment and the practice of removing plugs have offset this gradual elevating of putting surfaces.) Despite the problems inherent in topdressing, golf has enjoyed, from the very beginning, a mystical link with sand. Bunkers on the early links were formed as livestock trampled the grass and eventually wore away the turf as they sought shelter behind hillocks to protect them-

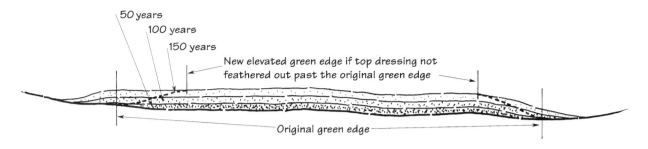

50 years
100 years
150 years

New elevated green edge if top dressing not
feathered out past the original green edge

Original green edge

RATE: ¼ inch minimum total accumulation
of top dressing per year

50 years—12.5 inches
100 years—25.0 inches
150 years—37.5 inches

FIGURE 3-7

An old green does not necessarily display what the original designer intended. Centuries, even decades of golf play, coupled with maintenance procedures and weather, can alter its character. Perhaps the practice of topdressing changed the original design most of all in the centuries before the introduction of aeration equipment.

selves from raging gales. Sandy scars arose because of the constant foot traffic, and these grassless areas aided the development of the game by creating interest, because the sand required a very different kind of shotmaking from grass.

Scotland's sheep, cattle, and rabbits were not the only ones responsible for creating the first sand hazards. Other bunkers were created as balls rolled into natural hollows. Recovery after recovery, with golfers continually swinging in the same spots, created even deeper scars that penetrated the turf and revealed the sandy subsurface (Figure 3-8). Ferocious rains further deepened the scars. Still other bunkers, including the notorious Hell on the 14th hole at St. Andrews, came about from the quarrying of seashells by villagers for use in their gardens.

FIGURE 3-8

Below this green in Ireland, the transition from disturbed sandy bank to a U-shaped maintained bunker is obvious. In time, if unchecked, erosion and traffic will destroy more turf and expose more sand. Another bunker will then be born.

GOLF HOLES ARE COMPOSITIONS

FIGURE 3-9

Erosion control on this bunker on a Scottish links shows vertical sod revetment, somewhat the worse for wear, and a near vertical wooden bulkhead. We assume that because the sod wasn't holding and needed constant replacement, the decision was made to use the wooden bulkhead.

The first greenkeepers soon found it necessary to stabilize the bunker walls with wooden bulkheads or vertical sod revetments (Figure 3-9). Indeed, the challenge of maintaining bunkers was one of the earliest greenkeeping practices, which persists to this day. Over the generations, it has had an impact on course design, partly because shapes and forms arose that became traditional, but also because the sand in the bunkers accented other features and affected the play and scores of golfers.

Bunkers were not the only components of the golf hole that evolved. Records show that golfers once simply teed balls one club's length from the preceding hole, presumably on the "green." In fact, soil displaced from the hole was utilized in the teeing process. It was not until 1874 that holes were first protected by metal cups at Crail Golfing Society in Scotland. Around the same time, separate teeing grounds were established and gradually developed into the architecturally crafted features we know today (Figure 3-10).

FIGURE 3-10

This is an interim phase of tee design. Rather than continuing to destroy the putting surface that doubled as the tee area, the tee was moved off the green. Later, it was moved to a more distant and safer location.

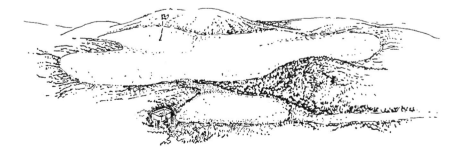

50

In summary, we believe that the earliest golf holes consisted of a fairway grazed short by cattle, a green grazed even shorter by sheep and rabbits, a hole occurring naturally or excavated by the golfers, and a teeing ground adjoining the hole. No earth was moved to create the green, though greens were slowly elevated through the process of topdressing. Grassless sandy scars dotted the landscape and enhanced the challenge. Early greenkeepers soon found it necessary to stabilize them.

Later, as the game spread far from Scotland, golf holes came about as designers sculpted the existing landscape. Yet, no matter the terrain or continent they worked on, these designers inevitably turned to linksland landforms for inspiration because it was on them that golf—its rules, customs, and playing equipment—had evolved.

The Heathlands Where Golf Course Architecture Was Truly Born

Not until the last decade of the 19th century, on the heathlands near London, were large quantities of earth moved to shape greens, tees, bunkers, ponds, and other features. Although their creation was truly and intrinsically golf course architecture, the "true classic" holes that served as models had mostly arisen before them, when little, if any, earth was moved. Today, with contemporary equipment, more can be done to sculpt the land. Still, linksland continues as the model for ever more striking compositions, with heathland architects first emulating their forms. It was on linksland that course architecture was conceived. On the heathlands, it became a reality.

Early Golf Course Architecture in America

Early American designers Devereux Emmet, Herbert Leeds, and Walter Travis, together with transplanted Scots, including Donald Ross and Tom Bendelow, followed the example of the heathland architects in England and adopted the practice of moving larger quantities of earth. But it was Charles Blair Macdonald, later recognized as the "father of American golf course architecture," who introduced the concept of adapting renowned holes to other sites. (The next chapter more fully describes his efforts.) Macdonald's work, along with that of the British heathland designers and others, led to a recognized art form: golf course architecture. It is also noteworthy that Macdonald coined the title.

In 1907, Macdonald published an article "seeking to compare the merits of various courses in hopes of defining the ideal." With the profession of course architecture becoming more recognizable and widespread, Macdonald felt, "There must be a criteria [sic] with which to judge one course against another." To this end, he devised a scorecard of sorts, providing a weighted means by which to dissect and evaluate a golf course. His intent was to examine the individual components of a golf course and establish ideals for each, as shown in Table 3-1. "I have tried to enumerate all essential features of a perfect course in accordance with enlightened criticism of the day and give each of these essential characteristics a value, the sum total of which is 100 or perfection," he wrote.

TABLE 3-1
Macdonald's "Scorecard"

Essential Characteristics		Merit
1. Course		33
a. Nature of the soil	18	
b. Perfection in undulating hillocks	15	
2. Putting greens		18
a. Quality of turf	10	
b. Nature of undulation	5	
c. Variety	3	
3. Bunkers and other hazards		18
a. Nature, size and variety	7	
b. Proper placing	11	
4. Length of hole		18
a. Best length of holes	12	
b. Variety and arrangement of length	6	
5. Quality of turf of fair green		8
6. Width of fair green of the course, 45 to 60 yards		3
7. Nature of teeing grounds and proximity to putting greens		2
Total		100

CLASSIC GOLF HOLE DESIGN

Macdonald emphasized that even the greatest of courses possess defects. Time and again he said, "An ideal course is something yet to be attained." A century later, many would still agree. Nevertheless, studying Macdonald's criteria for perfection provides an understanding of what the nuts and bolts of the trade meant to this golf architecture pioneer. And though Macdonald's concept of comparing one course against another is undeniably valuable, one wonders what the father of American golf architecture would say today regarding the infatuation that some, both designers and golfers, have developed with "course rankings" (though they are not parallel to his). We must point out that both these arbitrary top-100 lists and Macdonald's original formula can easily miss the intangible magic that resides in some holes and flows from them. Nevertheless, we agree that course ratings have created healthy competition among architects. Now the competitions have been extended to individual holes, and every golf hole is a composition planned in relation to the game and other holes in the circuit. The greatest of them reflect what Robert Trent Jones said: "Golf today, in all honesty, is what the golf course architects have made of it—a game of relaxed recreation and limitless enjoyment for millions and a demanding examination of exacting standards for those few who would seek to excel—depending on the requirements of the moment."

Aspects of Course Design

Many factors are involved in order to achieve testing qualities on each hole for the accomplished and, at the same time, provide a sense of well-being for the majority who seek it. Among these are strategy, the features of the hole (natural and created), its surroundings and distant vistas, and its setting in relation to them. The greensward and its conditioning also play a key role, while traditions are important on older layouts and soon become so on those newer courses destined to become renowned.

Nevertheless, course design includes what some may think are mundane aspects, but the dedicated designer finds them exciting and hopes they add to the player's interest. These include shapes, sizes, elevations, and grades of greens, tees, fairways, and roughs. They are part of the architect's palette and are indicated in Figures 3-11 and 3-12.

FIGURE 3-11

As golf grew and evolved, the names of golf hole parts remained almost constant. Here is contemporary vernacular.

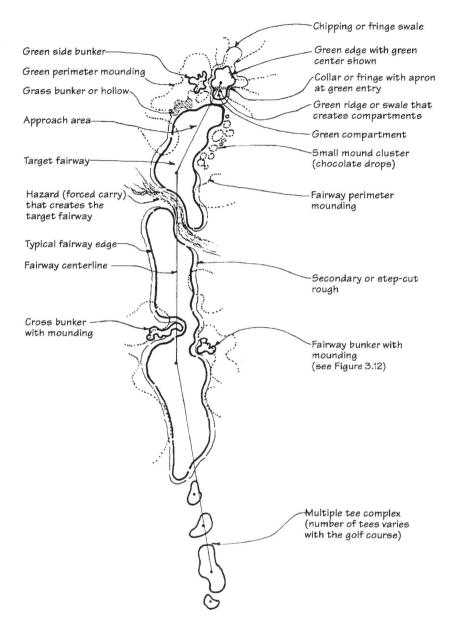

Chipping or fringe swale

Green side bunker

Green perimeter mounding

Grass bunker or hollow

Green edge with green center shown

Collar or fringe with apron at green entry

Green ridge or swale that creates compartments

Approach area

Green compartment

Small mound cluster (chocolate drops)

Target fairway

Fairway perimeter mounding

Hazard (forced carry) that creates the target fairway

Typical fairway edge

Fairway centerline

Secondary or step-cut rough

Cross bunker with mounding

Fairway bunker with mounding (see Figure 3.12)

Multiple tee complex (number of tees varies with the golf course)

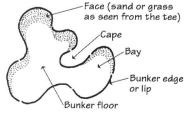

Face (sand or grass as seen from the tee)

Cape

Bay

Bunker edge or lip

Bunker floor

FIGURE 3-12

This enlargement of the fairway bunker in Figure 3-11 shows major components of a sand or grass bunker. The capes often extend from a mound and the bays from a swale. A similar concept can be used in green design.

The Magic of a Golf Hole

Landscape architect Kenneth Helphand has observed that any composition, golf holes included, can be dissected. Some may do this to determine whether the golf hole in question is interesting or dull, impressive or bland. Such quantitative dissections, however, overlook the magic inherent in some holes that defies analysis. An example is the 10th hole at Winged Foot West. In dissecting this hole, it's easy for its strategic merits to be obscured by its rather pedestrian setting in heavily populated Westchester County, New York. Seeing it for the first time, golf professional Ben Hogan is said to have described it as no more than a five-iron into somebody's bedroom. One wonders if his attitude changed after playing it.

It's obvious that the dramatic settings of the Devil's Cauldron at Banff Springs in the Canadian Rockies and the 15th and 16th holes at Cypress Point on the Monterey Peninsula enhance the experience for golfers. Even an unconscious dissection of these holes reveals not only strategic challenges but also scenic compositions that will be remembered forever. We're not saying that these holes would be without magic in less impressive settings, but Winged Foot's 10th has a magic of its own, as do many of the classic holes in Scotland and North America, whether sited in dramatic surroundings or in mundane locations.

4

THE TRADITION OF REPLICATING CLASSIC GOLF HOLES

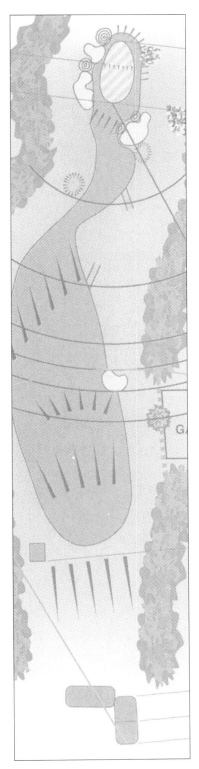

In 1998, Monet's *Basin aux Nympheas* sold at a London art auction for a record $44 million. The heavily impressionistic water lily painting, considered a classic by art aficionados, is now on sale by the tens of thousands at department stores around the world. Going rate: $19.99, frame included. What explains the dramatic difference in value for the same image? Through technology, it is now possible to inexpensively produce exact replicas of famous artwork, capturing their every detail with a high degree of accuracy. Yet it is only the original that's awarded the badge of "classic," which Webster's defines as "superior, of the highest class, being a model of its kind." The copies, though equally beautiful, are regarded as cheap knockoffs and relegated to use as wall coverings in college dormitories.

The opposite is true in golf course design due to the nature of its architecture and its intrinsic bond to the game. This forces the architect to replicate an original with his or her composition, exceeding the original more often than not.

The art of golf course design has its own classics, but replicas of these great holes are sometimes more revered than the originals. That is because the architects who have adapted them have struggled for, and succeeded in, enhancing their integrity, playing interest, and eye appeal.

The meaning of a "classic" golf hole has changed over the years. At one time, "classic" referred to renowned holes, many found originally on the links of Scotland but later adapted to other sites far from the homeland of the game. But golfers seemed to forget that use of the word and today use "classic" to describe any memorable hole. Even C. B. Macdonald, father of American golf course architecture and the first designer to adapt famous holes, eventually came to use "classic" in the modern sense. Nevertheless, throughout this book we use the word to describe holes of such greatness that their principles have been adapted totally or in part; in other words, we revert to the former meaning of "classic."

Efforts have been made on frequent occasion to copy famous golf holes, mostly those from the British Isles, and to copy them strictly without change. Despite their best efforts, however, designers have found that no two holes can ever be identical because a hole is part of the overall environment—geographic as well as socioeconomic—that surrounds it. Unlike paintings, which can be boxed in glass and hung on any wall, the art of golf course design takes place in the elements, and because they are organic, the resulting composition is forever undergoing change due to natural and other forces.

As golf spread around the globe from Scotland, courses were laid out on terrain where soil, winds, atmospheric conditions, and distant vistas were vastly different from those of the sparsely vegetated, widely undulating, windswept, sandy linksland. No earthmoving equipment—no matter how powerful—and no designer—no matter how imaginative—can exactly duplicate these external features. In a sense, that is fortunate, because the endless variety of holes is a major reason that the game of golf has remained fresh and popular. Nevertheless, every golf hole owes something tangible or intangible to one or more of its predecessors.

When determining what categories to study and researching those that would qualify as classics, we tended to concentrate on 18-hole layouts. Yet we did not mean to ignore nine-holers. For example, we found Royal Worlington and Newmarket Golf Club in Bury St. Edmunds, England, where Tom Dunn had designed nine holes in 1892 and H. S. Colt had remodeled them in 1906. It remains a nine-holer today, and what a great nine it is (Figure 4-1). Five of our major categories of potential classic holes are found there:

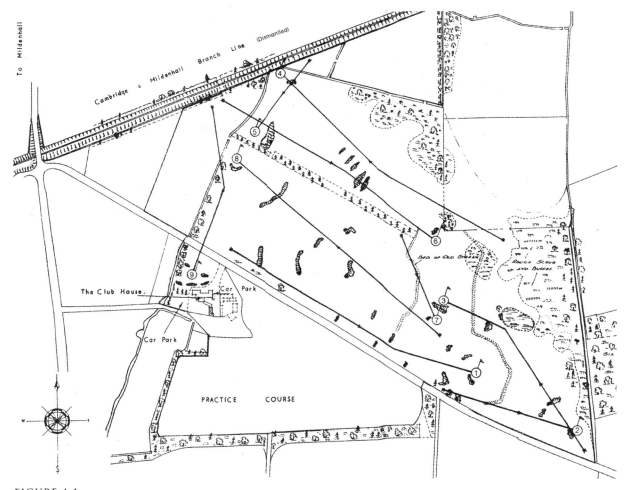

FIGURE 4-1
The plan of the Royal Worlington and Newmarket Golf Club, Bury St. Edmunds, England, provides a superb example of a nine-hole golf course. (Courtesy of Royal Worlington and Newmarket Golf Club.)

- Hole 2 has an inverted green.
- Hole 4 has a green sloping away from the shot.
- Hole 5 is a hogback green.
- Holes 3, 6, and 8 feature traditional cross bunkers.
- There are plenty of crossing holes: holes 2 and 3, holes 4 and 5, and holes 5 and 6.

In the 1930s, Bernard Darwin created a set of cigarette cards entitled "Three Jovial Golfers." Of the 18 holes included, two were from Royal Worlington and Newmarket, the third and the fifth holes. It was indeed an honor for a nine-holer to be included next to such greats as Gleneagles and Sunningdale. Herbert Warren Wind wrote a glowing description of each hole at Royal Worlington and Newmarket after stating: "I spent many happy days at Royal Worlington when John Langley and Willie Whitelaw made golf at Cambridge such a memorable pleasure." Wind continued for three pages extolling the virtues of the layout.

Adapting the Principles of Classic Golf Holes

Despite limitations inherent in attempting to copy a hole, the practice of replicating, or rather adapting, the *principles* of a classic golf hole has been prevalent and successful throughout the history of course design. This quest has taken several forms:

1. Adapting classic holes to other, even vastly different sites.

2. Attempting to produce accurate replications of the originals.

3. Adapting or copying more recent but nevertheless famous holes.

4. Accidental creation of a hole similar to an existing one. This has happened repeatedly.

5. Planning entire layouts, full length or short, where all 18 holes are adaptations of famous holes.

At times, the adaptation of a classic hole takes place consciously, as the architect studies the classic original and then attempts to translate its principles and shot values in a replica hole. Other times, the adaptation happens quite by accident in a subconscious manner. One example of the latter was observed on a recent tour of the newly completed Eagle Ranch Golf Course in the Canadian Rockies at Invermere, British Columbia, with its architect, William G. Robinson. The similarity of one hole on that course to the eighth at Pebble Beach (Figure 4-2) was striking. Robinson was familiar with the classic coastal California hole, but until the likeness of his hole to that one was brought to his attention, he had not been consciously aware that he had replicated it. No doubt, many adaptations arise in this manner, as planning procedures are more or less universal, and designers—as well as golfers—retain memories of impressive features both consciously and subconsciously.

FIGURE 4-2
This 1920s view of the eighth green at Pebble Beach Golf Links, Pebble Beach, California, was taken from the approach shot area after a well-placed drive. This was about the time that Chandler Egan was "perfecting" the course for the 1929 National Amateur.

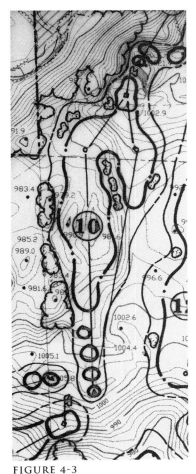

FIGURE 4-3
This routing plan of Erin Hills Golf Course, Milwaukee, Wisconsin, was the combined effort of the Hurdzan-Fry golf course architectural firm, together with writer and historian Ron Whitten, who incorporated several similarities to famous golf holes. For example, the 10th hole fits into the category of alternate routes. (Courtesy of Hurdzan-Fry.)

At the other extreme, entire layouts have been built in which all 18 holes result from a conscious effort to adapt famous golf holes. Outstanding examples, in addition to the Tribute Golf Club in Texas by Tripp Davis, include:

- Two separate courses, one in Dallas and one in Houston, which comprise Tour 18 in Texas, feature layouts with each hole designed to resemble a different hole from a famous course.
- Writer and historian Ron Whitten served as a consultant to golf architect Dr. Michael Hurdzan on the Erin Hills Golf Course, Milwaukee, Wisconsin, project. Whitten explains that the holes are not copies, but rather originals based on the styles of famous golf architects who practiced in that region; in his words, it's a "grandmaster" course (Figure 4-3).
- At the Boyne Highlands Donald Ross Memorial Course at Harbor Springs, Michigan, the goal was not necessarily to design every hole as a replica, but rather to employ the shot values and other principles of Donald Ross's design style.

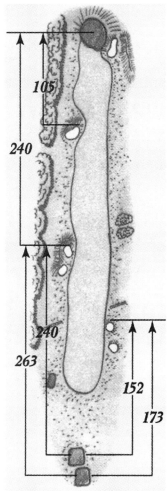

FIGURE 4-4

Stephen Kay's construction field book contains extensive photos, text, and sketches of characteristics and concepts to be incorporated into holes. For example, hole 1 at the Architects Golf Club, Phillipsburg, New Jersey, by Kay is called the Old Tom Morris hole. It utilizes design concepts that Old Tom would be gratified to know had been recognized.

- The Architects Golf Club, Phillipsburg, New Jersey (Figure 4-4), was designed by Stephen Kay (ASGCA), with Ron Whitten as consultant. This course starts with a hole in the Old Tom Morris style and ends with one in the manner of Robert Trent Jones, with holes in between expressed the way of other legendary architects. The holes are not adaptations. Rather, Kay and Whitten capture the philosophy and styles of the legendary designers by shaping features to their styles and by creating playing interest in the way that the traditional architects did.

- Ron Garl designed the course at Wooden Sticks Golf Club, Toronto, Ontario, to include 12 holes inspired by famous holes on other courses. "Eight of these holes pay homage to famous layouts, including St. Andrews and Augusta National, while four are based on features from Pine Valley in New Jersey," writer Amber Clarke explained in the official publication of the Canadian Golf Course Superintendents Association.

- Having restored Fox Chapel near Pittsburgh and Lookout Mountain near Chattanooga, two courses by Seth Raynor, course architect Brian Silva was architect of record for Cape Cod National at Brewster, Massachusetts, and Waverley Oaks in nearby Plymouth. Each embraced the principles and styles of Macdonald, Raynor, and Banks. After playing both these Massachusetts layouts, a group of members from Lookout Mountain retained Silva to plan a true Raynor course. This emerged as Black Creek in the Chattanooga area (Figures 4-5 and 4-6). It has attracted wide attention, partly because of its faithfulness to Raynor's style and principles. Yet Silva conceived his holes only after considering what Raynor would have done if he had had contemporary earthmoving equipment and know-how at his disposal.

- Jack Nicklaus's firm, Golden Bear International, is creating a course in Las Vegas called Bear's Best that will include Nicklaus's choice of 18 of his own holes. His company is also planning a similar course in Atlanta but with two holes from Scotland and one each from England and Ireland. On both courses, *exactness* is emphasized in contrast to the adaptation practiced by other course architects.

- Royal Links Golf Club by Perry Dye in Las Vegas, Nevada, was inspired by holes on venues at the Open (British). Table 4-1 lists those at Royal Links and the holes they replicated.

FIGURE 4-5
This modern Biarritz at Black Creek Country Club, near Chattanooga, Tennessee, is a rendition of the original hole in France that no longer exists.

FIGURE 4-6
The depth of the cross swale and the extensive effect it exerts on the putt are part of the challenge at the modern Biarritz at Black Creek Country Club, near Chattanooga, Tennessee. (Photo courtesy of Scott Wicker.)

TABLE 4-1
Holes at Royal Links and Holes They Replicated

Royal Links Hole Number and Yards	Hole Adapted From
1. 368, Par-4	No. 10, Royal Lytham and St. Annes
2. 372, Par-4	No. 7, Royal Troon
3. 170, Par-3	No. 2, Prestwick
4. 621, Par-5	No. 8, Royal Liverpool
5. 322, Par-4	No. 12, The Old Course, St. Andrews
6. 416, Par-4	No. 10, Royal Birkdale
7. 471, Par-4	No. 13, Royal St. George's
8. 153, Par-3	No. 8, Royal Troon (Postage Stamp)
9. 567, Par-5	No. 5, Muirfield
10. 466, Par-4	No. 17, The Old Course, St. Andrews (Road)
11. 324, Par-4	No. 6, Royal Cinque Ports
12. 471, Par-4	No. 6, Royal Birkdale
13. 348, Par-4	No. 15, Prestwick
14. 193, Par-3	No. 15, Turnberry (Ailsa Course)
15. 571, Par-5	No. 5, Turnberry (Ailsa Course)
16. 454, Par-4	No. 15, Carnoustie
17. 227, Par-3	No. 17, Royal Troon
18. 515, Par-5	No. 14, The Old Course, St. Andrews (Long)

TABLE 4-2

"Short Course" at Pine Valley: Full-Size Holes and Shorter Replicas

Short Course	Main Course
1	10
2	14
3	16
5	15
6	3
7	13
8	17
10	2

Par-3 courses often feature adapted, replicated, and copied golf holes. One famous example is Tom Fazio's 10-hole "Short Course" at Pine Valley; it includes eight holes that are skillful simulations of the shot to the green encountered on holes on the main course. Author and club historian Jim Finegan compares the full-size versions and shorter replicas as shown in Table 4-2.

On an even smaller scale, the "Little Old Course," a putting course at a senior center in Mission Viejo, California, was designed by Scott Miller to include a Swilcan Burn, a Road Hole, and emulations of Strath, Beardies, and Principal's Nose bunkers, all as miniaturized concepts borrowed from the Old Course at St. Andrews. At the other extreme, a less successful attempt was made in life-size proportions years earlier by golf architect Desmond Muirhead to reproduce the Old Course exactly on a site in Japan. Despite dogged determination, he found it impossible to do so.

Case Study: Macdonald Replicated Several Classic Holes at the National Golf Links

Even a cursory study of course design reveals that every hole on the Old Course at St. Andrews has been adapted in some form or another, as have nearly all the holes of the National Golf Links on Long Island. It was at this landmark course, opened in 1911, that architect Charles Blair Macdonald set forth to build "a classical golf course in America, one which would eventually compare favorably with the championship links abroad and serve as an incentive to the elevation of the game in America" (Figure 4-7, pages 66–67).

In his timeless book, *Scotland's Gift—Golf,* Macdonald wrote that "The courses in Great Britain abound in classic and notable holes and one has only to study them and adopt their best and boldest features. Yet in most of the best holes there is always some little room for improvement." This insight from the father of North American golf course architecture reveals just how profoundly the design principles of early links and other holes in Great Britain have shaped—and continue to shape—the art form of course design. This influence has remained constant even as golf has landed on distant shores with landscapes far removed from Scottish linksland, and even as every person who has ever laid out a golf course has incorporated his or her own ideas.

Despite his reverence for the early links holes, Macdonald was careful never to ransom his own design abilities, nor the specific attributes of the land, in an attempt to exactly copy these holes. Indeed, he once prepared a sequential list of 18 classic British holes and added his thoughts on how several could be improved. Thus, he differentiated between "classic" and "ideal" golf holes. Because it is one of the earliest efforts to list 18 of the greatest golf holes in a logical succession, the sequence is presented in Table 4-3 as it appeared in Macdonald's book for the benefit of the true student of course design.

Macdonald was not just theorizing with his list. By preparing it, he set the stage for the creation of the National Golf Links and was soon raising funds and assembling "maps, sketches and descriptions of famous holes in Great Britain." He set in motion an extensive search for the "ideal" property "on which it was possible to build the classic golf course." He was impressed by a site on Cape Cod, but felt it was too remote for many of his potential members. He then rejected land between Amagansett and Montauk on Long Island because it lacked sufficient topsoil. He next made an offer for a plot near Shinnecock Hills Golf Club far out on Long Island. His offer was rejected.

Finally, upon inspecting a large parcel on Sebonac Neck with frontage on Peconic Bay (also near Shinnecock Hills), Macdonald found what he was seeking. Though many felt the land was worthless, it took only a horseback tour of the site with Jim Whigham, his future (1909) son-in-law and scion of the famous Whigham golfing family of Prestwick, Scotland, to convince Macdonald he had found the perfect place to build his new and improved classic golf course. He completed a deal with the owners to purchase 205 acres and with renewed energy set out with Whigham to begin the design work. The duo quickly discovered specific areas on the newly acquired property that lent themselves to the creation of five classic Scottish holes, including the Alps (hole 17, Prestwick) (see Figure 4-17); the Redan (hole 15, North Berwick) (see Figure 4-10); the Eden (hole 11, "High-In," St. Andrews) (see Figure 4-14); the Sahara (hole 3, Royal St. George's) (see Figure 4-12); and the Road (hole 17, St. Andrews) (see Figure 4-13).

Macdonald and Whigham also discovered a superb site for a water hole. It would become the National Golf Links' 14th hole and was dubbed "the Cape" (see Figure 4-7). The concept was later employed by Macdonald and protégés Seth Raynor, Charles Banks, and Ralph Barton on many of their layouts. Perhaps the finest adaptation of the Cape is the fifth hole at Mid Ocean. Two other notable

ROYAL WEST NORFOLK GOLF CLUB

The very attractive centenary book of Royal West Norfolk Golf Club (1892–1992) says: "Late in 1891 a party of sportsmen on a drive along the coast from Heacham to Burnham, spotted what appeared to be unexplored and natural golf links land, between Hunstanton and Wells. Shortly thereafter, Royal West Norfolk Golf Club was born."

Apparently crossing holes were acceptable. The original layout, supervised by Horace W. Hutchinson, the "Great Horace," had holes 3 and 16 crossing. During the next 100 years, many changes were implemented, often because of the antics of neighboring marshlands and the incursions of the North Sea. The layout now incorporates two crossings, holes 2 and 17 and holes 4 and 5. Reading about those changes, we suspect the club was blessed with plenty of spare land that allowed for improvements and expansions.

In 1910, Bernard Darwin, writing in *The Golf Courses of the British Isles* about an enjoyable game of golf at a course in Brancaster, used many descriptive terms that will be found in later chapters of this book. They include "Maiden," deep bunkers, blind shots, plateaus, target or what he called "stepping stone" golf, steep-faced bunkers, and a course that penalized bad shots.

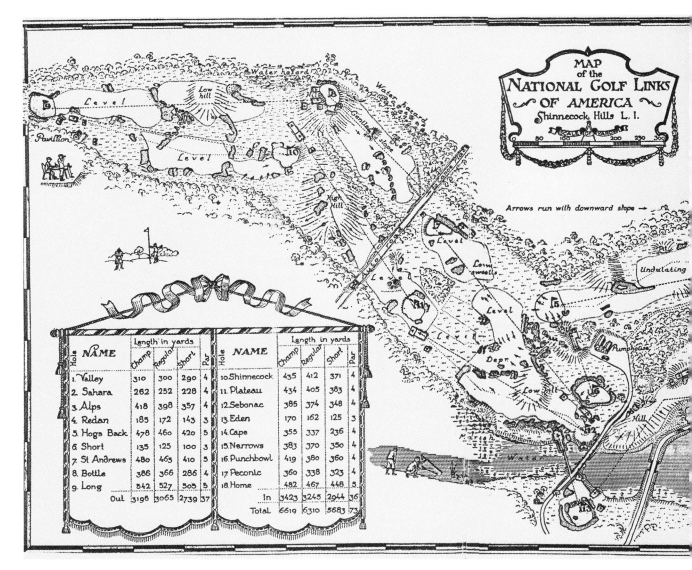

Map of the NATIONAL GOLF LINKS OF AMERICA Shinnecock Hills L. I.

SCALE OF YARDS 50 100 200 230

Arrows run with downward slope →

Hole	NAME	Champ	Regular	Short	Par
1	Valley	310	300	290	4
2	Sahara	262	252	228	4
3	Alps	418	398	357	4
4	Redan	185	172	143	3
5	Hogs Back	478	460	420	5
6	Short	135	125	100	3
7	St Andrews	480	465	410	5
8	Bottle	386	366	286	4
9	Long	542	527	505	5
	Out	3196	3065	2739	37

Hole	NAME	Champ	Regular	Short	Par
10	Shinnecock	435	412	371	4
11	Plateau	434	405	383	4
12	Sebonac	385	374	348	4
13	Eden	170	162	125	3
14	Cape	355	337	236	4
15	Narrows	383	370	350	4
16	Punchbowl	419	380	360	4
17	Peconic	360	338	323	4
18	Home	482	467	448	5
	In	3423	3245	2944	36
	Total	6619	6310	5683	73

FIGURE 4-7

The renowned National Golf Links of America, Southampton, New York, was planned by Charles Blair Macdonald to replicate or adapt the holes of famous British courses or the principles on which they were based. Its own holes have been copied widely. This course did the most to encourage interest in old but solid design concepts from Great Britain. (Copyright © by Erwin Raisz. Reprinted with permission by Raisz Landform Maps, 800-277-0047.)

examples include the third at Yale and the eighth at the St. Louis Country Club.

While the Cape was a Macdonald original (and later considered a classic), his true intent at the National Golf Links was to adapt and improve upon classic holes from the British Isles. He and partner Whigham felt that the location they had selected for the Alps hole at the National was superior to the original at Prestwick (see Figure 4-17). Macdonald was determined to surpass the original Alps hole, and many golfers have since testified that he did so. Prior to World War I, leading British golfers invariably chose the original Alps as the game's best two-shot hole. "This is curious because the second shot at the Alps is blind," wrote Macdonald and Whigham. "Not only is the green invisible, but the very difficult cross bunker in front of the green is

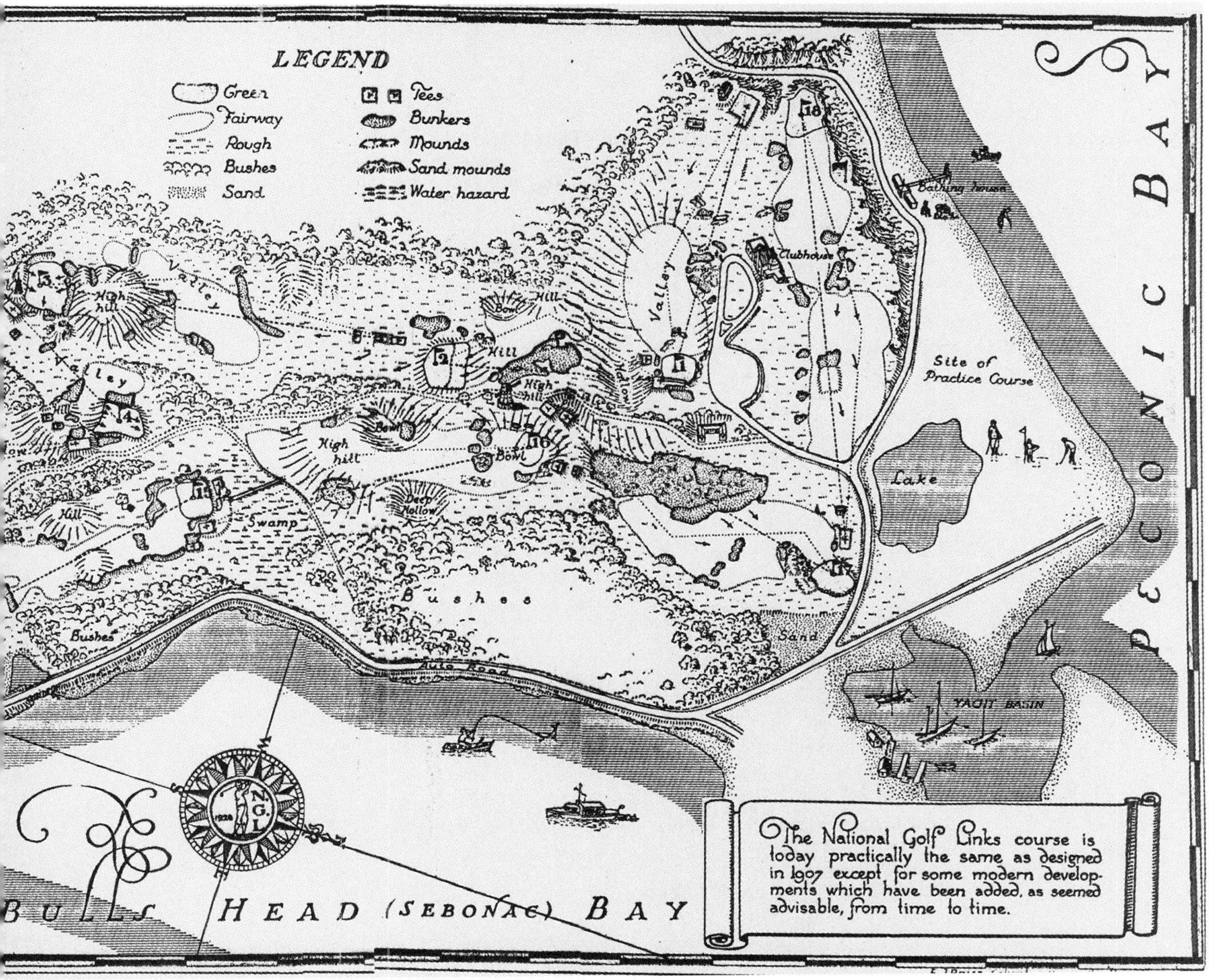
LEGEND
Green
Fairway
Rough
Bushes
Sand
Tees
Bunkers
Mounds
Sand mounds
Water hazard
PECONIC BAY
Bathing house
Clubhouse
Site of Practice Course
Lake
YACHT BASIN
Valley
High hill
Swamp
Deep Hollow
Bowl
Bushes
Sand
Auto Road
N.G.L.
BULLS HEAD (SEBONAC) BAY
The National Golf Links course is today practically the same as designed in 1907 except for some modern developments which have been added, as seemed advisable, from time to time.

hidden." They conclude that this hidden danger might be what makes the Alps so fascinating and add that "The popularity of the Alps is proof that not all blind holes are bad."

Macdonald adapted the Alps at the National so that the best line of play is to the right of a slope, where the ball rolls to a level and thus provides an easier second shot to the green (see Figure 4-7). Conversely, at Prestwick the best line of play is to the left of the direct path to the pin. The Alps hole at the National, therefore, is not a replica that repeats every feature and nuance, but rather an interpretation that takes advantage of an ideal site.

Likewise, Macdonald believed he had found a perfect natural site for the Redan (see Figure 4-7). (Ben Sayers, widely known professional from Scotland, would later say he felt it was better than the

TABLE 4-3

The Holes at the National Golf Links and the Classic Holes That Inspired Them

Hole	Length	Suggested By	Macdonald's Comments for Improvement as Interpreted by the Authors
1	370	Bottle hole at Sunningdale (Figure 4-8)	Replace ditch with deep graduated bunkers. Rebunker the green.
2	340	A composite hole with the first shot similar to that of the 14th (Perfection at North Berwick) with the green guarded by bunkering similar to the 15th at Muirfield.	
3	320	No. 3, the Old Course at St. Andrews (Figure 4-9)	
4	187	No. 15, the Redan at North Berwick (Figure 4-10)	A hole similar to the Redan, but not a replica. Perhaps Macdonald's Redan at the National Golf Links, then not in existence, was what he envisaged.
5	560	No.16, Littlestone, Kent, England, a dogleg	The shortest route to the green arises from "cutting the corner." This should be made excessively difficult as at the fourth on the Lido (NLE).
6	400	No. 4, Royal St. George's, Sandwich, England (Figure 4-11)	
7	130	No. 5, Brancaster[a]	Raise tee for complete visibility of flagstick.
8	420	No. 9, Leven, Scotland	
9	350	No. 9, Brancaster[a]	
10	240	No. 3, the Sahara at Royal St. George's, Sandwich, England (Figure 4-12)	Make the long direct carry 175 yards with shorter alternative routes.
11	450	No. 17, the Road hole on the Old Course at St. Andrews (Figure 4-13)	
12	160	No. 11, St. Andrews (the Eden) (Figure 4-14)	
13	400	No. 3, the Cardinal hole at Prestwick (Figure 4-15)	
14	490	No. 14, Long hole at St. Andrews (Figure 4-16)	Make the green larger and ease the run-up to it.
15	210	No. 12, Biarritz, France	
16	300	No. 7, Leven	Lengthen hole. Guard green with mounds and change stream so that is on a bias to the green.
17	380	No. 17, the Alps at Prestwick, resemblance only (Figure 4-17)	
18	380	No. 8 at St. Andrews (Figure 4-18)	

[a]Probably Royal West Norfolk; see sidebar reprinted from *The Royal West Norfolk Centenary Book 1892–1992.*

CLASSIC GOLF HOLE DESIGN

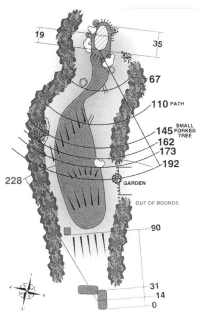

FIGURE 4-8

Most bottleneck holes are in a straight alignment. This early one at the Old Course, Sunningdale Golf Club, Berkshire, England, has a kink in the bottle's neck. (Copyright © DuCam Marketing (UK) Ltd.)

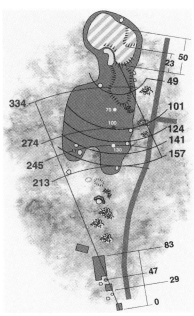

FIGURE 4-9

Cartgate hole at the Old Course at St. Andrews, Scotland, refers to a long-gone gate for cart or pedestrian access to the links. (Copyright © DuCam Marketing (UK) Ltd.)

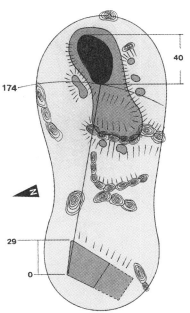

FIGURE 4-10

Much is written about this hole, the Redan, at North Berwick Golf Club, Scotland, one of the best known holes in golf. (Copyright © DuCam Marketing (UK) Ltd.)

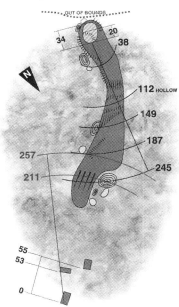

FIGURE 4-11

Hole 4 at Royal St. George's Golf Club, Sandwich, England, is a classic design. C. B. Macdonald found no way to improve on this long and difficult par-4 when emulating it. (Copyright © DuCam Marketing (UK) Ltd.)

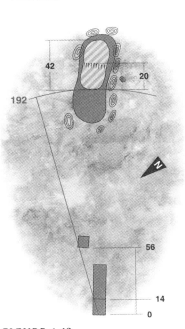

FIGURE 4-12

The Sahara, hole 3 at Royal St. George's Golf Club, Sandwich, England, is another classic. The space between tee and green is a terrifying mix of sandy hills and valleys. (Copyright © DuCam Marketing (UK) Ltd.)

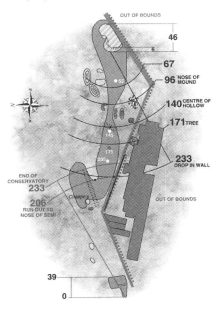

FIGURE 4-13

This renowned hole, the Road, the 17th on the Old Course at St. Andrews, Scotland, is seldom copied exactly today because hitting over or even near buildings and occupied territory could lead to liability. Yet that is the main feature off the tee. Elsewhere trees and hills have sometimes been substituted for the building. (Copyright © DuCam Marketing (UK) Ltd.)

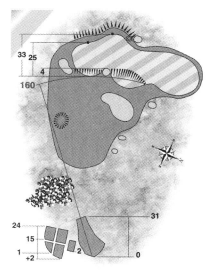

FIGURE 4-14

The Eden, the 11th hole at the Old Course at St. Andrews, Scotland, is another widely publicized and adapted hole. One feature that can't be seen could be the golfer's major concern: the beach behind the green makes for a difficult recovery if the wind or wrong club selection carries the shot too far. (Copyright © DuCam Marketing (UK) Ltd.)

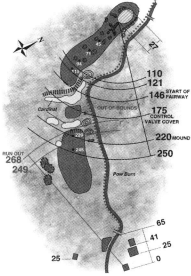

FIGURE 4-15

The Cardinal, the third hole at Prestwick Golf Club, Prestwick, Scotland, takes its name from the huge bunker complex midway through the hole. The out-of-bounds along the entire right side makes play even more interesting. (Copyright © DuCam Marketing (UK) Ltd.)

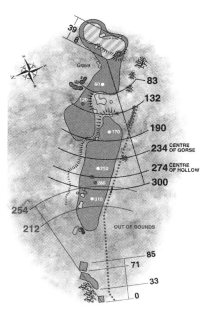

FIGURE 4-16

The Long, the 14th on the Old Course at St. Andrews, Scotland, is the longest hole on the Old Course. (Copyright © DuCam Marketing (UK) Ltd.)

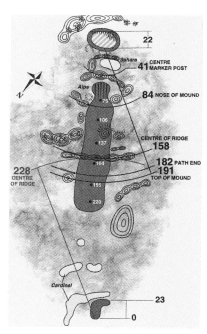

FIGURE 4-17

The Alps, the 17th at Prestwick Golf Club, Prestwick, Scotland, is a classic hole. C. B. Macdonald later suggested improvement to this hole by emphasizing play to the right. Though today blind holes are frowned on, this one lives on. Excitement is generated by trudging up the hill to see where your shot has landed. (Copyright © DuCam Marketing (UK) Ltd.)

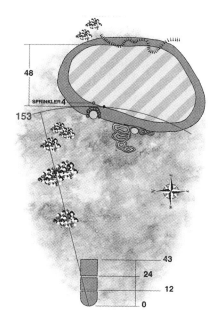

FIGURE 4-18

The eighth hole on the Old Course at St. Andrews, Scotland, is the original Short but not the one that became a classic. Not really a short hole by today's standards, the eighth is now a bit longer than the 11th. Many replications now tend to be very short. (Copyright © DuCam Marketing (UK) Ltd.)

original.) While they felt they had improved the setting for this hole, both Macdonald and Whigham argued that the original Redan design provided more options than any other short hole and conceded that its principles for a 180-yard hole could not be improved upon.

The Eden (High-In), the 11th hole at the St. Andrews Old Course (see Figure 4-14), had, at the time, been voted the best one-shot hole in the British Isles, although critics had pointed out that it was possible to top one's tee shot and still reach the green. True to his promise to improve the classics, Macdonald solved this problem at the National by providing a 75-yard carry over water and rough to a green identical to the original in Scotland.

To adapt the Sahara hole from Royal St. George's (a short par-4 that was altered in the 1970s to a par-3) (see Figure 4-12), Macdonald created a smaller, but still substantial bunker resembling the Sahara Desert (see Figure 4-7). While not exactly replicating the original 200-yard sandy wasteland in front of the tee, both the Sahara in England and that on Long Island "force the golfer to adopt the same strategy," according to Macdonald. Both are excellent examples of the principle of risk and reward.

In addition to adapting these notable classics, other holes at the National were Macdonald originals. Later, he and his protégés adapted both his interpretations and originals on other sites (see Appendixes A and B).

On completion, his National Golf Links of America did, in fact, include 18 holes of an exemplary nature. To create them, Macdonald had moved large quantities of earth, far more than for other layouts of the day, and he had sought the advice of leading experts in their fields so that his design assured that golfers must think at each hole before they swing.

Macdonald's lofty concepts were achieved at the National. Cornish and Whitten wrote, "It was like no other course in the country, and every player, every writer, every course designer who viewed it, marveled. British golfers and writers were astonished at what an ideal links creation Macdonald had wrought."

The National Golf Links was truly in a class by itself. It was a true landmark and a classical course. It revolutionized the architecture of new courses and forced many existing layouts to be rebuilt. Although not the only designer to introduce the concept of adapting design principles of renowned British holes to those in North America, Macdonald defined the process for aspiring designers and brought classics to the attention of golfers. Indeed, the exaggerated drop-offs around

FIGURE 4-19
The edge of this green at Tamarack Country Club, Greenwich, Connecticut, provides a striking example of the exaggerated drop-off.

greens and bunkers emphasized classic features to those golfers who studied terrain (Figure 4-19).

Carrying on Macdonald's Legacy: Raynor and Banks

Macdonald designed 15 more courses. Each included a Redan, an Eden, and a Cape, the last a Macdonald original. In developing the National, Macdonald had employed Seth J. Raynor as surveyor and engineer. Impressed by Raynor, Macdonald hired him as a partner on all projects that followed. Later, Raynor entered into the practice of course architecture on his own, and all his designs included versions of British classics and Macdonald's originals. It is also noteworthy that Raynor designed an early version of Cypress Point on the Monterey Peninsula, but his plan was never executed because of his early death at age 46 in 1926.

Five years earlier, Raynor had employed Charles Henry Banks, an English instructor and track coach at Hotchkiss School in Connecticut. Banks finished Raynor's uncompleted layouts and planned several more on his own. Nicknamed "Steamshovel Banks" or "Steamshovel Charlie," he moved prodigious quantities of earth to construct his features, often as much as 10,000 to 15,000 cubic yards per green. The designs for his greens and holes followed the principles of the classics or the Macdonald originals. Historians of golf architecture theorize that one of Banks's objectives in moving immense quantities of earth was to emphasize the features of the classics that he was adapting and to bring them to the attention of golfers to a degree that his mentors, Macdonald and Raynor, may never have done.

Banks passed away in 1931 also at an early age of 48. His major contribution to course design is his massive greens and bunkers that emphasize the features of the classics in an exaggerated way. Golfers did, in fact, recognize them, and their design kept alive the practice of emulating famous holes during the hiatus of almost a quarter century of Depression and war when course architecture was at a low ebb. But even in the recovery years, when funds were still limited, golf architects continued to be aware of adaptations. Then, as course construction accelerated, the classics again predominated in the art form. Surely this was due in part to Charles Banks's unique, massive features, which continued to pique the interest of golfers and draw their attention to an earlier era. Members of clubs that contain Banks's courses are protective of their unique features and resist remodeling except in periods of economic downturn, when some find costs of maintaining them too high.

Appendix A presents a partial list of Macdonald, Raynor, and Banks layouts. Appendix B provides an analysis of the forms and principles that Banks followed, based on the legacy of Macdonald and Raynor, in his ingenious adaptations of classic golf holes.

> **CHARACTERISTIC TRAPEZOIDAL BUNKERS**
>
> Ron Whitten, celebrated architectural editor of *Golf Digest*, described the Macdonald-Raynor features and presumably those of Banks, which were even more pronounced, as "trapezoidal bunkers, duckwalks across the landscape, their sand as flat as a bath mat, their sides as steep as the sides of a bathtub. The huge pedestal greens have right-angled corners so precise that the superintendents edge them with a T-square. The bunkers' features are so vast and broad that depth perception is thrown out of kilter."

APPENDIX A

COURSES BY MACDONALD, RAYNOR, AND BANKS

Charles Blair Macdonald (1856–1939), born in Niagara Falls, Ontario, Canada, is known as the father of American golf course architecture. Macdonald created some 15 layouts in addition to his masterpiece, the National Golf Links on Long Island, New York. With only one exception, Downers Grove in the Chicago area, all his layouts included:

1. Replicas of classic holes
2. Holes that include classic features of British holes
3. Replications of his own originals, notably the Cape

Two protégés, Seth J. Raynor (1874–1926), who had been retained by Macdonald as engineer and surveyor at the National Golf Links, and

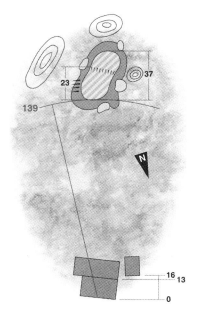

Charles Banks (1883–1931), a former teacher at Hotchkiss School in Connecticut, carried on this tradition alone and in collaboration with each other. Macdonald was also assisted by his son-in-law H. J. Whigham (1869–1954), a writer and scion of a renowned Scottish golfing family. Whigham also practiced course design on his own, as did another associate, Ralph Barton (1875–1941), a college professor who worked with the triumvirate and later on his own.

Macdonald's, Raynor's and Banks's layouts, with few exceptions, included a Valley, an Eden, an Alps, a Redan, a Biarritz with its Valley of Sin, a Short, a Long, a Road, a Maiden (Figure 4-20), a Punch Bowl (Figure 4-21), and sometimes a Sahara and a Bottleneck. They also included one or more exceptionally deep bunkers that sometimes bore the name "Purgatory" and a high cone-shaped mound called "Chocolate Drop" (Figures 4-22 through 4-24).

FIGURE 4-20

The present sixth hole at Royal St. George's Golf Club, Sandwich, England, is the Maiden today. The play, once over the sand hill left of the green, was changed by Alister Mackenzie because it was a blind shot over a horrifying bunker. (Copyright © DuCam Marketing (UK) Ltd.)

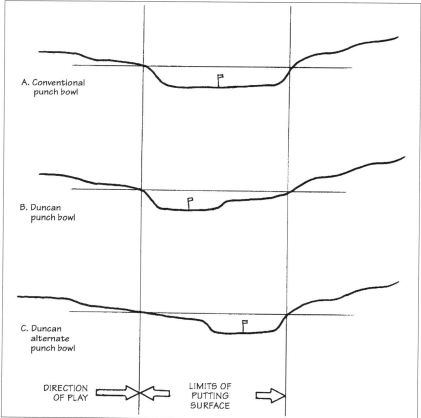

FIGURE 4-21

The Punch Bowl is a name assigned to different green sites, some almost buried beneath steep hillsides and others perched on hillsides. Most are similar to the three examples shown here.

CLASSIC GOLF HOLE DESIGN

FIGURE 4-22
Chocolate Drops can take many forms. This hole at Tamarack Country Club in Greenwich, Connecticut, shows one popular way to use the single mound.

FIGURE 4-23
Hayden Lake Country Club, Hayden Lake, Idaho, sports a cluster of Chocolate Drops, another popular concept from the early 1900s.

FIGURE 4-24
With geometric shapes for green and bunker and Chocolate Drops or Dragon's Teeth lined up symmetrically, golf on this hole at Highland Country Club, Indianapolis, Indiana, becomes a tee square and triangle world. This is an early Tom Bendelow design. (Courtesy of Ron Whitten.)

In adapting classic holes, Macdonald, Raynor, and Banks, but most of all the last, tended to accentuate grades to make the classic features clearly recognizable; the work of other architects was often more subtle, with classic features merely suggested. The trio tended toward repetition, unlike most course designers, who seek variety.

Table 4-4 includes courses created alone or in collaboration with each other. Note terminology: Use of the word "with," for example; "Macdonald with Raynor," indicates true collaboration, while "assisted by" implies major contributions to design but not true collaboration. NLE stand for "no longer exists." FKA means "formerly known as."

TABLE 4-4
Courses Created by Macdonald, Raynor, and Banks

Course and State	Designer and Year of Opening
Annapolis Roads GC, Maryland	Charles Banks [date unknown]
Augusta CC, Georgia	Seth Raynor, revised 1926
Babson Park G&YC (NLE), Florida	Seth Raynor, 1921
Bayside CC (NLE), Rhode Island	Seth Raynor, 1920
Bellport CC, New York	Seth Raynor, 1916
Blind Brook Club, New York (Figure 4-25)	Macdonald with Raynor, assisted by George Low, 1915
Blue Mound G&CC, Wisconsin	Seth Raynor, 1924
Bon Air Vanderbilt Hotel GC (Lake Course) (NLE), Georgia	Seth Raynor [date unknown]
Brookville CC, New York	Seth Raynor, 1922
Camargo Club, Ohio	Seth Raynor, 1921
Caracas CC, Venezuela	Charles Banks, 1931
Castle Harbour GC, Bermuda (now Tucker's Point GC)	Charles Banks, 1932
Cavalier G&YC, Virginia	Charles Banks, 1930
Charleston CC of South Carolina	Seth Raynor, 1922
Chicago GC, Illinois	Macdonald, 1895; revised by Raynor, 1923
Cold Spring Harbor CC, New York	Seth Raynor, 1923
(The) Creek Club, New York	Macdonald assisted by Raynor, 1925
Deepdale GC (NLE), New York (Figure 4-26)	Macdonald assisted by Raynor, 1925
Downer's Grove GC (first known as Chicago GC), Illinois	Macdonald, 1893
Essex County Club (West Course), New Jersey	Charles Banks, 1930
Everglades Club, Florida	Seth Raynor, 1919 and 1926

(continued on page 78)

CLASSIC GOLF HOLE DESIGN

FIGURE 4-25
C. B. Macdonald and Seth Raynor collaborated to create beautiful Blind Brook Club, Purchase, New York. Like the hole shown here, the whole course retains much of its original character.

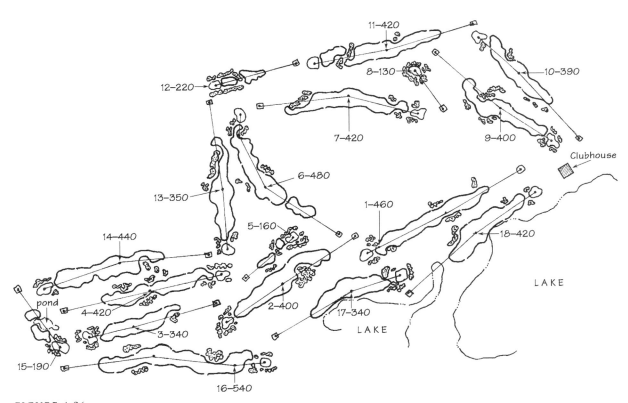

FIGURE 4-26
In The Missing Links, *author Daniel Wexler observes that Deepdale Golf Club, Great Neck, New York, in its 30 years of existence, included eight U.S. Golf Association presidents in its membership.*

THE TRADITION OF REPLICATING CLASSIC GOLF HOLES

Course and State	Designer and Year of Opening
Fairfield CC, Connecticut	Seth Raynor, 1921
Fishers Island GC, New York	Seth Raynor, 1912
Forsgate CC (East Course), New Jersey (Figure 4-27)	Charles Banks, 1931
Fox Chapel GC, Pennsylvania	Seth Raynor, 1925
Gardiner's Bay CC, New York	Seth Raynor revised nine and added nine, 1915
Gibson Island CC (NLE), Maryland (Figure 4-28)	Macdonald with Raynor, 1922
Green Park—Norwood GC (NLE), North Carolina	Seth Raynor [date unknown]
Greenbrier GC (Old White), West Virginia	Macdonald assisted by Raynor, 1915
Hackensack CC, New Jersey	Charles Banks with assistance from Macdonald, 1930
Hotchkiss School GC, Connecticut	Seth Raynor assisted by Charles Banks, then on staff at Hotchkiss, 1921

(continued on page 80)

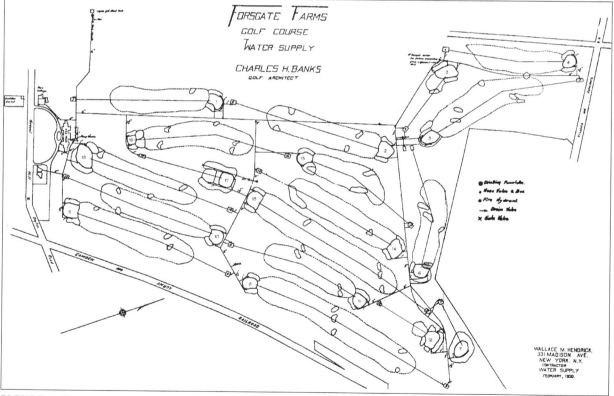

FIGURE 4-27

Bob Ribbans gave us this 1930 drawing of Forsgate Farms Golf Course, Jamesburg, New Jersey, prepared by Charles H. Banks. A working drawing of the water system, it shows many golf course features important in developing this book. (Courtesy of Forsgate Farms Country Club, an RDC Golf Group Facility.)

CLASSIC GOLF HOLE DESIGN

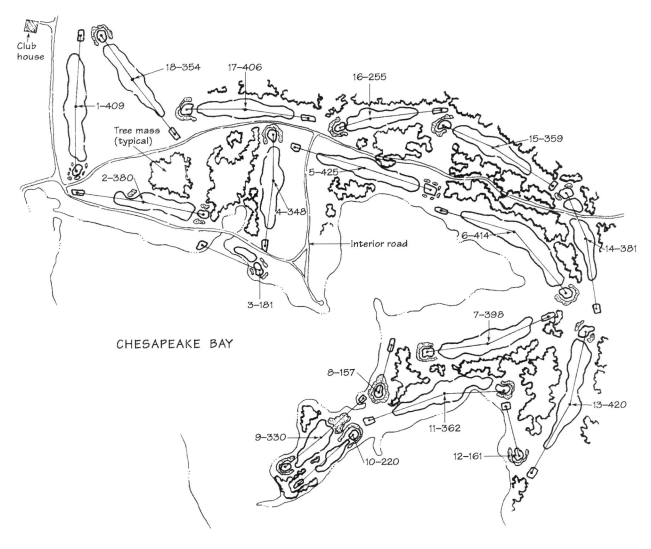

FIGURE 4-28
Gibson Island Country Club, Gibson Island, Maryland (which no longer exists), is a fine example of every golfer's dream. Author Daniel Wexler says, "Buy an island, build the ideal course, and then invite all one's friends to come visit, to play, to build houses and stay awhile."

Course and State	Designer and Year of Opening
Junko CC, Venezuela	Charles Banks, 1931
Knoll CC, New Jersey	Charles Banks, 1929
Lido GC (NLE), New York (Figure 4-29)	Macdonald assisted by Raynor, 1917
(The) Links (NLE), New York (Figure 4-30)	Macdonald assisted by Raynor, 1919
Lookout Mountain GC (FKA Fairyland GC), Tennessee	Seth Raynor assisted by Charles Banks, 1925
Mid Ocean Club, Bermuda	Macdonald assisted by Raynor, Banks, and Barton, 1924
Mid Pacific CC, Hawaii	Seth Raynor with Charles Banks, 1927
Midland Hills CC, Minnesota	Seth Raynor, 1915
Minnesota Valley GC, Minnesota	Seth Raynor [date unknown]
Montclair GC, New Jersey	Charles Banks, added fourth nine, 1930
Monterey Peninsula GC (Dunes C), California	Seth Raynor assisted by Charles Banks, 1926
Moore Estate GC (NLE), New York	Macdonald assisted by Raynor
Morris County GC, New Jersey	Originally by Tom Bendelow; revised by H. J. Whigham; then Seth Raynor revised and added 12, 1923
Mountain Lake Club, Florida	Seth Raynor [date unknown]
National Golf Links of America, New York	Macdonald assisted by Whigham, 1911
Otto Kahn Estate GC, New York	Macdonald assisted by Raynor, 1925
Piping Rock Club, New York	Macdonald assisted by Raynor, 1913
Rock Spring CC, New Jersey	Charles Banks, 1927
Roselle CC, New Jersey	Seth Raynor [date unknown]
Shoreacres GC, Illinois	Seth Raynor, 1921
Sleepy Hollow GC, New York	Macdonald assisted by Raynor, 1914
Somerset CC, Minnesota	Seth Raynor [date unknown]
Southampton GC, New York	Seth Raynor with Charles Banks, 1927
St. Louis CC, Missouri	Macdonald assisted by Raynor, 1914
Tailer's Ocean Links (NLE), Rhode Island	Seth Raynor, 1920
Tamarack CC, Connecticut (Figure 4-31)	Charles Banks, 1929
Thousand Islands Club, New York	Seth Raynor, 1927
University of Minnesota GC, Minnesota	Seth Raynor assisted by Ralph Barton, 1921
Waialae CC, Hawaii	Seth Raynor with Charles Banks, 1925
Wanumetonomy CC, Rhode Island	Seth Raynor, 1922

(continued on page 83)

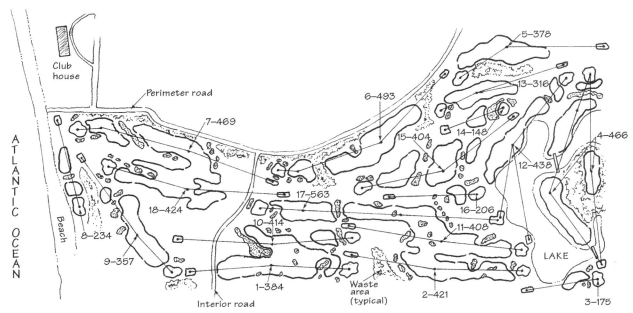

FIGURE 4-29

Bernard Darwin called the Lido Golf Club, Lido Beach, New York (which no longer exists), the finest course in the world. This may have been the first time swampland, now called wetlands, was used for a golf course. The site is now occupied by a municipal golf course and condominiums.

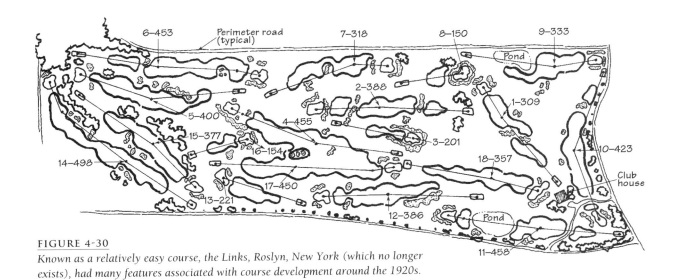

FIGURE 4-30

Known as a relatively easy course, the Links, Roslyn, New York (which no longer exists), had many features associated with course development around the 1920s. They include cross bunkers, greens surrounded by bunkers, or nearly so, as well as modified versions of Alps, Biarritz, Short, Redan, and Eden.

THE TRADITION OF REPLICATING CLASSIC GOLF HOLES

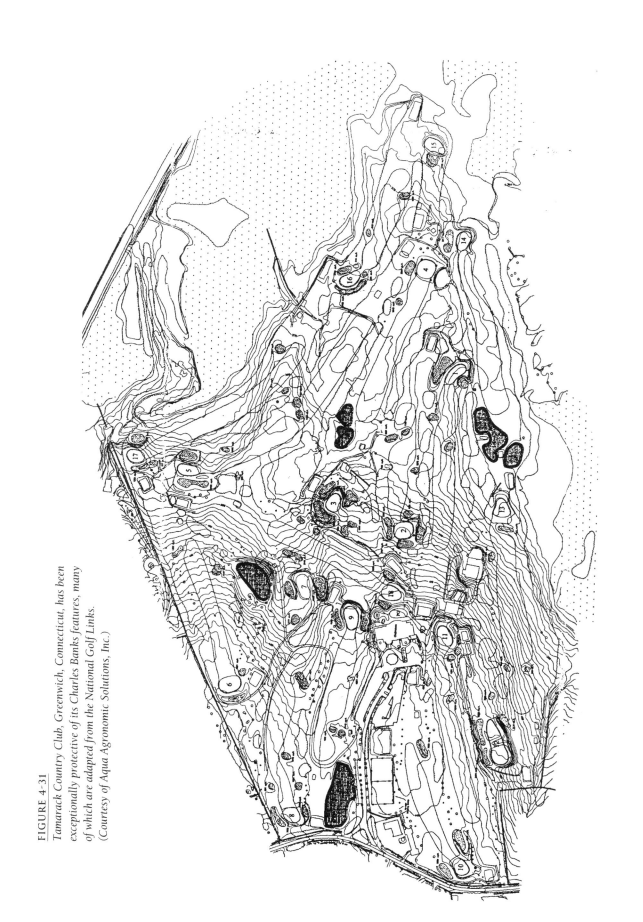

FIGURE 4-31
*Tamarack Country Club, Greenwich, Connecticut, has been
exceptionally protective of its Charles Banks features, many
of which are adapted from the National Golf Links.
(Courtesy of Aqua Agronomic Solutions, Inc.)*

Course and State	Designer and Year of Opening
Westhampton CC (Oneck Course) (NLE), New York (Figure 4-32)	Charles Banks, 1929
Westhampton CC, New York	Seth Raynor, 1914
Whippoorwill Club (a total revision of an existing Donald Ross course)	Charles Banks, 1927
Whitney Estate GC (NLE), New York	Macdonald assisted by Raynor, 1917
Wyantenuck GC, Massachusetts	Charles Banks revised three, including the unique raised Punch Bowl
Yale University GC, Connecticut	Macdonald with Raynor, assisted by Banks and Barton, 1926
Yeaman's Hall Club, South Carolina	Seth Raynor, 1922

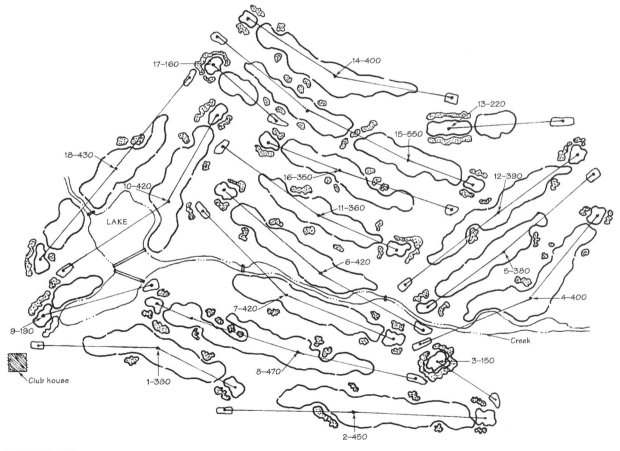

FIGURE 4-32

The Oneck Course at Westhampton Country Club, Westhampton, New York, is a Charles Banks project that did not survive Depression and war. Calling upon all he had learned from Macdonald and Raynor, Banks created a superior golf course with an oceanfront setting that is now home sites.

THE TRADITION OF REPLICATING CLASSIC GOLF HOLES

APPENDIX B

BANKS'S GENIUS IN ADAPTING GOLF HOLES

In recent years, increasing study has been given to the works of Charles Banks. A paper entitled "Charles Henry, 'Steamshovel Banks'" by Fred Rosenberg features holes designed by Banks at Forsgate Country Club in New Jersey (see Figure 4-27). A book-length publication by George Bahto, a writer and historian who has researched the lives and works of Banks, Macdonald, and Raynor—some say more thoroughly than anyone else—features holes at Knoll Country Club, another Banks layout in New Jersey.

By abstracting and augmenting the outstanding work of Rosenberg and Bahto, we have prepared Table 4-5, which details Banks's adaptation of holes at the two golf courses. Banks tended to exaggerate rises, drop-offs, humps, and hollows to emphasize features in his adaptations. The table also shows that the forms and principles of adapted holes result in part from the genius of the adapter.

TABLE 4-5
An Analysis of Banks's Adaptation of Holes at Forsgate Farms and Knoll Country Club

Hole	Forsgate Farms	Knoll Country Club
1	*Preparatory*: A forgiving hole that provides the golfer a warm-up. Rosenberg notes that the name was often given to opening holes in Scotland (see Figures 4-27 and 4-33).	*Valley*: An unforgiving hole from an elevated tee. The drive is into a lower level referred to as a valley. The putting surface is tightly bunkered with two prominent mounds that can deflect the ball off the green (Figure 4-34).
2	*Narrows*: A tight and narrow driving hole. It is an adaptation of Macdonald's 15th at the National Golf Links (see Figure 4-27).	*Maiden*: A long par-4 with the tee shot across water to a plateau green described by Bahto as a Maiden Green.
3	*Eden*: This hole resembles the 11th on the Old Course at St. Andrews (High-In). It features the Strath and Cockleshell bunkers of the original (see Figures 4-27, 4-35, and 4-36).	*Redan*: An adaptation of the Redan at North Berwick, Scotland, but with modifications typical of those used by Macdonald on his Redan, the fourth at the National Golf Links (Figure 4-37).
4	*Hogsback*: Forsgate's hogback features a ridge in the putting surface. On some courses a hogback features both a ridge on the fairway and one on the green (see Figure 4-27).	*Hogback*: The green only is hogbacked. The words *hogback* and *hogsback* were used interchangeably by Banks.

CLASSIC GOLF HOLE DESIGN

FIGURE 4-33

Hole 1, or Preparatory hole, at Forsgate Farms Golf Course, Jamesburg, New Jersey, looking from the rear of the green to the distant tee, is a Reverse Redan style of green. (Courtesy of Forsgate Farms Country Club, an RDC Golf Group Facility.)

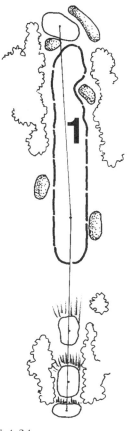

FIGURE 4-34

Many golf holes have been named "Valley," including the first hole at Knoll Country Club, Parsippany, New Jersey. Some of these had an elevated tee where you hit down to a depressed landing area that was not necessarily a valley.

Hole	Forsgate Farms	Knoll Country Club
5	*Punch Bowl:* Rosenberg mentions the relationship of this hole to the ninth at Hoylake in England. Banks had a Punch Bowl on almost all his courses, as did Macdonald and Raynor (see Figure 4-27).	*Cape:* Knoll's Cape is a par-5 Cape with a dogleg right off the tee and with the bite-off across bunkers arranged at a diagonal to the shot. Most Capes are par-4s.
6	*The Knoll:* The second shot of this hole is partially blind. The hole is probably an original at Forsgate and not an adaptation (see Figure 4-27).	*Short:* This is a short par-3 to a green surrounded by sand with a horseshoe-shaped ridge in the putting surface. It is a true adaptation of the sixth at the National Golf Links. Except for length, it bears little relationship to Short, the eighth on the Old Course.

(continued on page 87)

FIGURE 4-35

Though many golf course designers have adapted the Eden hole at the Old Course at St. Andrews, Scotland, there is no Eden River or adjacent beach in most replicas, including the third hole at Forsgate Farms Golf Course, Jamesburg, New Jersey, shown here. (Courtesy of Forsgate Farms Country Club, an RDC Golf Group Facility.)

FIGURE 4-36

This is a reverse photo shot of the third-hole Eden showing the fifth hole in the background at Forsgate Farms Golf Course, Jamesburg, New Jersey. (Courtesy of Forsgate Farms Country Club, an RDC Golf Group Facility.)

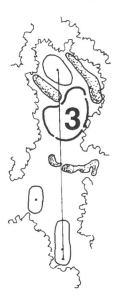

FIGURE 4-37

The centerline of this hole and the angle of the green on the third hole at Knoll Country Club, Parsippany, New Jersey, resemble the Redan at North Berwick Golf Club, Scotland. Other bunkering varies, however.

CLASSIC GOLF HOLE DESIGN

Hole	Forsgate Farms	Knoll Country Club
7	*Redan*: Here Banks has introduced the Macdonald version of the 15th at North Berwick (see Figures 4-27 and 4-38).	*Drive-Pitch*: This is truly a Redan. The name describes the hole. It is something of a breather except for a carrying bunker off the tee and deep greenside bunkers (Figure 4-39).
8	*Long*: Adapted from the 14th on the Old Course at St. Andrews (see Figure 4-27).	*Bottle*: Adapted from the "classic" Bottle hole. Here the neck is at the 100-yard mark from the green, unlike the Bottle at the National Golf Links, where it comes into play on the tee shot.
9	*Plateau*: This hole has two plateaus, one in the fairway and the green itself (see Figures 4-27 and 4-40).	*Plateau*: The typical Plateau green on this hole arose from modifications. After the course had been in play, the green was moved back to an existing plateau (Figure 4-41).

(continued on page 88)

FIGURE 4-38
This Reverse Redan is shown in the camera shot from the seventh green back to the tee at Forsgate Farms Golf Course, Jamesburg, New Jersey. (Courtesy of Forsgate Farms Country Club, an RDC Golf Group Facility.)

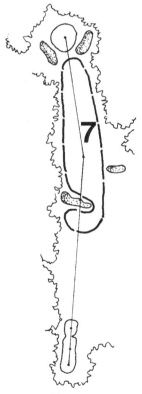

FIGURE 4-39
This short par-4 uses a cross (carrying) bunker to add penal design flair at the seventh hole, a Redan, at Knoll Country Club, Parsippany, New Jersey.

FIGURE 4-40
*This photo shows the ninth green, a Plateau, at Forsgate Farms Golf Course,
Jamesburg, New Jersey, in the foreground and directly in back of it the 10th tee
and 18th green. (Courtesy of Forsgate Farms Country Club, an RDC Golf Group
Facility.)*

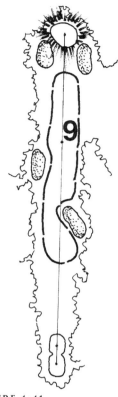

FIGURE 4-41
*In our research, we discovered
hundreds of Plateau greens, like hole
9 at Knoll Country Club, Parsippany,
New Jersey. Some were barely raised
above ground level. Many were much
higher.*

Hole	Forsgate Farms	Knoll Country Club
10	*Valley*: Named after the opening hole at the National Golf Links, it is typical of starting holes on many Macdonald, Raynor, and Banks layouts. One wonders if it was intended as the first on a preliminary layout, with the nines reversed in later plans (see Figures 4-32 and 4-42).	This hole has been revised since opening and is probably a Knoll original and not an adaptation (Figure 4-43).
11	*Steamshovel*: Named for Charles Banks's nickname, "Steamshovel Charlie" or "Steamshovel Banks" (see Figure 4-27)	A long par-4 with no fairway bunker, this hole plays to a uniquely contoured green. It is not an adaptation.
12	*Horseshoe*: Completely surrounded by sand, this is the hole often referred to on other courses as "Short." The putting surface is characterized by a distinct horseshoe-shaped undulation (see Figure 4-27).	Originally a 358-yard par-4, this hole has been lengthened by 30 yards, while the deep-bunkered putting surface has been reduced in size.

CLASSIC GOLF HOLE DESIGN

FIGURE 4-42

Hole 10, a Valley, at Forsgate Farms Golf Course, Jamesburg, New Jersey, reminds us of the Reverse Redan. It has an interesting semicircular roll, somewhat like the horseshoe or thumbprint terrace of the Short at the National Golf Links. (Courtesy of Forsgate Farms Country Club, an RDC Golf Group Facility.)

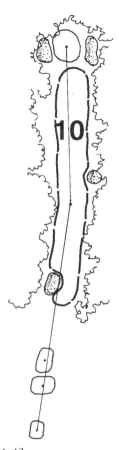

FIGURE 4-43

A standard par-4, hole 10 at Knoll Country Club, Parsippany, New Jersey, has a carrying bunker that penalizes the short hitter or topped shot.

Hole	Forsgate Farms	Knoll Country Club
13	*Southwind*: An uphill par-5 into the south wind. When the wind is from that direction, it is a true three-shotter. With a north wind, many golfers can reach home on their second shot (see Figure 4-27).	*Biarritz*: An adaptation of Macdonald's versions of the Biarritz. The front part of the putting surface has long been maintained as fairway. Originally, the green was 225 feet deep and divided by the "Valley of Sin."
14	*Northwind*: A straightaway par-4 with a wide fairway (see Figures 4-27 and 4-44).	*Road*: Only 430 yards in length, this hole bears only scant resemblance to the original at St. Andrews. Yet there is resemblance with trees on the right replacing the hotel and bunkers at the green placed in the same manner as those on the Old Course (Figure 4-45).

(continued on page 90)

FIGURE 4-44
The 14th green, the Northwind, at Forsgate Farms Golf Course, Jamesburg, New Jersey, is almost a Reverse Redan with a Purgatory-type bunker. (Courtesy of Forsgate Farms Country Club, an RDC Golf Group Facility.)

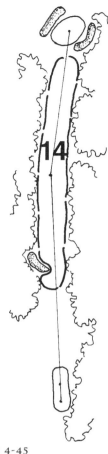

FIGURE 4-45
Called the Road after the original at the Old Course at St. Andrews, Scotland, the 14th hole at Knoll Country Club, Parsippany, New Jersey, has no building to carry and no road when you get to the green. Note that a deep greenside bunker left of the green takes the place of the Road.

Hole	Forsgate Farms	Knoll Country Club
15	*Chocolate Drop*: Surrounded by sand, a high cone-shaped mound is found on many of Banks's layouts. One example is the left greenside bunker on the 14th at Tamarack in Connecticut (see Figure 4-27).	A par-5 dogleg right. The principles of this hole are found on other Banks layouts.
16	*North Berwick*: The three-tiered green was adapted from the 16th at North Berwick, Scotland. The tiered green was used by Macdonald on his 11th (the Plateau) hole at the National Golf Links (see Figures 4-27 and 4-46).	A 370- to 380-yard hole, this can't be recognized as an adaptation. Yet the Banks objective is recognizable (Figure 4-47).

FIGURE 4-46
The 16th hole at Forsgate Farms Golf Course, Jamesburg, New Jersey, is a fairly standard hole with a heavily bunkered and terraced green. It is based on the 16th hole at North Berwick Golf Club, Scotland. (Courtesy of Forsgate Farms Country Club, an RDC Golf Group Facility.)

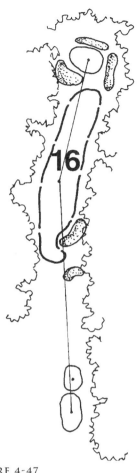

FIGURE 4-47
Two carrying bunkers lie in wait for the unwary or unlucky at the 16th hole at Knoll Country Club, Parsippany, New Jersey. There are also bunkers to control the approach shot.

Hole	Forsgate Farms	Knoll Country Club
17	*Biarritz*: A typical Macdonald, Raynor, Banks adaptation of Willie Dunn's Biarritz hole in France (see Figures 4-27 and 4-48).	*Eden*: Banks's adaptation of Macdonald's Edens. They, in turn, were adaptations of the 11th hole at St. Andrews. A huge bunker behind the green, which symbolized the beach of the Eden River, has been removed (Figure 4-49).
18	*Purgatory*: The exceedingly deep greenside bunker, as found on the right, is a characteristic of many Banks layouts (see Figures 4-27 and 4-50).	A 435-yard finishing hole, whose green originally extended from a plateau down a slope to a lower level. Now it is a Redan-type green situated entirely on the plateau (Figure 4-51).

FIGURE 4-48

As often happened, Biarritz greens were eased by maintaining the front portion as a fairway, though this eliminated an exciting golfing experience. Fortunately, the huge side bunkers often remained intact, as shown here at the 17th hole at Forsgate Farms Golf Course, Jamesburg, New Jersey. (Courtesy of Forsgate Farms Country Club, an RDC Golf Group Facility.)

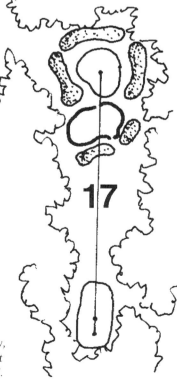

FIGURE 4-49

The Eden, hole 17, at Knoll Country Club in Parsippany, New Jersey, lacks a river and beach. The huge bunker at the rear of the green simulates them but is now removed.

CLASSIC GOLF HOLE DESIGN

FIGURE 4-50
The Purgatory bunker at the 18th hole at Forsgate Farms Golf Course, Jamesburg, New Jersey, awaits the golfer who places a shot to the right of the green. Golfers can spend many minutes (hours?) trying to extricate themselves from it. The left-side bunker is also a monster. (Courtesy of Forsgate Farms Country Club, an RDC Golf Group Facility.)

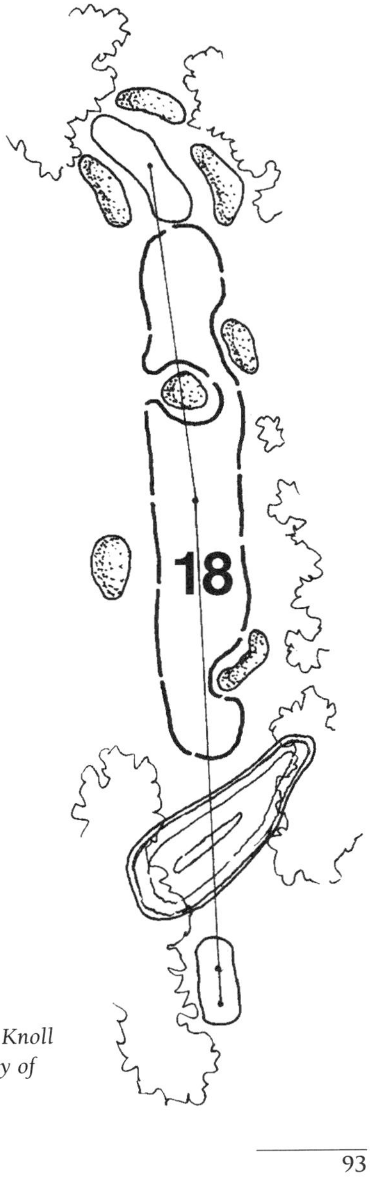

FIGURE 4-51
The pond off the tee has been removed from the 18th hole at Knoll Country Club, Parsippany, New Jersey. Still, there are plenty of problems with carry bunkers and a closely guarded green.

THE TRADITION OF REPLICATING CLASSIC GOLF HOLES

5

BROAD CRITERIA FOR CLASSIC GOLF HOLES

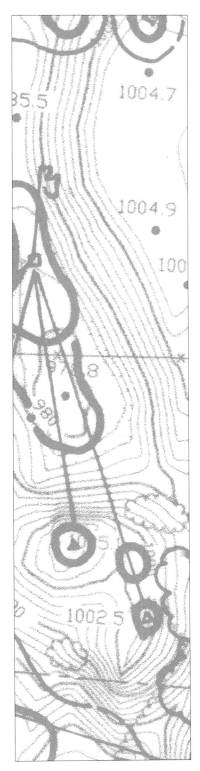

Golf holes are different, with each offering its own unique challenge and diversity. Yet all holes can be grouped into a few broad categories: Holes are straight or doglegged; uphill, downhill, or level; short, long, or medium in length. They are located in settings ranging from the world's most spectacular landscapes to the dullest (including reclaimed town dumps) and are played into or against or at an angle to the prevailing wind. Whatever the categories to which a hole belongs and wherever it is located, it is an artistic composition arising from the genius, great or small, of its designer, who has used the paints and brushes of the art form to produce it.

The practice of adapting well-known golf holes, which we refer to as "classics," has permeated the art form of golf course design and has had an impact on the game itself. Nevertheless, resemblances between the classics and their adaptations often verge on the nebulous, making it difficult to uncover and select a hole as a bona fide adaptation. For example, erudite golf editor Dr. Bradley Klein has observed that the sixth hole at Augusta National bears many of the features of the Redan (the 15th at Berwick), while at least five other holes at Augusta resemble holes on the Old Course at St. Andrews (Figures 5-1 and 5-2).

Unlike his peers Macdonald, Raynor, and Banks, Augusta National designer Alister Mackenzie is not known for his adaptations of classics, but, as Klein observes, he practiced this form of architec-

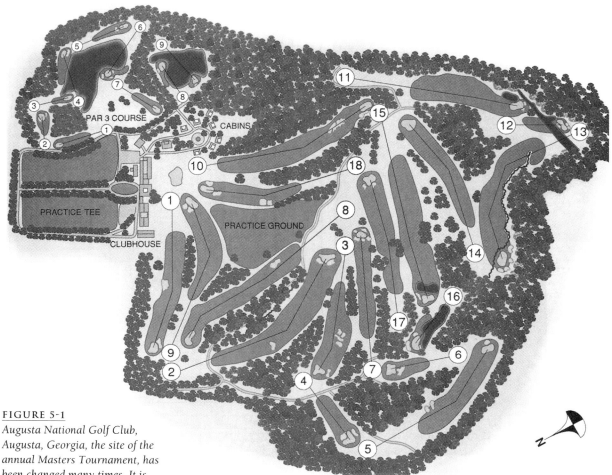

FIGURE 5-1
Augusta National Golf Club, Augusta, Georgia, the site of the annual Masters Tournament, has been changed many times. It is therefore difficult to compare the present layout shown in a recent yardage booklet to the original. Most feel it gets better and better. (Copyright © DuCam Marketing (UK) Ltd.)

ture, albeit in a more subtle manner. Time and abundant modifications required to accommodate Augusta's world-famous tournament have obscured these resemblances still further. That explains why the adaptation of classic holes on this course has largely escaped the attention of golf architects and writers who cover the profession. It also demonstrates precisely why it can be difficult, at best, to identify adaptations and therefore to name true classics.

Undaunted by vagueness, we have set out to present the best possible study of the intriguing and important subject of adaptations of classic holes. At times, we wondered how many adaptations were required to make a hole a classic and how precise these adaptations must be to count. Seeking answers, we researched all sources of records; we visited old and new golf courses on both sides of the "pond"; and we tapped the memories of golf writers and our own col-

CLASSIC GOLF HOLE DESIGN

FIVE HOLES AT AUGUSTA NATIONAL RESEMBLE CLASSICS ON THE OLD COURSE AT ST. ANDREWS

According to the golf writer Dr. Bradley Klein, five other holes at Augusta National resemble (or once did) those on the Old Course: the 205-yard 4th with bunkers sited similarly to "Cockleshell" and "Strath" on the 11th (High-In); the 365-yard 7th, with features similar to the 18th, although greenside bunkers have been added, which mask the resemblance; the 405-yard 14th with similarities to the 6th and the 17th; where the green is said to be a reverse of the green on the 14th (Long); and the 435-yard 17th resembling the Road hole, but with trees emulating the stationmaster's house (other course architects have also used trees when replicating this hole) (see Figures 4-13, 4-14, 4-16, 5-57, 6-54A, and 5-3 through 5-6).

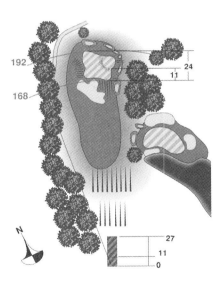

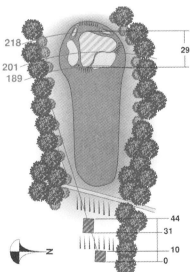

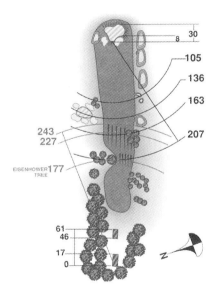

FIGURE 5-2

Although there are resemblances to the 15th at North Berwick, Scotland, the classic Redan, the critical angle between centerline and green axis is missing on hole 6 at Augusta National Golf Club, Augusta, Georgia. For the practiced eye, there is still a vague resemblance to the Reverse Redan, despite modifications since designer Alister Mackenzie's day. (Copyright © DuCam Marketing (UK) Ltd.)

FIGURE 5-3

Comparing the bunkering on the fourth hole at Augusta National Golf Club, Augusta, Georgia, to the Eden is now a stretch, though there were many similarities at one time. (Copyright © DuCam Marketing (UK) Ltd.)

FIGURE 5-4

Comparing the 17th hole at Augusta National Golf Club, Augusta, Georgia, which has no buildings and no road, to the Road at the Old Course at St. Andrews, Scotland, is a difficult task. This hole is straight, whereas the classic Road plays as a slight dogleg. (Copyright © DuCam Marketing (UK) Ltd.)

ARE HOLES AT CYPRESS POINT ADAPTATIONS?

Course architect Seth Raynor was selected to design Cypress Point on the Monterey Peninsula but died before his plans were complete. Alister Mackenzie replaced him. It has been speculated that Raynor's layout would have included the Alps, Biarritz, Eden, and others he invariably used, with his obvious style. Amid the sandy setting of Cypress Point, that style might not have been apparent. Yet it is possible that several of Mackenzie's holes are, in fact, adaptations of classics, but rendered in a very subtle manner.

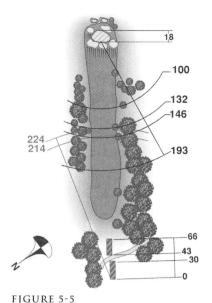

FIGURE 5-5

With bunkering at the green, the seventh hole at Augusta National Golf Club, Augusta, Georgia, is now quite different from the 18th on the Old Course, and there is now no Valley of Sin at Augusta. (Copyright © DuCam Marketing (UK) Ltd.)

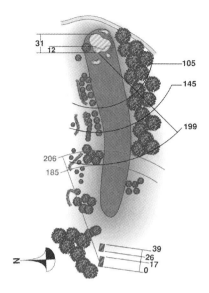

FIGURE 5-6

Comparisons are hard to make, but the 14th hole at Augusta National Golf Club, Augusta, Georgia, is said to include features of three holes on the Old Course at St. Andrews, Scotland. (Copyright © DuCam Marketing (UK) Ltd.)

leagues. We uncovered dozens of potential classics, some of which truly qualify, some with characteristics that might qualify them, and many that walked the line between rough interpretation and readily recognizable.

Always we were at risk in our adventure because golf holes change over the years due to natural forces or, as at Augusta National, the constant yearning of our species for perfection and something newer and more challenging. Designers also change the length of holes, alter their sequence in the round, add hazards, delete hazards, and so on. In addition, maintenance practices such as topdressing can elevate green heights, and mowing practices can change the size and shape of nearly every feature on the course. Trees are planted and mature while distant vistas are changed by development or other forces. Despite the sedentary and peaceful appearance of a golf course, it is a living, changing landscape. That adds to the challenge of identifying adaptations and classic golf holes.

Our original list of a few dozen categories of classic golf holes or features grew into a list of thousands. This proliferation occurred despite constant and ruthless elimination as our research continued. Yet it showed that every golf hole owes something to history. Eventually, we selected only a handful as true classics. All those we selected have, in one way or another, profoundly influenced the architecture of the playing fields of the game. A review of the criteria we considered in naming our selections is necessary to fully understand the exact merits of each classic golf hole and the reasons for its inclusion here.

Classic Sites, Routings, and Extremes

Searching for the classics, we were forced to decide whether we were looking for classic courses, holes, or features. Certainly, there are classic courses, the two best known being the Old Course at St. Andrews and the National Golf Links on Long Island. Yet several of the heathland courses, for example, Sunningdale and Wentworth, can be considered classics, as can the landmark courses of America. And there are classic features galore. Three outstanding examples are the Hell bunker on the 14th and the Valley of Sin on the 18th at St. Andrews, together with the Cardinal bunker on Prestwick's 3rd.

As described in this and the next chapter, we focused our search for the most part on classic holes. We often found that a classic feature was part of a classic hole, so it is necessary to review categories before focusing on individual holes.

Classic Sites

We decided to present the following settings as "classic sites": true linksland; coastal bluffs and other coastlines that are not truly links; open meadows; pastures; prairies; and foothills, both timbered and open, together with valley and parkland (land that is sparsely but not heavily wooded). While these describe the classic sites of golf courses, it should be noted that, by the end of the 20th century, golf courses were being developed on other, far less traditional sites. These include town dumps, quarries, and other derelict lands that are not suitable for golf but must be modified.

DESIGNING FOR 18

Some believe that two designers, one a Scot and one a Canadian of Scottish descent, considered it a cardinal sin to play only 9 holes when 18 were available. Donald Ross and Stanley Thompson were among those who often went against the trend. Ross and Thompson, it has been said, made it one of their design objectives to have the ninth as far from the clubhouse as possible so that golfers would have to play 18 as they headed home. Nevertheless, we suspect that their paramount reason for doing so was to gain the best holes from the existing terrain rather than compromising great holes by favoring two loops of nine.

Classic Routings

As discussed in Chapter 1, 9 or 18 holes are the standard for golf courses, although there were 3-, 6-, and 12-hole routings. Early examples of courses with varying numbers of holes included Bruntsfield Links with 6, North Berwick with 7, Gullane with 13 (later 15), Musselburgh with 5 to 7, and Montrose with an amazing 25. In fact, the Old Course had 22 holes before two were eliminated in 1764. (Holes were played out and in; hence the elimination of two reduced the total number by four.) It wasn't until 1764 when the Old Course finally evolved into 18 holes that the standard was set.

The practice of designing two loops of nine holes each (both starting at and returning to the clubhouse) may have begun in India at the Royal Calcutta Golf Club as early as 1829. By the last half of the 19th century, numerous examples existed of courses with the two 9-hole-loop design. These included an early version of Royal Montreal, Australian Golf Club (Figure 5-7), Royal County Down (Figure 5-8), and Royal Selangor in Malaysia (Figure 5-9). While returning nines have, in general, become the standard, it is a certainty that some layouts would have had more character if the designer had not been charged with bringing the ninth back to the clubhouse. (The convenience for golfers who want to play just nine holes is perhaps foremost among the reasons for this common requirement. But it must be noted that the constant need for golfers to return "home" for reasons of their own encourages it.)

Other early golf courses of note with two 9-hole loops include Glenview Country Club in Illinois (Figure 5-10), designed in 1904 by

FIGURE 5-7
The Australian Golf Club, Sydney, Australia, has the returning nines with the 7th and 11th holes also returning close to the clubhouse. (Copyright © DuCam Marketing (UK) Ltd.)

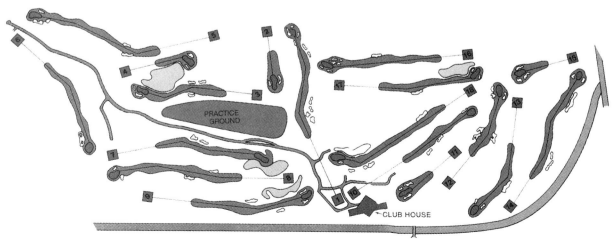

CLASSIC GOLF HOLE DESIGN

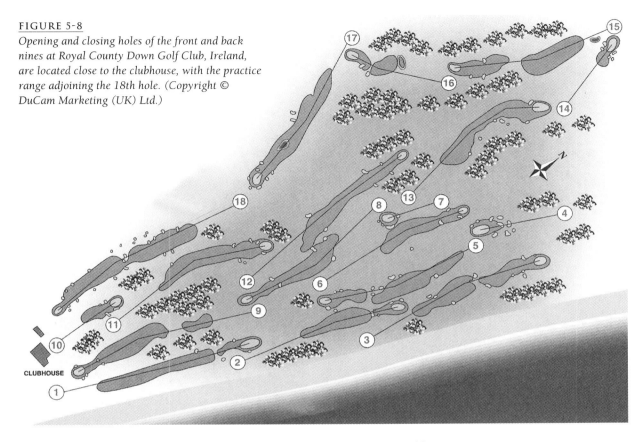

FIGURE 5-8
Opening and closing holes of the front and back nines at Royal County Down Golf Club, Ireland, are located close to the clubhouse, with the practice range adjoining the 18th hole. (Copyright © DuCam Marketing (UK) Ltd.)

H. J. Tweedie, and Burlington Country Club in Vermont, designed by Donald Ross with Walter B. Hatch in 1924.

Also of interest, Carnoustie Golf Links in Scotland, originally designed in part by Allan Robertson, features two 18-hole loops working out of one clubhouse (Figure 5-11). There are also examples of courses with three 9-hole loops from one clubhouse. Two include Prince's Golf Club in England, designed by three different golf course architects (Figure 5-12), and Stratton Mountain Country Club in Vermont by Geoffrey Cornish and Bill Robinson (Figure 5-13). Accommodating three loops requires pushing opening tees and finishing greens farther from the clubhouse for safety's sake. Yet it is not unusual in contemporary developments.

Consecutive Par-3s and Par-5s

While Chapter 1 introduced the subject of back-to-back par-3s and par-5s, it's been a rule of thumb for at least several decades that this practice should be avoided. Fortunately, true artists ignore such gen-

FIGURE 5-9

At Royal Selangor Golf Club, Kuala Lampur, Malaysia, holes 1, 9, and 18 are close to the clubhouse. However, the site shape required that the 10th hole be more remote. (Courtesy Octopus Publishing Group Ltd.)

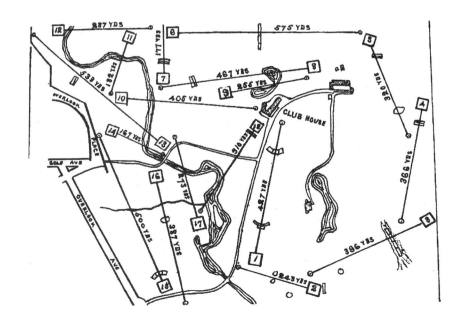

FIGURE 5-10

The concept of returning nines was utilized early at the venerable Glenview Country Club, Glenville, Illinois. (Courtesy of Tree Wolf Productions.)

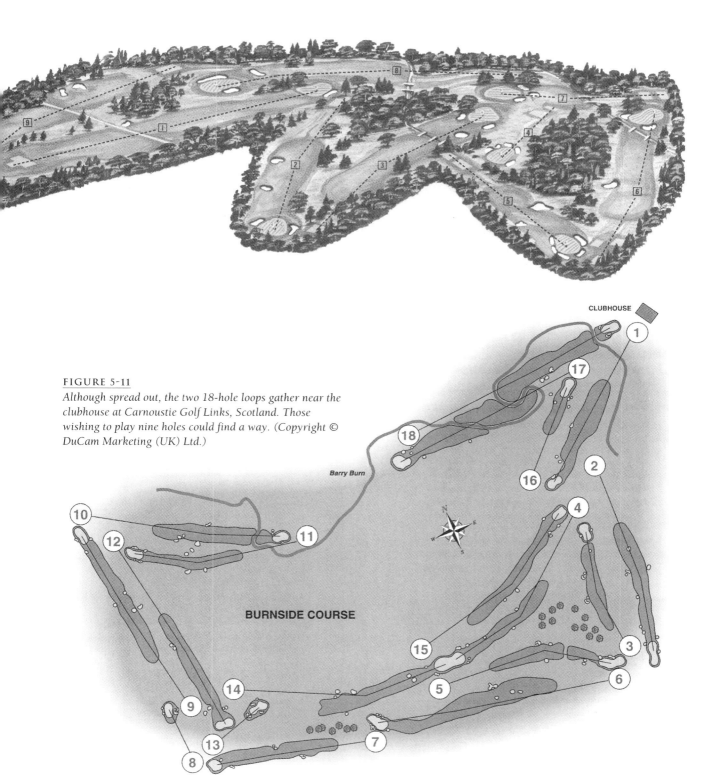

FIGURE 5-11
Although spread out, the two 18-hole loops gather near the clubhouse at Carnoustie Golf Links, Scotland. Those wishing to play nine holes could find a way. (Copyright © DuCam Marketing (UK) Ltd.)

CLUBHOUSE

Barry Burn

BURNSIDE COURSE

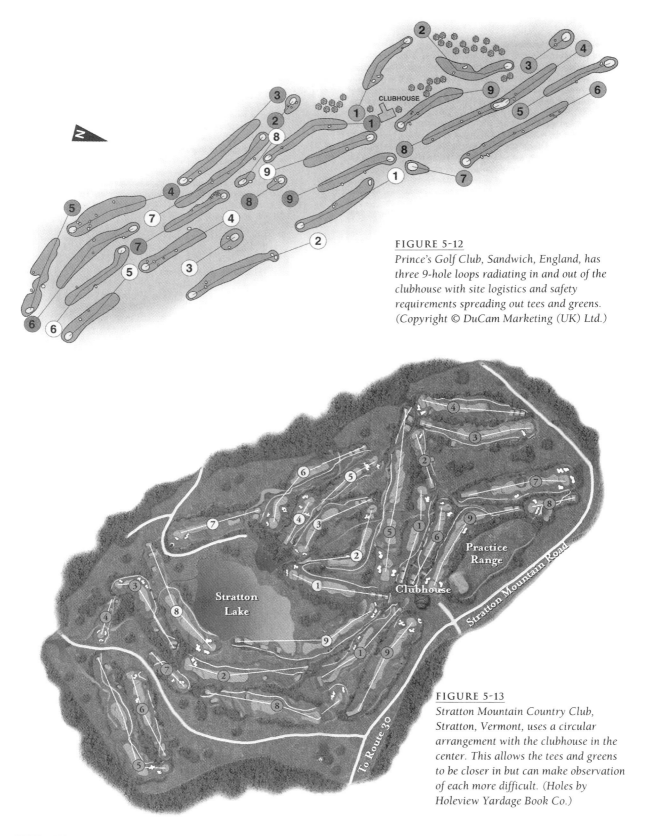

CLUBHOUSE

FIGURE 5-12
Prince's Golf Club, Sandwich, England, has three 9-hole loops radiating in and out of the clubhouse with site logistics and safety requirements spreading out tees and greens. (Copyright © DuCam Marketing (UK) Ltd.)

Stratton Lake

Practice Range

Clubhouse

Stratton Mountain Road

To Route 30

FIGURE 5-13
Stratton Mountain Country Club, Stratton, Vermont, uses a circular arrangement with the clubhouse in the center. This allows the tees and greens to be closer in but can make observation of each more difficult. (Holes by Holeview Yardage Book Co.)

CLASSIC GOLF HOLE DESIGN

eralized rules if they in any way compromise their compositions. Course designers, being artists, have proven on many occasions they won't hesitate to use consecutive par-3s and par-5s if doing so will result in superior holes.

Some examples of consecutive par-3s and par-5s include:

- Royal Lytham and St. Annes in England: Holes 6 and 7, opening around 1886, played at 486 and 551 yards, respectively, with their directions varying by about 45 degrees (Figure 5-14).
- Royal Antwerp in Belgium by Willie Park, Jr.: Holes 14 and 15 played at 486 and 551 yards, respectively, but with a 90-degree difference in orientation (hole 14 is a dogleg, while hole 15 is a straightaway).
- Royal West Norfolk Golf Club in England: Opened in 1891, this course sported two consecutive par-5s: holes 7 and 8, with lengths of 477 and 485 yards, respectively. These holes varied

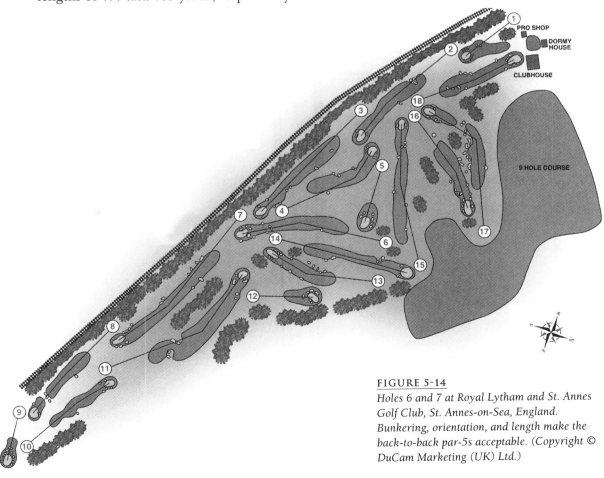

FIGURE 5-14
Holes 6 and 7 at Royal Lytham and St. Annes Golf Club, St. Annes-on-Sea, England. Bunkering, orientation, and length make the back-to-back par-5s acceptable. (Copyright © DuCam Marketing (UK) Ltd.)

in direction by some 45 degrees, and there was little resemblance in playing characteristics, as hole 8 was a target-style hole, while hole 7 was quite open.

- Ballybunion in Ireland: There are two consecutive par-5s on this course, built around 1896. Holes 4 and 5 vary by only 4 yards but are oriented at much different angles.

Some of the better-known consecutives in the United States today include Baltusrol's 17th and 18th; Seminole's 14th and 15th (Figure 5-15); Riviera's 1st and 2nd; Cherry Hills' (Denver) 17th and 18th (Figure 5-16); and Town and Country Club's (St. Paul) three par-5s: the 15th, 16th, and 17th (Figure 5-17).

Two courses that stand out for the quality of their consecutives and for taking the format a step farther are Prince's Golf Club in Sandwich, England (see Figure 5-12), and Cypress Point on the Monterey Peninsula in California (see Figure 1-8). Prince's had a pair of consecutive par-5s, the 1st and 2nd and the 14th and 15th, until golf architect Howard Swan changed the numbering of the existing layout when he added nine holes to this venerable layout. Despite a limited variation in yardage between these holes, the difference in orientation and other features distinguish each. Cypress Point offers two consecutive par-5s and two consecutive par-3s. The long holes, 5 and 6, are 490 and 521 yards, respectively. They are oriented at nearly 90 degrees

FIGURE 5-15
With entirely different orientations on holes 14 and 15, and with 15 a double fairway, there is not much chance of monotony on back-to-back par-5s at Seminole Golf Club, Palm Beach, Florida. (Courtesy Octopus Publishing Group Ltd.)

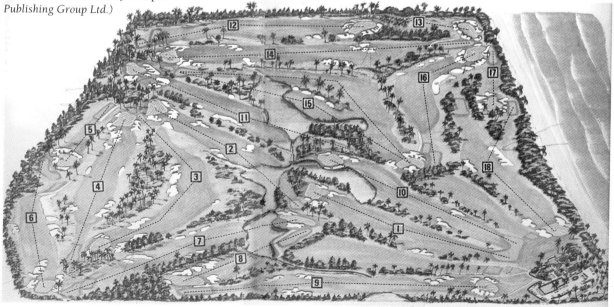

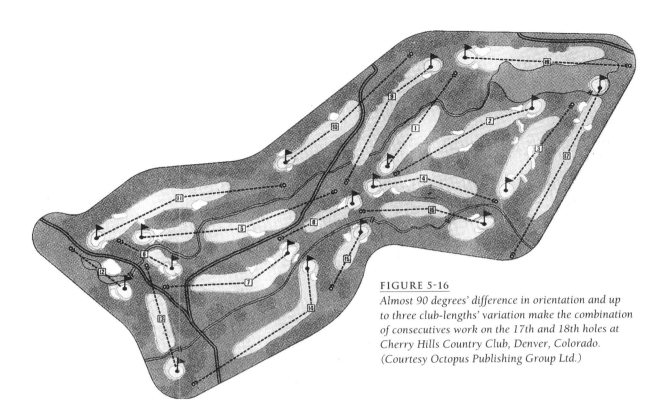

FIGURE 5-16
Almost 90 degrees' difference in orientation and up to three club-lengths' variation make the combination of consecutives work on the 17th and 18th holes at Cherry Hills Country Club, Denver, Colorado. (Courtesy Octopus Publishing Group Ltd.)

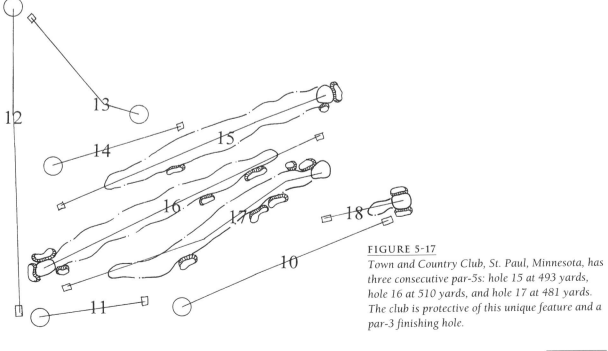

FIGURE 5-17
Town and Country Club, St. Paul, Minnesota, has three consecutive par-5s: hole 15 at 493 yards, hole 16 at 510 yards, and hole 17 at 481 yards. The club is protective of this unique feature and a par-3 finishing hole.

from each other. The consecutive one-shotters at Cyprus Point vary greatly in length (139 yards and 233 yards) and are oriented some 60 degrees apart.

Opening Par-3s

Players and architects have long condemned the use of a par-3 as the opening hole. Many feel strongly that a one-shotter slows play; in practice, it often does. Disadvantages then follow: most notably a crowd of impatient golfers at the first tee. (At daily-fee courses, golfers driving to the pro shop may see the backlog building on the first tee and leave to find a less crowded layout.) Yet par-3s are not the only holes susceptible to slow play. Exceptionally short par-4s that can be reached from the tee by long hitters and short par-5s that force those going for the green in two to wait for the putting surface to clear can have a similar effect on play. What's more, while a par-3 first hole may tend to hold up play on the first tee, architects have observed that it can lead to a more even flow on subsequent holes.

We found a number of courses with opening par-3s. In fact, a par-3 designed by one of the authors at the private Brooklake Country Club (Figures 5-18A and 5-18B) in New Jersey has proven to be a fine starting hole despite a carry over water. It evens out play on the holes that follow. Other opening par-3s can be found in England at West Cornwall (229 yards) and Hayling (189 yards), while La Moye Golf Club in the Channel Islands has a 165-yard starting hole, and the widely known starting hole at Royal Lytham and St. Annes is a par-3 (Figures 5-19 and 5-20). In 1891, Muirfield, originally designed by Old Tom Morris, had an opening par-3 that was altered around 1920 to speed play.

It is more common to see a par-3 tenth than a par-3 first hole, although players often start on the back side on busy days. Committees have also frequently and permanently switched the order of the nine-hole loops after the architect has completed the project. There are numerous par-3 tenth holes in the world of golf. One of the best known in the United States can be found at Prairie Dunes in Hutchinson, Kansas (Figure 5-21), where Press Maxwell added nine holes in 1957 to his father Perry's original nine. Abroad, Dick Wilson's Lagunita Country Club in Venezuela, built in 1956, has an outstanding par-3 tenth. Par-3 tenth holes are, in fact, common.

Southport and Ainsdale Golf Club in Lancashire, England (Figure 5-22), has par-3s on both its first and tenth holes. Obviously, the

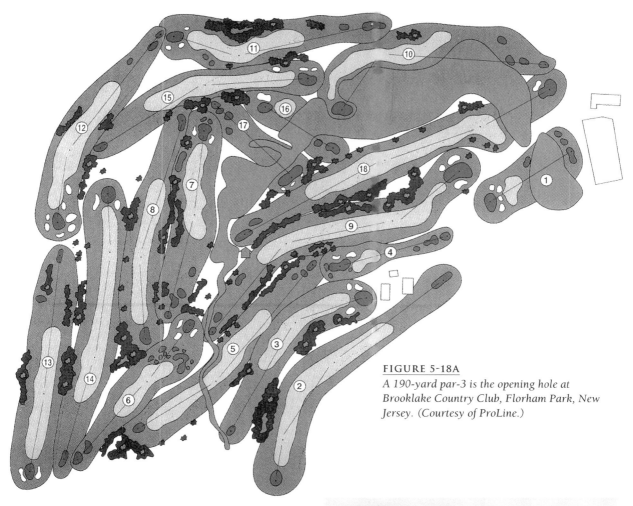

FIGURE 5-18A
A 190-yard par-3 is the opening hole at Brooklake Country Club, Florham Park, New Jersey. (Courtesy of ProLine.)

FIGURE 5-18B
A first hole with water and an array of four pot bunkers at Brooklake Country Club, Florham Park, New Jersey, gets the golfer off to an interesting start. (Courtesy of ProLine.)

BROAD CRITERIA FOR CLASSIC GOLF HOLES

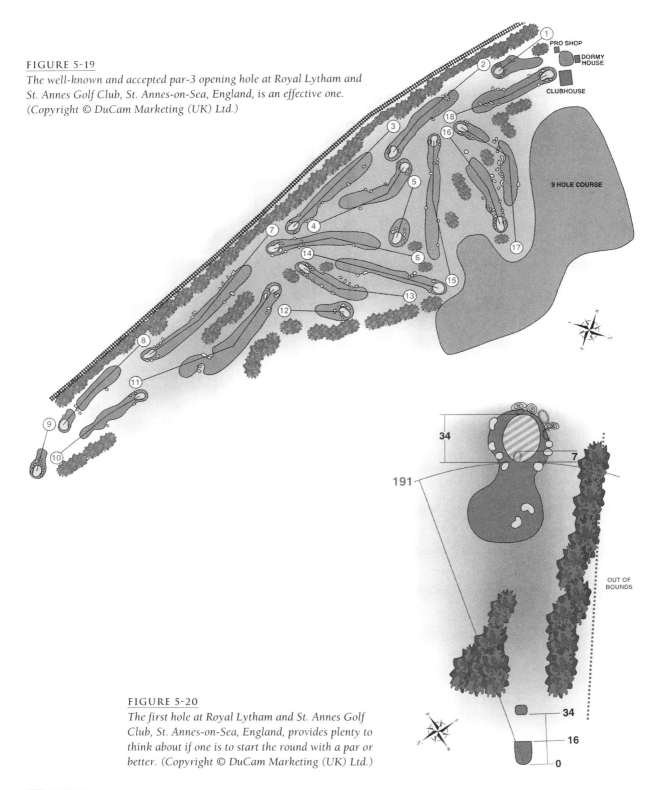

FIGURE 5-19

FIGURE 5-19

The well-known and accepted par-3 opening hole at Royal Lytham and
St. Annes Golf Club, St. Annes-on-Sea, England, is an effective one.
(Copyright © DuCam Marketing (UK) Ltd.)

PRO SHOP

DORMY HOUSE

CLUBHOUSE

9 HOLE COURSE

FIGURE 5-20

The first hole at Royal Lytham and St. Annes Golf
Club, St. Annes-on-Sea, England, provides plenty to
think about if one is to start the round with a par or
better. (Copyright © DuCam Marketing (UK) Ltd.)

OUT OF
BOUNDS

CLASSIC GOLF HOLE DESIGN

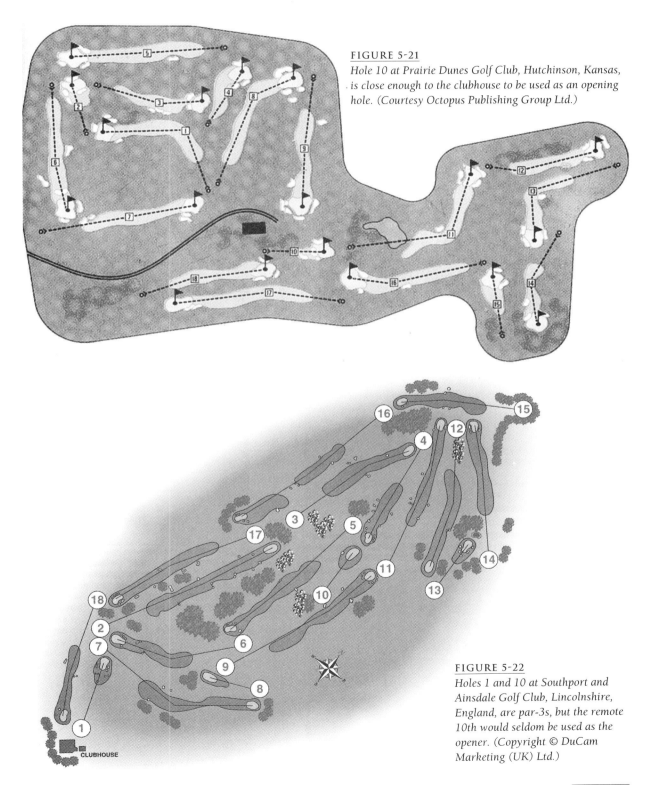

FIGURE 5-21

Hole 10 at Prairie Dunes Golf Club, Hutchinson, Kansas, is close enough to the clubhouse to be used as an opening hole. (Courtesy Octopus Publishing Group Ltd.)

FIGURE 5-22

Holes 1 and 10 at Southport and Ainsdale Golf Club, Lincolnshire, England, are par-3s, but the remote 10th would seldom be used as the opener. (Copyright © DuCam Marketing (UK) Ltd.)

BROAD CRITERIA FOR CLASSIC GOLF HOLES

WINNERS OF EARLY OPENS BECAME LEADING COURSE DESIGNERS

Reviewing the leaders of the early opens, one sees that nearly all were or became leading course designers, including Willie Park, Sr., Tom Morris, Sr., Mungo Park, Willie Fernie, Willie Park, Jr., and Harry Vardon.

designer of the first nine in 1906 (the famous James Braid) and the designer of the second nine in 1922 (the less well known James Steer) were unconcerned by par-3 starting holes, but the tenth at this course is located almost a thousand yards from the clubhouse and would be barely suitable as a starting hole. Back in America, the Wachusett Country Club (Massachusetts) quite intentionally added an opening par-3 to its Donald Ross course during an in-house renovation project. It survived for decades but was eventually altered. Unlike par-3 tenth holes, opening par-3s are not common, but neither are they rare, and many have commendable attributes.

Positioning a par-3 as the lead hole brings both risk and reward for the architect, the club, and the golfer. Our study reveals that the practice of having par-3 first and tenth holes was more common prior to World War II and has since fallen off in popularity, leading us to believe that experience proved too many problems arise because of them.

Crossing Holes

Perhaps not surprisingly, holes that cross one another are uncommon today. The best known cross in existence today is probably that of the 7th and 11th on the Old Course at St. Andrews (Figure 5-23), a crossing that dates far back into history and is now known to golfers from every continent. Crossing holes were once very common along the eastern seaboard of the United States, and fairly common elsewhere in the country. Such a design saved space and decreased the acreage of turfgrass that needed to be maintained. However, by the beginning of the 20th century, with the arrival of the hard-core ball, more crowded courses, and an increasingly litigious society, many crossing holes were abandoned.

Looking back to the last half of the 19th century, we see that Prestwick Golf Club (Figure 5-24), with its 12 holes, was cross-routed entirely until around 1882. This demonstrates that crossing holes were not found simply on lesser known, more rudimentary courses; Prestwick was the venue of the first British Open Championship in 1860 and hosted it annually until 1872. Playing the 12 holes three times was at one period considered an official round.

Other examples of crossing holes in the United Kingdom include:

- Holes 3 and 18 at Elie Golf House Club, as revised by Tom Morris in 1895 (Figure 5-25)

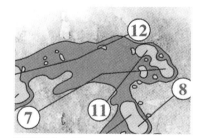

FIGURE 5-23
If the earliest known golf course has crossing holes (the 7th crosses the 11th), can they be all bad? Although acceptable at the Old Course at St. Andrews, Scotland, for centuries, the idea has almost died out. But there are exceptions. (Copyright © DuCam Marketing (UK) Ltd.)

CLASSIC GOLF HOLE DESIGN

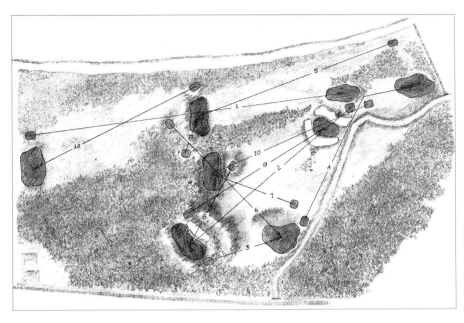

FIGURE 5-24
The 12 holes at Prestwick Golf Club, Prestwick, Scotland, were cross-routed from 1851 to 1882. Cross routing was common in those days.

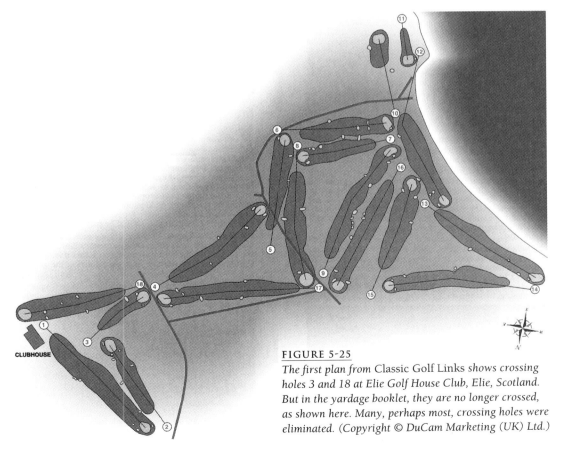

FIGURE 5-25
The first plan from Classic Golf Links shows crossing holes 3 and 18 at Elie Golf House Club, Elie, Scotland. But in the yardage booklet, they are no longer crossed, as shown here. Many, perhaps most, crossing holes were eliminated. (Copyright © DuCam Marketing (UK) Ltd.)

- Holes 5 and 15 at Aberdovey in Wales, opening in the 1880s
- Holes 9, 10, and 11 at Crail Golfing Society, originally opened in 1786 (Figures 5-26)
- Holes 2 and 10 at Royal Jersey in the Channel Islands
- Holes 4 and 9 at Moray Golf Club in Scotland (Figure 5-27)
- Holes 3 and 16 at Machrihanish Golf Club in Scotland (Figure 5-28)

In the United States in Oakland, California, there are two courses with crossing holes. One is the Sequoyah Country Club, revised in 1921 by Herbert Fowler, with holes 15 and 16 crossing (Figure 5-29). The second is Claremont Country Club, discussed below.

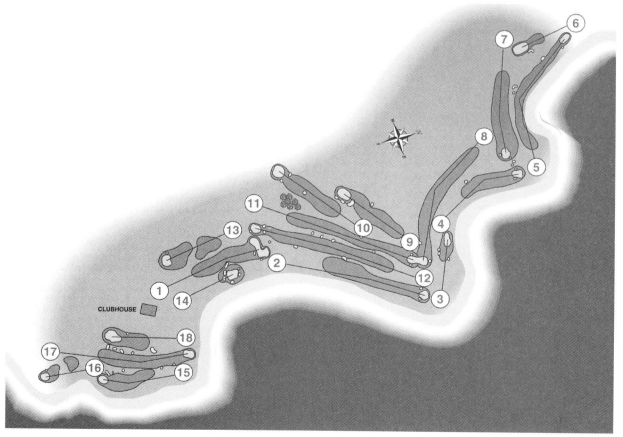

FIGURE 5-26
At Crail Golfing Society, Scotland, there's a difference between the original routing as shown in the book Classic Golf Links *and a recent yardage booklet. The changes in holes 9, 10, and 11 are substantial in order to uncross them. (Copyright © DuCam Marketing (UK) Ltd.)*

CLASSIC GOLF HOLE DESIGN

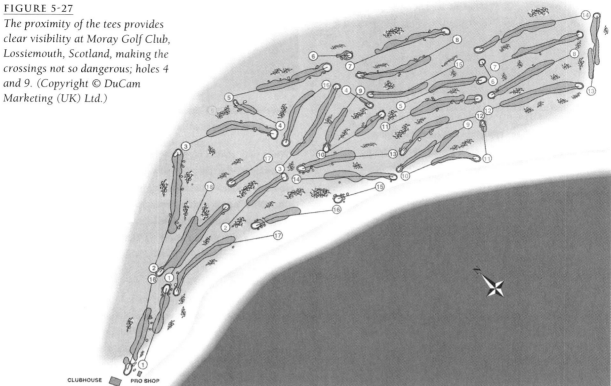

FIGURE 5-27
The proximity of the tees provides clear visibility at Moray Golf Club, Lossiemouth, Scotland, making the crossings not so dangerous; holes 4 and 9. (Copyright © DuCam Marketing (UK) Ltd.)

CLUBHOUSE PRO SHOP

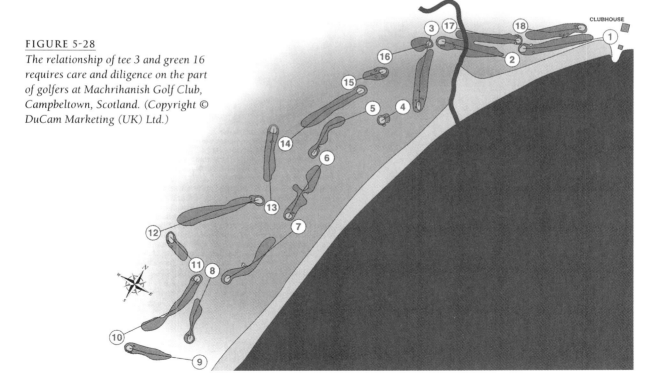

FIGURE 5-28
The relationship of tee 3 and green 16 requires care and diligence on the part of golfers at Machrihanish Golf Club, Campbeltown, Scotland. (Copyright © DuCam Marketing (UK) Ltd.)

CLUBHOUSE

BROAD CRITERIA FOR CLASSIC GOLF HOLES

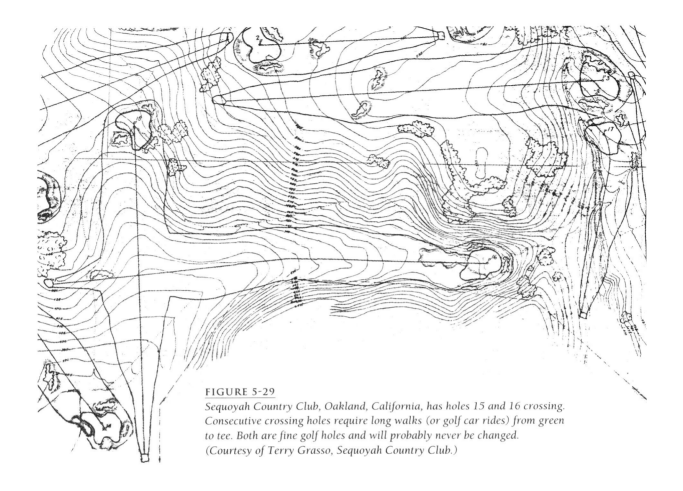

FIGURE 5-29
Sequoyah Country Club, Oakland, California, has holes 15 and 16 crossing. Consecutive crossing holes require long walks (or golf car rides) from green to tee. Both are fine golf holes and will probably never be changed. (Courtesy of Terry Grasso, Sequoyah Country Club.)

Not all crossing holes are simple examples of two fairways intersecting each other.

- In Ireland, Lahinch Golf Club, opened in 1893, has hole 18 crossing holes 5 and 6 (Figure 5-30).
- At Ballybunion, the shot from the fourth tee plays over the third green.
- A nine-hole municipal course in Ritzville, Washington, developed in the 1940s, has two crossings (Figure 5-31).
- Claremont Country Club has holes 8 and 18 crossing, while hole 7 crosses both holes 4 and 5 (Figure 5-32). This club has devised an interesting way to control traffic and to avoid accidents. The player on the highest numbered hole has the right-of-way. This method has been quite successful to date.
- Bellerive Country Club, designed by Robert Trent Jones, Sr., in 1960 (Figure 5-33), has an alternate tee for hole 3. When used, the tee shot from hole 12 plays over it.

CLASSIC GOLF HOLE DESIGN

FIGURE 5-30

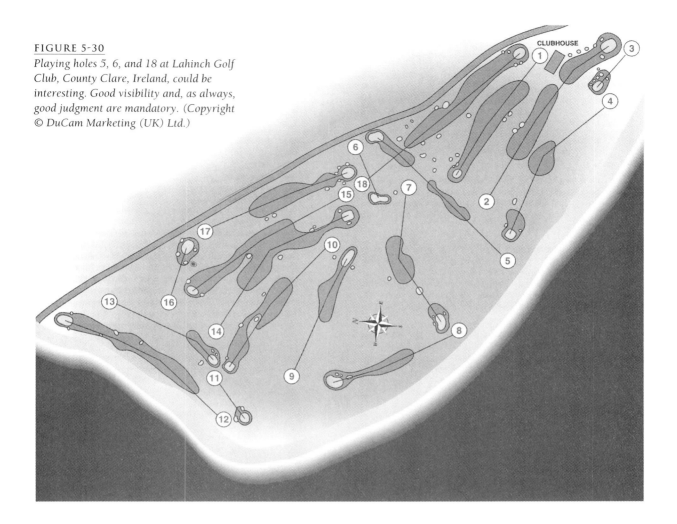

FIGURE 5-30
Playing holes 5, 6, and 18 at Lahinch Golf Club, County Clare, Ireland, could be interesting. Good visibility and, as always, good judgment are mandatory. (Copyright © DuCam Marketing (UK) Ltd.)

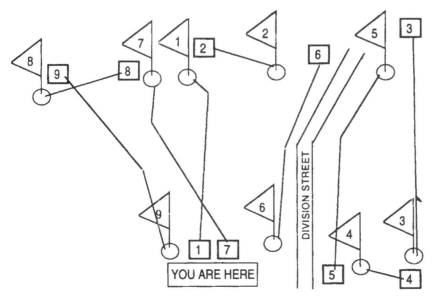

FIGURE 5-31
Designed in-house shortly after World War II, the nine-hole municipal course in Ritzville, Washington, has prospered despite two crossings. (Courtesy of Ritzville Golf Course.)

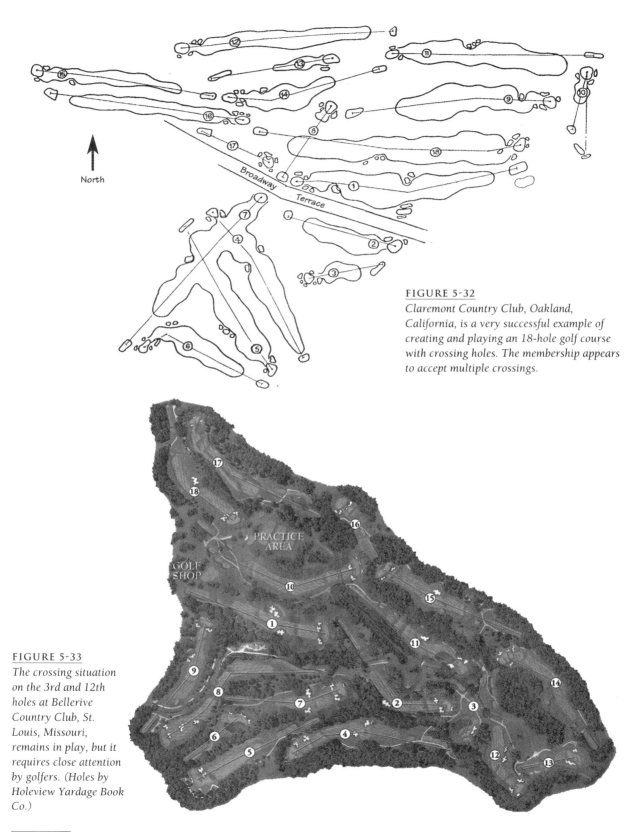

Broadway

Terrace

FIGURE 5-32
Claremont Country Club, Oakland, California, is a very successful example of creating and playing an 18-hole golf course with crossing holes. The membership appears to accept multiple crossings.

PRACTICE AREA

GOLF SHOP

FIGURE 5-33
The crossing situation on the 3rd and 12th holes at Bellerive Country Club, St. Louis, Missouri, remains in play, but it requires close attention by golfers. (Holes by Holeview Yardage Book Co.)

All the foregoing courses have endured and compensated for a lack of space. Yet, with more people playing golf and the attendant liability, the concept of crossing holes is probably doomed for the foreseeable future. One notable exception is on estate courses (par-3 and otherwise), where play is restricted to the owner's guests and where a necessary objective is to make limited space suffice. It is noteworthy, too, that Alister Mackenzie's popular Jockey Club par-3 layout at San Isidro in Argentina included several shots over greens to other holes.

Extremes (Length)

For better or worse, ours is a species prone to experimenting, and course designers are certainly not immune from the urge to achieve something different and hopefully better. Indeed, it is their desire to exceed perfection to produce the outstanding. Thus, in certain cases, once-extreme holes have become classics.

One way golf architects have pushed past the status quo is in the constant lengthening of golf courses. At one extreme is the world's longest course: the famous International Golf Club, Bolton, Massachusetts (Figure 5-34). Originally designed by Geoffrey Cornish, the layout was later modified by Robert Trent Jones and his son, Rees, and again by Brian Silva and Mark Mungeam with help from Cornish. Ini-

FIGURE 5-34

Opened in 1959 as the world's longest golf course, Surprenant National, Bolton, Massachusetts, designed by Geoffrey Cornish, has gone through several names and is now International Golf Club. It has preserved its avowed purpose as the world's longest course by periodic lengthening. The originator and original owner, Albert H. Surprenant, felt as early as 1953 that length was the "wave of the future."

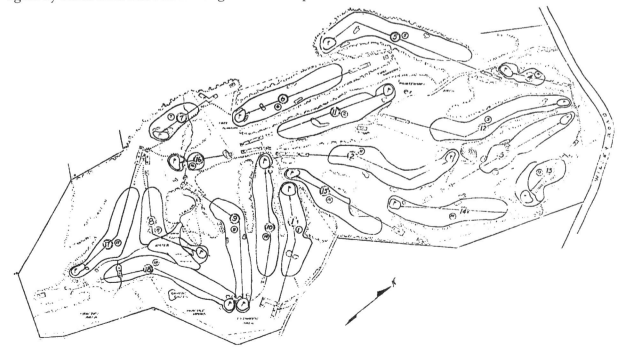

tially, a major objective at International (then Runaway Brook) was simply to create the world's longest course. We suspect this was because the avowed philosophy of the owner, Albert H. Surprenant, inventor and manufacturer, tended toward endless experimenting. He was heard to say that if Americans had remained in the middle of the road, they would still be living in a few colonies on the East Coast. His long course was a clear success, and though there were several sets of tees with shorter yardages, many golfers wanted to try the world's longest course. They played from the long tees, then called the "tigers." These long yardages still exist and, in fact, have been extended from the original 8005 yards to the present 8325 yards. (Shorter tees are available that play to 7138, 6547, 5742, and 5163 yards.) Table 5-1 shows the present International Long Course card.

On the other hand, extremely short holes have been created. Some examples of both long and short have become potential classics. Eminent writer Rich Skyzinski, in a well-illustrated piece, describes several such holes. In Table 5-2, we have compiled the Skyzinski list and added others.

The length of a golf hole has traditionally been a critically important factor. In fact, it is the largest single factor in determining a hole's

TABLE 5-1
International Golf Club; Pines Course; Long Card

Hole	Yards	Par	Hole	Yards	Par
1	405	4	10	440	4
2	460	4	11	590	5
3	674	5	12	567	4
4	180	3	13	250	3
5	715	5	14	437	4
6	530	4	15	487	4
7	277	3	16	270	3
8	412	4	17	440	4
9	535	4	18	656	5
OUT	4188	36	IN	4137	36
			OUT	4188	36
			TOTAL	8325	72

TABLE 5-2
Extremes Both Short and Long

Hole	Course	Yards	Par	Architect's Rationale
11	Silver Spring Golf Club	120	3	Downhill, this "wisp of a hole" was needed by course architect George Fazio for linkage.
7	Pebble Beach (Figure 5-35)	120	3	Wind plays a major role on this Grant-Neville-Egan hole.
1	Wake Forest Golf Club, Wake Forest, NC	711	5	Once the world's longest par-5, architect Gene Hamm planned it as a marketing tool. Golf tags were available that proclaimed, "I parred the longest par-5 in the world."
12	Meadow Farms Golf Club, south of Washington, DC, in Virginia	841	5	Designed by owner Bill Meadows in the early 1990s, it has been successful in providing publicity.
3	Pawleys Plantation, Pawleys Island, SC (Figure 5-36)	69	3	Opened in 1988, with Jack Nicklaus as architect, this hole has provided a very exacting par-3.
1	La Cantera Golf Club, San Antonio, TX	666	5	A Morrish-Weiskopf course, opened in the 1990s. Tiger Woods reached the green with a driver and a two-iron.
	Lake Chabot Golf Club, Oakland, CA (see Figure 3-2A)	678	6	William Lock, original designer. The hole provides a relatively easy par because it is downhill.
7	Satsuki Golf Club, Sano, Japan	964	5	The rationale for its extreme length is not known, but is suspected to be to achieve the world's longest hole.

FIGURE 5-35
This 1929 photo shows the seventh hole at Pebble Beach Golf Links, Pebble Beach, California, prior to a national championship tournament.

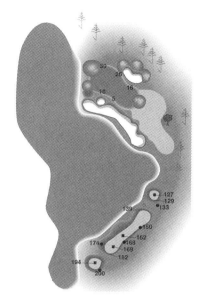

FIGURE 5-36
Many problems must be solved as you play on the complicated par-3 3rd hole at Pawleys Plantation Golf and Country Club, Pawleys Island, South Carolina. (Copyright © Pro's Yardage Caddy, Columbia, SC.)

LENGTHENING HOLES

At the time this book was written, plans are under way to lengthen Augusta National, while several holes on the Old Course at St. Andrews were recently lengthened, as were several at International.

difficulty. Skyzinski includes the following comments on the subject, each offered by prominent members of the American Society of Golf Course Architects:

Bobby Weed: "Length is not the determining factor anymore. . . . Donald Ross created angle turns at 600 feet. Then it went to 700, 750, 800 and now we are at 850. . . . The way to equalize is to tighten the landing areas at 300 yards."

Steve Smyers: "Five hundred yards used to be two good whacks. Now 500 or below is a par-4 for many, unless climate or topography dictate otherwise. I think good architects utilize wind to their advantage." Smyers adds that the game is "changing, maybe fundamentally, and course architecture needs to respond."

Tom Fazio: "If you are playing against the wind, a 375-yard hole can be hard; if you're playing downwind, a 430-yarder can be easy." (Fazio also notes that elevation above sea level affects the tee shot, with the second shot also affected when a wood or long iron is called for.)

Jay Morrish: "You can't make a hole long enough these days." (Hearing of a proposed 841-yard hole, Morrish at first dismissed the idea, saying, "Someone's just trying for some publicity." Thinking for a moment, he added, "Hey, 20 years from now we may not be laughing about that.")

At the start of the new century, length continues to be a subject of concern to course architects. Is International's unabashedly long course the wave of the future? Or will the solution to ever-evolving technology and bigger, stronger players be found in tightening landing areas, using the prevailing wind to the utmost, creating more mounding, and adding other problems around the course, such as enhancing the trend to more exciting approaches, grading fairways into challenging landing areas, and creating strategic patterns through mowing practices? Perhaps the ultimate solution will be found in a combination of all these factors and allowing long "unreachable" holes to fit into a balance that includes short- and medium-length holes.

Extremes (Other Than Length)

Extremes other than length are also apparent when searching for classic golf holes. But they are understandably controversial. However, golf architects have rarely had a problem with such controversy.

Canadian architect Stanley Thompson, for one, felt that one controversial hole on each course would add to its overall interest. History has been kind to many of Thompson's extremes, which include the Devil's Cauldron at Banff Springs (Figure 5-37), the eighteenth at Capilano, the fifth at Jasper Park Golf Course in Alberta, and the ninth at Highland Links on Cape Breton in Nova Scotia. All have been accepted and have become popular. Can any golfer play the Devil's Cauldron successfully and not feel a profound sense of achievement? Yet, in its early days, Thompson was almost censured for creating it, as was Dr. Mackenzie in the first weeks following the opening of the 16th at Cypress Point (Figure 5-38).

Despite these successes, controversial holes can also verge on the ridiculous. (The difference between greatness and foolishness can be surprisingly close.) One hole cited by some as ridiculous was the 14th at Wentworth by the Sea Golf Club in Portsmouth, New Hampshire. Here, one of the authors created a 415-yard par-4 that is intrinsically a Cape hole but with a Redan green that drops off left into the Atlantic Ocean. The fairway, carved out of bedrock, was undulating to an exaggerated degree, with uphill, downhill, and sidehill lies, but with

FIGURE 5-37
The highly publicized eighth hole, called the "Devil's Cauldron," at Banff Springs, Alberta, in the Canadian Rockies, has so awesome a setting that it is hard to concentrate on golf. (Courtesy Octopus Publishing Group Ltd.)

FIGURE 5-38
An X marks the spot for the future 16th green at Cypress Point Golf Club, Pebble Beach, California, which, since its opening in 1918, has become probably the best-known par-3 in the golf world.

three distinct level areas from which fair shots to the green were possible. A combination of golfers not thinking strategically and shots not landing where intended caused many who played the hole to miss these choice areas. The hole was therefore altered after 30 years of play by architect Brian Silva, ironically the partner of its creator. Many said the 14th helped keep the Wentworth Hotel in business because golfers from far and wide wanted to try it (they stayed at the hotel during the economic downturn of the 1970s) (Figure 7-35).

Perhaps this example proves that extreme—even ridiculous—holes can be destined for greatness if the public eventually accepts them. Outstanding examples of those that have become renowned, despite an initial storm of protest, include:

- The fourth hole at Woking Golf Club, England, that features a bunker in the middle of the landing area.
- Mackenzie's finishing hole at Sitwell Park in England, with its wildly undulating putting surface (Figure 5-39). Mackenzie himself said it met with a storm of protest on opening day.
- The aforementioned Stanley Thompson holes, and many others by leading course designers, including (but certainly not limited to) several by Robert Trent Jones and Pete Dye, two of the most renowned of all.
- The "Flower Hole" at Sentry World in Wisconsin, where glorious eye appeal has compensated for other problems.

FIGURE 5-39
The 18th hole at Sitwell Park Golf Club, England, is the epitome of a rolling green. (Courtesy of Geoff Shackelford.)

CLASSIC GOLF HOLE DESIGN

Doglegs, Blind Holes, and Double Fairways

Holes in three specific categories warrant special attention: doglegs, blind holes, and double fairways.

Doglegs

We think that most early holes were generally straight, incorporating few if any profound bends. In the homeland of the game, and in those countries to which it spread, the practice of bending holes gradually became more common as ideal sites became less and less available. In *Classic Golf Links,* Donald Steel writes that the fourth hole at Prestwick, by Old Tom Morris, probably introduced the principle of the dogleg. Other holes at Prestwick are doglegs, though none are 90 degrees (the inside angle). The Cardinal, hole 3, is a double dogleg.

In *Golf Courses of the British Isles*, Bernard Darwin labels Prince's Golf Club in England as "the apotheosis of the dog-legged or round-the-corner holes." At Royal Antwerp in Belgium, architect Tom Simpson introduced doglegs on 11 holes, but none approached 90 degrees. Doglegs nearing 90 degrees, created before World War II, included the 14th at Royal Melbourne (1926) (Figure 5-40), the 3rd at New South Wales (1928), and the 11th at Wack Wack in the Philippines (1933). Club Zur Vahr in Bremen, Germany, has two early dogleg holes, both close to 90 degrees (Figure 5-41), as does Vallescondido Golf Club in Mexico City (4th and 10th) (Figure 5-42). Tryall Golf and Beach Club in Jamaica has two sharp doglegs (holes 3 and 13) dating from 1956, while hole 9 at the Tobago Golf Club in Trinidad and Tobago, holes 16 and 17 at Ballybunion (Figure 5-43), and hole 18 at Royal Dublin (Figures 5-44A and 5-44B) all are close to being right-angle doglegs.

Some short right-angle doglegs tempt a golfer to try to carry the angle. For example, the 17th at Stockbridge Golf Club in the Berkshire Mountains of Massachusetts offers a direct shot of 280-plus yards across out-of-bounds and a woodlot. The carry was attempted (though rarely successfully) a generation ago, but is now nearly impossible owing to a maturing forest (Figure 5-45).

Another type of right-angle dogleg can be seen, among other places, at St. Johnsbury Country Club in Vermont, a Cornish-Havers addition to a Willie and Mungo Park layout. This 350-yard hole is an exciting finish to the round because it demands accurate tee shot

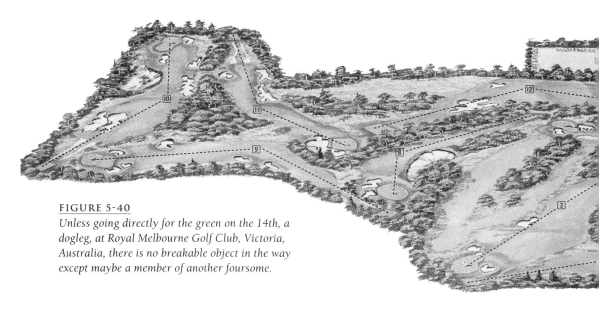

FIGURE 5-40
Unless going directly for the green on the 14th, a dogleg, at Royal Melbourne Golf Club, Victoria, Australia, there is no breakable object in the way except maybe a member of another foursome.

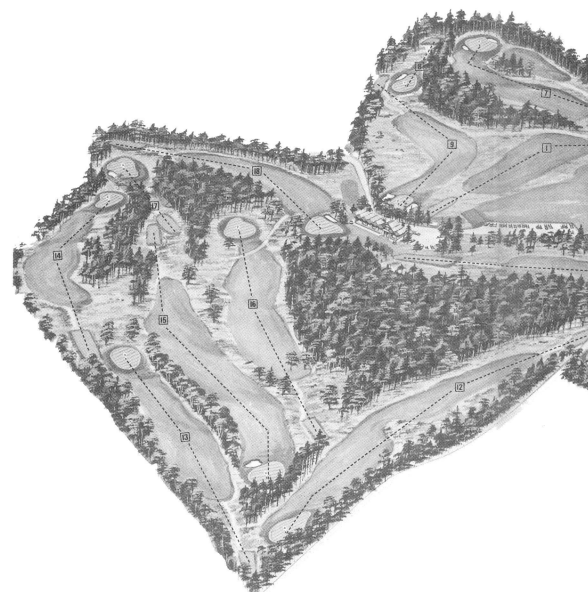

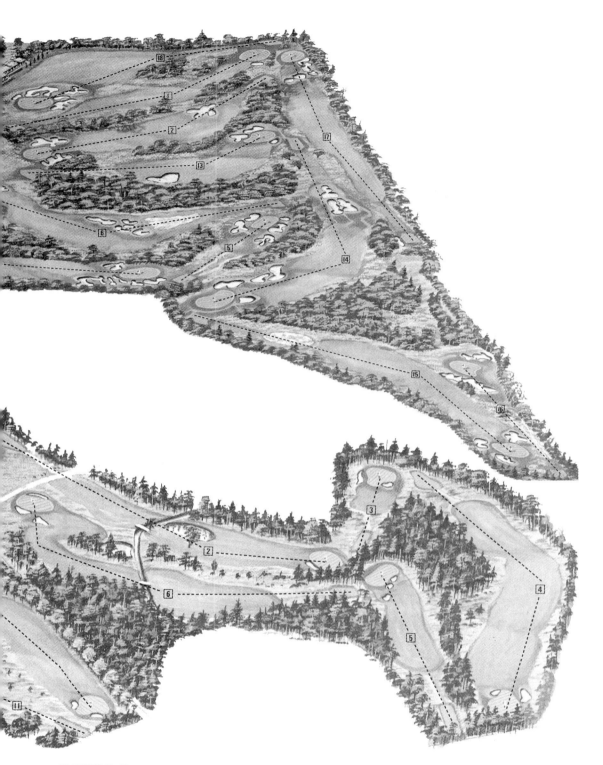

FIGURE 5-41
Two doglegs right out of the box at Club Zur Vahr, Bremen, Germany, can be challenging when you are still a bit cold. Fortunately, they aren't very severe. (Courtesy Octopus Publishing Group Ltd.)

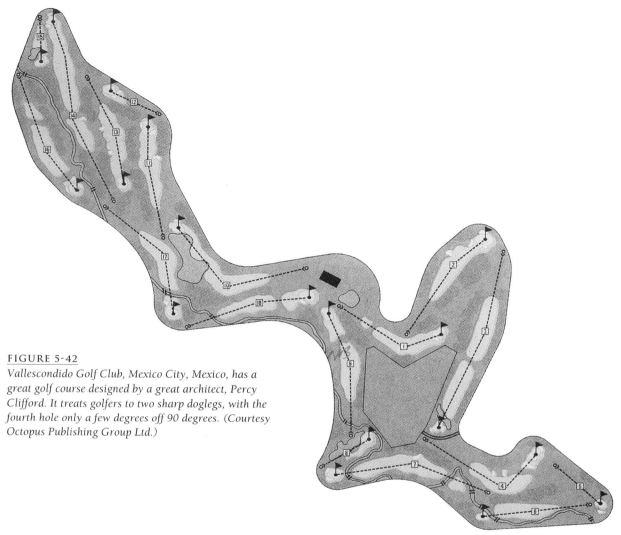

FIGURE 5-42
Vallescondido Golf Club, Mexico City, Mexico, has a great golf course designed by a great architect, Percy Clifford. It treats golfers to two sharp doglegs, with the fourth hole only a few degrees off 90 degrees. (Courtesy Octopus Publishing Group Ltd.)

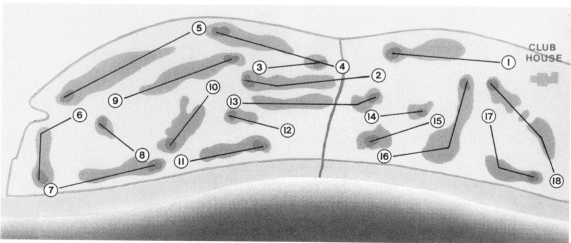

FIGURE 5-43
The 16th and 17th holes at Ballybunion Golf Club, County Kerry, Ireland, are a pair of fairly sharp doglegs set amidst the usual links environment. (Courtesy of Chrysalis Books.)

CLASSIC GOLF HOLE DESIGN

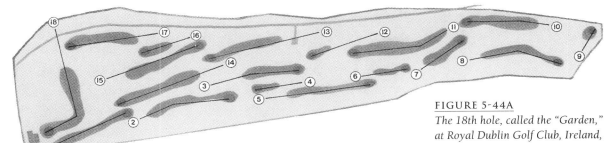

FIGURE 5-44A

The 18th hole, called the "Garden," at Royal Dublin Golf Club, Ireland, combines a near-90-degree dogleg with out-of-bounds; that's a strong test for a finishing hole. (Courtesy of Chrysalis Books.)

FIGURE 5-44B

In this aerial shot of Royal Dublin Golf Club, Ireland, you can trace the boundary of the practice ground which is the right side of the 18th fairway. (Courtesy of Peter Barrow, photographer, Dublin, Ireland.)

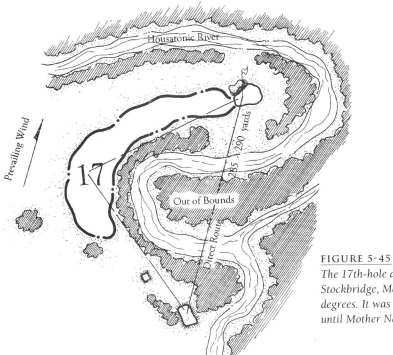

FIGURE 5-45

The 17th-hole dogleg at Stockbridge Golf Club, Stockbridge, Massachusetts, is even sharper than 90 degrees. It was tempting on this hole to try to cut the corner until Mother Nature stepped in and grew a forest.

placement in order to chip to an elevated green (see Figure 5-46). The seventh hole at Avon Country Club in Connecticut (Figure 5-47) is another 350-yard par-4, but in this case by cutting across the angle the green can be reached on the drive, *if* the wind is behind the golfer.

The longer the hole, the more critical is a 90-degree dogleg. Hence, on par 5s they can be more of a problem to the golfer wishing to cut the corner. On the first two illustrations, tree masses can often make the shortcut impossible (Figures 5-48 and 5-49). On the third illustration, one must play two long and brave shots or risk ending in the water or sand (Figure 5-50).

Despite the early popularity and proliferation of doglegs, the Roaring Twenties saw a reduced emphasis on penal design, including sharp doglegs. (A sharp dogleg was considered penal if it imposed a "wasted" second shot simply to align the ball with the next leg of the hole or if the driver couldn't be used on the tee.) Ninety-degree doglegs also tended to slow play, and in some cases the trees between the tee and green disappeared, resulting in a ridiculous hole where players could easily cut the corner and even reach the green from the tee. For all

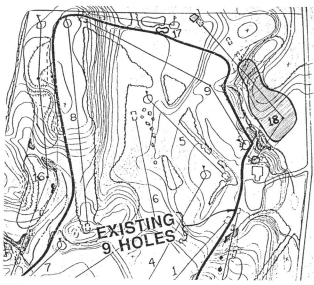

FIGURE 5-46
As the routing study shows, the 18th hole at St. Johnsbury Country Club, St. Johnsbury, Vermont, requires a tee shot across rough terrain and accurate placement to make the next shot easier.

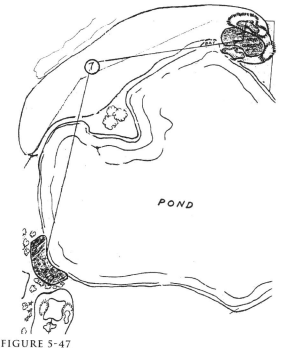

FIGURE 5-47
A preliminary study shows that the sharp dogleg on the seventh hole at Avon Country Club, Avon, Connecticut, doubles as a Cape hole—all carry over water, if you dare.

CLASSIC GOLF HOLE DESIGN

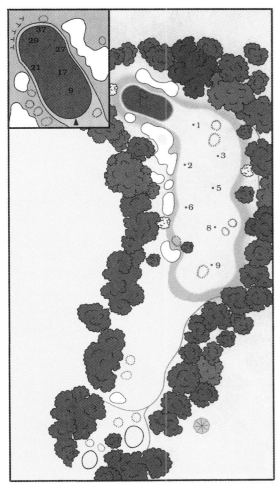

FIGURE 5-48

The 12th hole at Pine Valley Golf Club, Pine Valley, New Jersey, with a short second leg, makes the tee shot placement very critical. Otherwise, your second shot can leave you a dangerous route home.

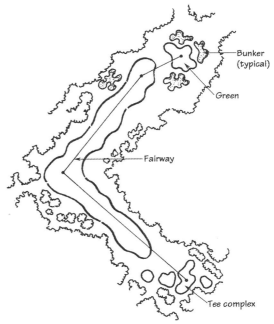

FIGURE 5-49

The third hole on the Timber nine at Port Ludlow Golf Course, Port Ludlow, Washington, is an exciting, steeply downhill shot to a 90-degree corner. Cutting the corner is nearly impossible due to tree cover.

FIGURE 5-50

The 18th hole at Meadow Course at Country Clubs of Fox Meadow, Medina, Ohio, a 556-yard par-5, has a 90-degree dogleg between the second and third shots. The bend occurs at about 467 yards off the back tee when the golfer takes the safe option of not crossing any water (A). The bolder golfer can effectively play the hole at somewhere between 470 and 480 yards by hitting a drive down the right half of the fairway, flirting with the sand and water on that side, then playing the remaining distance over the lake and the 5- to 6-foot bunker that wraps around in front of the green (B). (Courtesy of Steve Burns.)

BROAD CRITERIA FOR CLASSIC GOLF HOLES

these reasons, sharp doglegs have become less common. Still, less severe dogleg holes abound and have become an integral part of the game.

Double Doglegs

It wasn't long after the acceptance of dogleg holes that imaginative designers discovered that double doglegs on par-5s can prove exceptionally interesting. While the number of doglegs now in play is legion, only a few are double. Generally, these holes are accepted, unless the golfer is penalized for a long drive. (This happens when the second leg of the hole is too short for the player to use a club other than a short iron, resulting in a shot that is considered wasted.) As was pointed out quite clearly in the authors' earlier text on golf course design, the golfer complaining of a "wasted" shot was simply paying the price for not executing the prior shot effectively.

Scotland's Prestwick Golf Club was one of the first courses to have several pronounced doglegs, namely on holes 4, 9, 10, and 18. But more notably, Prestwick also has a double dogleg, namely the 482-yard third hole, the Cardinal (Figure 5-51). We consider it to be a potential classic. Another potential classic double dogleg was the fifth hole at Donald Ross–designed St. Charles Country Club in Winnipeg, Canada (Figure 5-52). This hole played wonderfully well for decades, but ever-increasing driving distances began to create a penal situation before course architect C. E. Robinson corrected the problem by merely removing trees, thus making it possible for the long hitter to go for the green on the second shot. One example of this type of hole that has enjoyed acceptance from opening day is the double-dogleg finishing hole at Cranberry Valley on Cape Cod (Figure 5-53). Here the golfer is not punished for a long drive, and the second shot provides the ideal length.

There are two styles of the double dogleg. One angles in the same direction both times (Figure 5-54) and one angles in two different directions (Figure 5-55).

As we proceeded through this study, it became obvious that the potential classic "Cardinal," although named for the Prestwick hole 3 bunker, is really synonymous with a double dogleg. Ideally, an adaptation would dogleg twice in the same direction and have a formidable hazard area (unplayable or out of bounds) inside the dogleg(s). In addition, it was felt that regardless of the direction of the doglegs, the

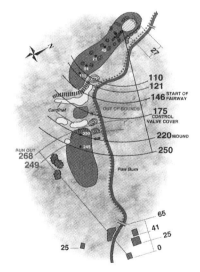

FIGURE 5-51

The double dogleg on the third hole, called the "Cardinal," at Prestwick Golf Club, Prestwick, Scotland, is the critical element of this hole, which was the predecessor to many that followed. The bunker by the same name has an even greater reputation. (Copyright © DuCam Marketing (UK) Ltd.)

CLASSIC GOLF HOLE DESIGN

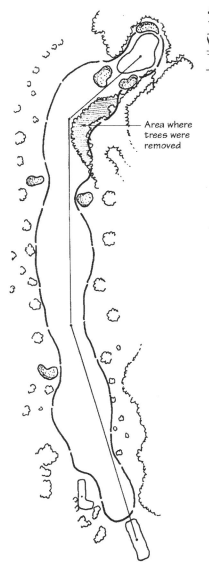

FIGURE 5-52

On the fifth hole at St. Charles Country Club, Winnipeg, Manitoba, the golfer must balance carefully between the angles and leg lengths of the double dogleg and the trees, hazards, or obstacles that affect the shots (such as the buildings at Road hole at the Old Course at St. Andrews, Scotland).

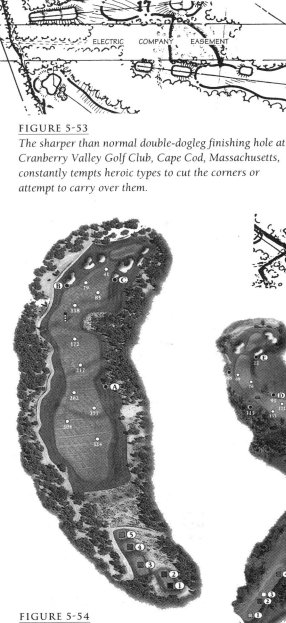

FIGURE 5-53

The sharper than normal double-dogleg finishing hole at Cranberry Valley Golf Club, Cape Cod, Massachusetts, constantly tempts heroic types to cut the corners or attempt to carry over them.

FIGURE 5-54

Both doglegs on hole 15 at Paako Ridge Golf Club, Sandia Park, New Mexico, designed by Ken Dye, angle right, making the slicer a happier person at least for one hole. On another hole, they could both go left as well. (Holes by Holeview Yardage Book Co.)

FIGURE 5-55

On the 4th hole at Dorado Beach Golf Club, Dorado Beach, Puerto Rico, hookers, slicers, drawers, or faders all get their chance at glory on one leg or another. (Holes by Holeview Yardage Book Co.)

double dogleg, coupled with the inside hazards, would qualify as a potential "Cardinal."

Blind Holes

Innumerable holes are blind from one position or another, whether these positions are reached intentionally or through wayward shots. We consider a hole to be legitimately blind only if:

1. A player anywhere on the tee or fairway cannot see where to properly advance the ball.

2. A player cannot see the group ahead when it is within distance of the next shot.

At one time, the degree of blindness on the approach to the green was categorized by holes:

1. Where the putting surface was entirely visible (Figure 5-56A).
2. Where the flag only could be seen (Figure 5-56B).
3. Where the green was totally invisible (Figure 5-56C).

The above designations were based solely on the position of the ball, not by the player or caddy moving one way or another to see the target before returning to the ball.

As happened with crossing holes, since golf courses have become increasingly crowded and society increasingly litigious, the popularity of blind holes has diminished. However, a fair number of

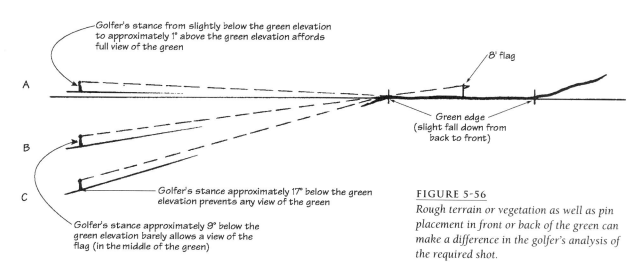

FIGURE 5-56
Rough terrain or vegetation as well as pin placement in front or back of the green can make a difference in the golfer's analysis of the required shot.

such holes are still built, and many early blind holes continue the tradition of this near-classic type of hole.

On the Old Course at St. Andrews, players can find themselves behind a hump or in a hollow and therefore in a blind position on holes 6, 12, 13, and 17. These continue the tradition of blind holes on a site that might be called "flat," despite its wild, erratic, but gentle undulations (Figures 5-57 through 5-60). And at Prestwick, the tee shots on holes 5 and 7 must surmount the famous Himalayas, while the 17th is called the "Alps" due to a rise in front of the green making it blind (Figures 5-61 through 5-63). Royal St. George's in Sandwich, England, had a total of four blind shots—on holes 1, 3, 4, and, perhaps most famously, 6, known as the "Maiden" (Figures 5-64 through 5-67). After these holes were altered, Bernard Darwin said, "The whole art of golf no longer consisted of hitting a ball over a sandhill and then running to the top to see what had happened on the other side." Darwin also describes two blind holes that were developed in the 1880s at Aberdovey and Harleck, both in Wales. He adds that there were once six blind one-shot holes at Burnham and Berrow in

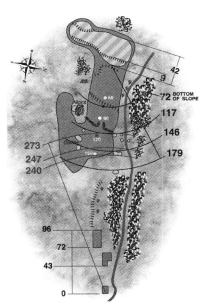

FIGURE 5-57
A ridge off the tee on hole 6 at the Old Course at St. Andrews, Scotland, can screen the view into the fairway, while a ridge in front of the green can be quite misleading. (Copyright © DuCam Marketing (UK) Ltd.)

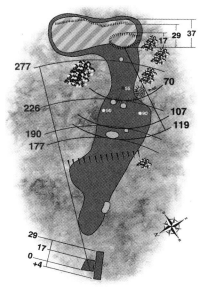

FIGURE 5-58
A ridge can hide the green on the 12th hole at the Old Course at St. Andrews, Scotland, but so can many small hillocks or hollows, if you're in the wrong spot. (Copyright © DuCam Marketing (UK) Ltd.)

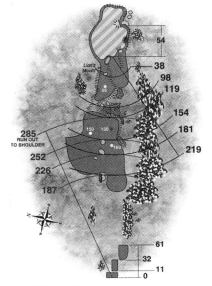

FIGURE 5-59
More humps and hollows, both grassy and sandy, along with many bunkers on hole 13 at the Old Course at St. Andrews, Scotland, can hide the green or the golfer at times. (Copyright © DuCam Marketing (UK) Ltd.)

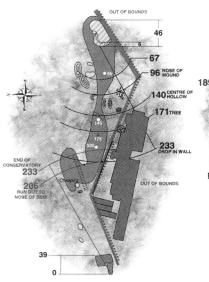

FIGURE 5-60

It takes X-ray vision to see the green through the buildings from the tee on the 17th hole, the Road, on the Old Course at St. Andrews, Scotland. A relatively short first leg, if played straight away, prompts many to cut the corner over the buildings. The knowledgeable player picks his or her spot and hits away. Others find their ball, but no solace, in the hotel pool or garden. (Copyright © DuCam Marketing (UK) Ltd.)

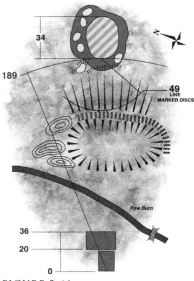

FIGURE 5-61

The renowned Himalayas make the fifth hole at Prestwick Golf Club, Prestwick, Scotland, a blind, one-shot hole. Excitement reigns until you get a look at where your tee shot landed. (Copyright © DuCam Marketing (UK) Ltd.)

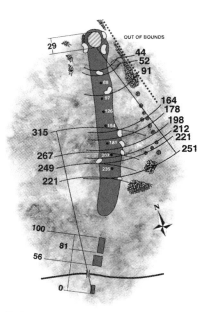

FIGURE 5-62

You have your work cut out with hills, valleys, and many bunkers to deal with on the seventh hole at Prestwick Golf Club, Prestwick, Scotland. (Copyright © DuCam Marketing (UK) Ltd.)

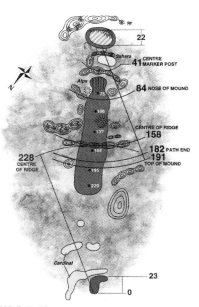

FIGURE 5-63

Called the "Alps," the 17th hole at Prestwick Golf Club, Prestwick, Scotland, is probably the most well-known blind par-4 in golf history. Though the Alps would not be acceptable these days, no real golfer would abide removing the hill, so it stays. (Copyright © DuCam Marketing (UK) Ltd.)

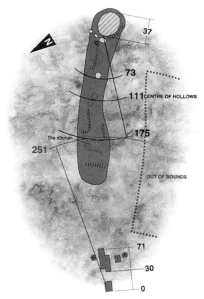

FIGURE 5-64

Hole 1 at Royal St. George's Golf Club, Sandwich, England, called the "Kitchen," has a blind shot off the tee. Then you deal with the usual humps and hollows. (Copyright © DuCam Marketing (UK) Ltd.)

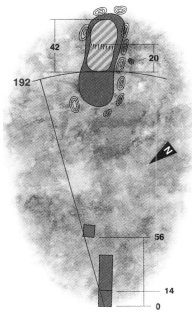

FIGURE 5-65
Scurry around to get a glimpse of the green on the third hole at Royal St. George's Golf Club, Sandwich, England, or let your caddy give you a line. (Copyright © DuCam Marketing (UK) Ltd.)

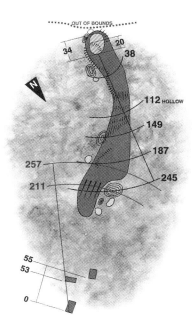

FIGURE 5-66
On hole 4 at Royal St. George's Golf Club, Sandwich, England, typical links terrain can hide your landing area, your ball, or you. (Copyright © DuCam Marketing (UK) Ltd.)

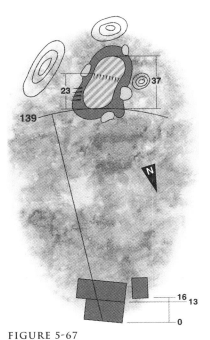

FIGURE 5-67
Hole 6 at Royal St. George's Golf Club, Sandwich, England, is better known for a large hill, called the "Maiden," than the present hole layout. In the old days, one hit over the Maiden, a truly blind shot. (Copyright © DuCam Marketing (UK) Ltd.)

Somerset, England, "to say nothing of several longer holes where the approach shot is played merely at a guide flag waving upon a hilltop."

One famous and long-lived blind hole is the Dell, the sixth at Lahinch (Figure 5-68) in Ireland. None of the green is visible from the tee because the putting surface sits in a small valley behind a steep hill. A caddy, who by this point in the round has had ample opportunity to evaluate a golfer's swing, attitude, and ability, will select a club and provide the line. Not until the player has proceeded to the green is it possible to know the result of the tee shot. In adapting the Dell, modifications have been practiced. Three are depicted in Figures 5-69 through 5-71. The objectives of modifying the Dell include introducing visibility while retaining the principles of the hole.

The blind nature of certain targets and hazards on a golf course is part of the game and not likely to earn the sympathy of fellow golfers should one be fooled. For example, Americans playing for the first time at St. Andrews, who rebuke their caddy for failing to mention a

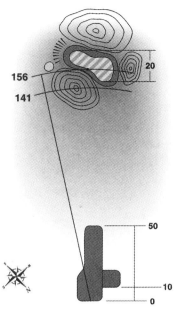

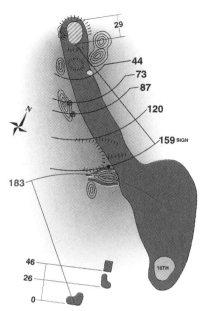

FIGURE 5-68
All you see from the tee on the sixth hole at Lahinch Golf Club, County Clare, Ireland, the original "Dell," is your caddy pointing to a target rock. Take his advice and hit away. (Copyright © DuCam Marketing (UK) Ltd.)

FIGURE 5-69
With the green somewhat depressed and a large hump just in front of it on the third hole at Burnham and Berrow Golf Course, Somerset, England, the golfer won't see much of the target. Though it may be difficult to see on the diagram, the large mound creates a Dell effect. (Copyright © DuCam Marketing (UK) Ltd.)

FIGURE 5-70
Golf architect Steve Durkee achieved visibility on the 12th hole at Dorset Field Club, Dorset, Vermont, in that the green is hidden from parts of the tee. Yet the golfer can move around and take a peek at it. (Copyright © Bob Labbance.)

CLASSIC GOLF HOLE DESIGN

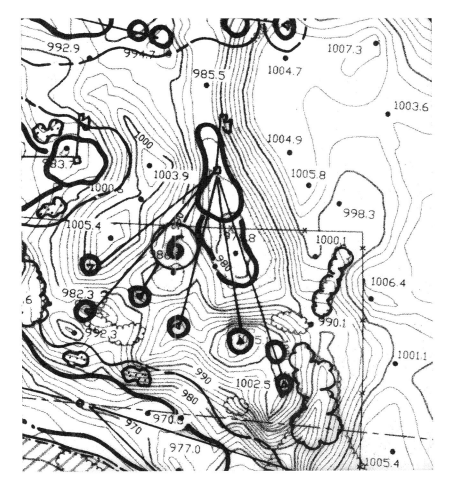

FIGURE 5-71
This routing for the par-3 hole 6 at Erin Hills Golf Course, Milwaukee, Wisconsin, features a multiple tee complex. The three tees on the left, or west side, leave a blind shot, creating a "Dell" style hole with all the excitement and intrigue of the original. (Courtesy of Hurdzan Fry.)

hidden bunker where their ball has come to rest, can expect the retort: "It's been there for 500 years; you should have known about it." Due to the fame of such holes as the Dell, and the inherent added challenge, some golfers feel that blind shots, if not overdone, are acceptable. Designers likewise continue to create them if the blindness adds something to the hole.

Double Fairways

Strategic golf course design, offering alternate routes from the tee to the green (Figure 5-72), is more common than penal golf (Figure 5-73), which requires compulsory carries over hazards and tends to punish any shot that is less than perfect. A third, less common design is the "bite-off" or "heroic" type (Figure 5-74), where the player decides how much of the hazard to carry.

A

B

C

FIGURE 5-72

The golfer has the option on the tee shot at the eighth hole on the West Course at Magnolia Creek Golf Links, League City, Texas, to take the straight, shorter but more perilous route or go the long way to the right and hopefully ignore the bunkers (A). Photographs in B and C show how this interesting hole looks. (Courtesy of Ault, Clark & Associates, Ltd.)

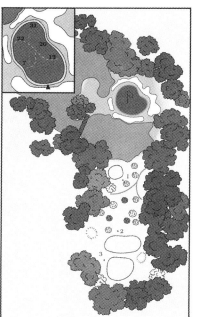

FIGURE 5-73

Pine Valley Golf Club, Pine Valley, New Jersey, offers many penal shot situations. The par-3 14th hole is all carry to the green.

FIGURE 5-74

On the fourth hole at Dorado Beach Golf Club, Dorado Beach, Puerto Rico, there are two chances to be a hero. Carry the water across the corner off the tee. Then carry the water again to the green. Normal golfers will play the Z game to the green. (Holes by Holeview Yardage Book Co.)

CLASSIC GOLF HOLE DESIGN

There are also holes with two separate fairways (Figure 5-75). These are not to be confused with still another type of hole that provides "target golf." Dr. Alister Mackenzie's plan of a distinctive hole won a competition sponsored by *Country Life*. Published in the July 25, 1914, issue, it is truly the apotheosis of a hole with alternate routes, and it helped Mackenzie achieve global fame after World War I, although he had designed several courses before entering the competition.

Other Distinctive Types of Holes

There are a number of other types of challenging and exciting holes. Hogbacks (hogsbacks), optical illusions, drop shots, water holes, bottlenecks or bottles, valleys, and compulsory carries are discussed in this catchall category.

Hogback (or Hogsback) Holes

Many early hogback fairways arose because the sites sat atop ridges rather than in valleys. Holes 2, 14, and 16 at England's famed Rye Golf Club (designed by H. S. Colt and Douglas Rolland, 1894) were referred to as hogbacks, as was the 17th hole at Royal Dublin in Ireland

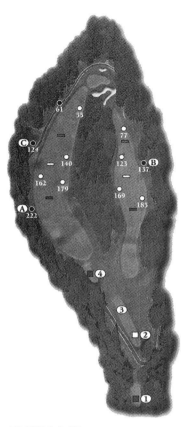

FIGURE 5-75
Hole 14 at Kayak Point Golf Course, Stanwood, Washington, designed by Thompson, Wolveridge, and Fream, has two distinct fairways to consider. The straighter appears to be narrower. (Holes by Holeview Yardage Book Co.)

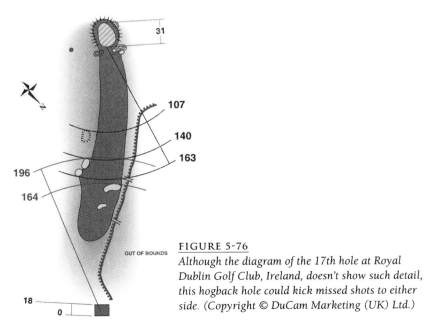

FIGURE 5-76
Although the diagram of the 17th hole at Royal Dublin Golf Club, Ireland, doesn't show such detail, this hogback hole could kick missed shots to either side. (Copyright © DuCam Marketing (UK) Ltd.)

(Figure 5-76). Another more recent example is the 13th at Chalk Mountain Golf Course in California, where one of the authors laid out the hole along an existing ridge in order to get from the 12th to the 14th hole (Figure 5-77).

It is also not uncommon for architects to intentionally plan hogback fairways. Canadian Stanley Thompson, for one, often created this prominent feature by building linear stone dumps in the center of his holes. This would result in a grassed ridge that sometimes ran the entire length of the hole. Dividing the hole longitudinally, the ridge provided landing areas on both sides and necessitated a variety of shots into the green. Sometimes the green might be hogbacked, forcing golfers to decide while still on the tee which side of the ridge to play in order to have the best shot into the hogback green.

Hogback greens are probably more common now than hogback fairways, but hogback greens are not a new creation. Tom Dunn's Royal Worlington and Newmarket in England had a hogback green (the 5th) as early as 1890. The 18th at Merion near Philadelphia also has one, while Trevose Golf and Country Club (Figures 5-78A and 5-78B) in

FORCES BEYOND THE ARCHITECT'S CONTROL

Certainly, hogback greens can be planned by the architect and precisely installed during construction, but hogbacks and other green shapes may also arise from forces beyond the architect's control or intentions. For an example we look to Pete Dye before he became an eminent course architect. At the conclusion of World War II, Dye awaited discharge orders at Fort Bragg. During that time, he worked at the fort's golf course and was allowed to play Pinehurst No. 2 daily for six months. Interested even then in course design, he ascertained that Pinehurst had instituted a topdressing program on its greens, dating back to the mid-1930s when they were converted from sand to grass. The program involved ¼-inch of sand per week during the growing season. By 1945, according to Dye's estimate, the elevation of the greens was at least 14 inches higher than when grassed in the mid-1930s. This, rather than the architect's intentions, contributed to the notorious dome shapes of the greens of Donald Ross, often referred to as the grandmaster of course design.

Similarly, it has been noted that the greens at St. Andrews rose several feet in elevation from their inception in the middle of the 19th century until use of aerating equipment, over a century later, began to compensate by removing plugs. Sand topdressings, if applied when the turf is dormant, can also be blown into ridge forms. As these enlarge, they, too, can take on interesting forms, including hogbacks.

CLASSIC GOLF HOLE DESIGN

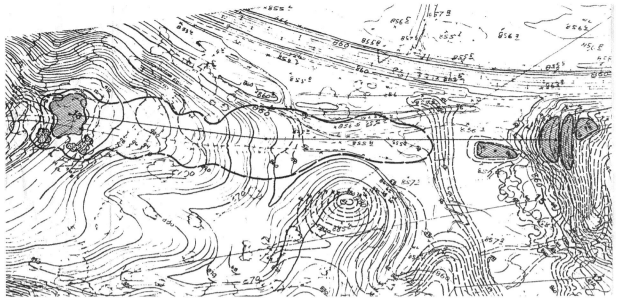

FIGURE 5-77

The hogback ridge on the 13th hole at Chalk Mountain Golf Course, Atascadero, California,
was the only logical route to tie the golf course routing together in a smooth, flowing manner,
but it's a relatively tough hole for the regular, once-every-week, public golfer. Hole 13 climbs
the ridge, virtually untouched until about 100 yards off the green. A swale was cut in for visibility.
The green is perched on the upper part of the ridge.

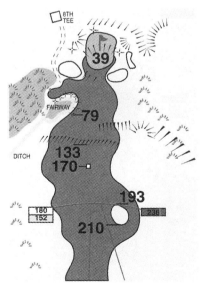

FIGURE 5-78A

The hogback is centered in the front
portion of the green and extends to all
sides on the seventh hole at Trevose
Golf and Country Club, England.
(Hole diagram by King, with
permission of Eagle Promotions Ltd.)

FIGURE 5-78B

The very subtle hogback on the seventh hole at Trevose Golf and Country Club,
England, is barely discernible at the front of the green, then moving downward to the
flagstick. (Courtesy of Trevose Golf and Country Club.)

England, designed by H. S. Colt, had a lateral hogback green, hole 7, according to golf architect and author Don Steel in *Classic Golf Links*. Famed designer Donald Ross was noted, not necessarily correctly, for mounding his greens in the form of an inverted saucer. He also built a number of true hogback greens, including the 18th of his 1917 version of Oakland Hills and several at Pinehurst.

Optical Illusion Holes

Alister Mackenzie, the "father" of wartime camouflage, never hesitated to obscure a problem for the less alert or less observant. On several occasions, he observed that camouflage and course design had aspects in common. One way he achieved an optical illusion was to place bunkers across the fairway 100 feet or more short of the green (Figure 5-79). This obscured the area between them and the putting surface. Yet this was by no means a Mackenzie first; Donald Ross practiced the same technique on scores of his holes before and after World War I, while the Spectacles on the 14th at Carnoustie achieve somewhat the same result (Figure 5-80).

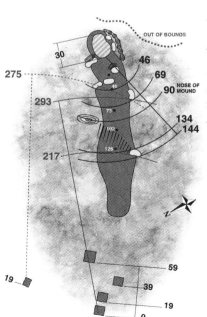

FIGURE 5-79
The bunkers well short of the green at the 14th hole, called the "Goosedubs," at Prestwick Golf Club, Prestwick, Scotland, are certain to trick the unwary into misclubbing. (Copyright © DuCam Marketing (UK) Ltd.)

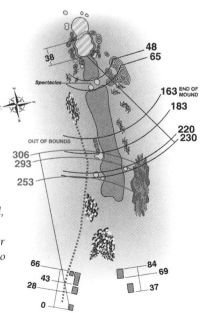

FIGURE 5-80
The Spectacles, hole 14 at Carnoustie Golf Links, Scotland, are famous simply because of their appearance. However, their placement can cause the golfer to misjudge the distance to the green. (Copyright © DuCam Marketing (UK) Ltd.)

CLASSIC GOLF HOLE DESIGN

Drop Shots

From a tee elevated 75 feet or more above the green, an interesting par-3 may result, as can a drop shot to a fairway tightly bunkered at the landing area (see Figures 3-2A and 3-2B, page 46).

Water Holes

Water can be the most exciting and memorable hazard on the course. According to the *Rules of Golf*, "a water hazard is any sea, lake, pond, river, ditch, surface drainage ditch, or other open water." Holes with water abound; yet they are not necessarily classic in themselves. One category of water hole that does fit our definition of a classic is the island green. It will be described more fully in the next chapter.

Related to water holes are wetlands, which force the golfer to skirt or play across them in the same manner as when encountering water. The crossing can be perpendicular, the skirting of the wetland, or play across it on a diagonal (as a bite-off). Another interesting water hole is created by use of a stream to bring the hazard into play twice (Figure 5-81).

Bottleneck or Bottle Holes

Any hole where the route is restricted by bunkers or other means is called a "bottleneck." On many such holes, the restriction creates a bottle shape, often with the narrow end nearest the green (Figures 5-82 and 5-83). But there are other "bottlenecks" as well. Golf architect William B. Langford, in a piece later reprinted in *Masters of the Links* by Geoffrey Shackelford, describes a bottleneck design on a 360-yard hole, with the restriction placed around the landing area for long hitters (Figure 5-84). Two other types of bottlenecks are shown in Figures 5-85 and 5-86.

Apparently, Alister Mackenzie was not an admirer of bottlenecks. He wrote in *The Spirit of St. Andrews* that "Charles Ambrose, an able golfer, writer and critic, has been advocating that the way to limit the flight of the golf ball is to penalize everyone who drives over a certain distance." Mackenzie contended that a gust of wind or draft could unfairly destroy the golfer's calculations, causing him or her to drive into the bottleneck. Yet, in making such a statement, the eminent Dr. Mackenzie seems to be objecting to one of the many superb characteristics of linksland—that variety is enhanced by constantly changing winds.

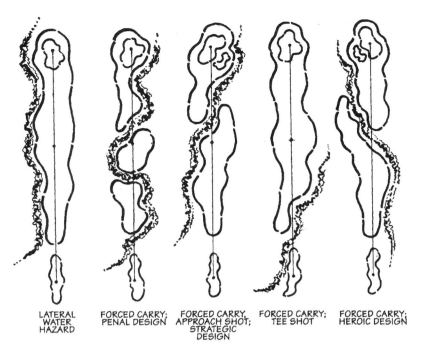

LATERAL WATER HAZARD

FORCED CARRY; PENAL DESIGN

FORCED CARRY, APPROACH SHOT; STRATEGIC DESIGN

FORCED CARRY; TEE SHOT

FORCED CARRY; HEROIC DESIGN

LAKES (AND OTHER SIMILAR FEATURES)

NOTE: WETLANDS CAN BE ASSOCIATED WITH CREEKS, OR LAKES, SWAMPS, BOGS, VERNAL POOLS, OR OTHER SIMILAR FEATURES. ALL NORMALLY PLAY AS WATER HAZARDS EXCEPT UNDER SOME LIMITATIONS—GOLFERS ARE NOT ALLOWED TO ENTER OR PLAY FROM WITHIN THESE FEATURES.

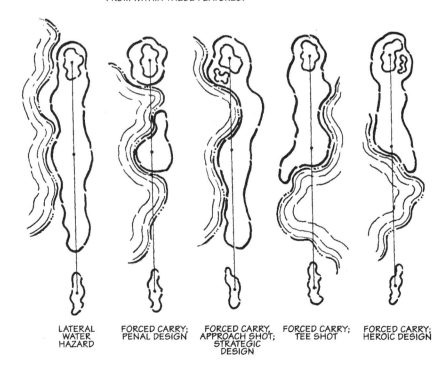

LATERAL WATER HAZARD

FORCED CARRY; PENAL DESIGN

FORCED CARRY, APPROACH SHOT; STRATEGIC DESIGN

FORCED CARRY; TEE SHOT

FORCED CARRY; HEROIC DESIGN

CREEKS

FIGURE 5-81
This diagram from Golf Course Design shows 10 different ways to use water to inspire or infuriate the golfer. There are probably hundreds of additional adaptations based on these concepts.

CLASSIC GOLF HOLE DESIGN

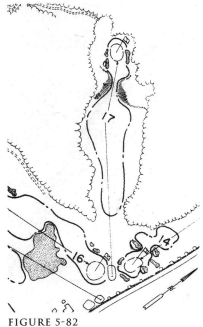

FIGURE 5-82
This very narrow bottleneck on the 17th hole at Essex County Club, Manchester, Massachusetts, is formed by constricting slopes. (Courtesy of Phil Wogan.)

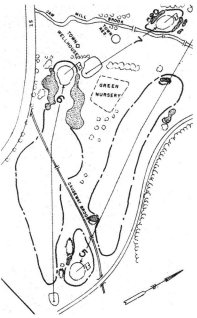

FIGURE 5-83
Also at Essex County Club, Manchester, Massachusetts, the neck of the bottle on hole 6 is formed by hazards on both sides. (Courtesy of Phil Wogan.)

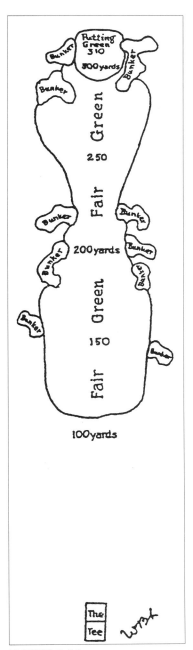

FIGURE 5-84
Golf architect William B. Langford used an ever-constricting bunker complex to create a bottleneck on this simulated hole. (Courtesy of Geoff Shackelford.)

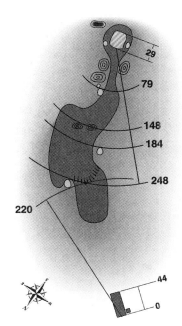

FIGURE 5-85
With the neck of the bottle offset to the right side, the golfer's problems are further complicated at hole 14 on Lahinch Golf Club, County Clare, Ireland. (Copyright © DuCam Marketing (UK) Ltd.)

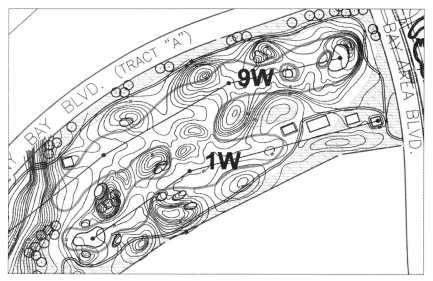

FIGURE 5-86
The first hole on the West Course at Magnolia Creek Golf Links, League City, Texas, designed by Ault, Clark & Associates, features a narrow bottle to begin with. Then the neck wiggles its way to the green, giving the golfer lots to think about en route. (Courtesy of Ault, Clark & Associates, Ltd.)

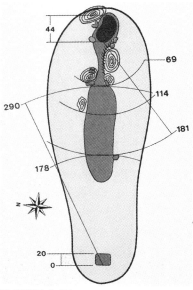

FIGURE 5-87
Old Tom Morris used mounding to create the neck of the bottle on the third hole at Muirfield Golf Course, Scotland. (Copyright © DuCam Marketing (UK) Ltd.)

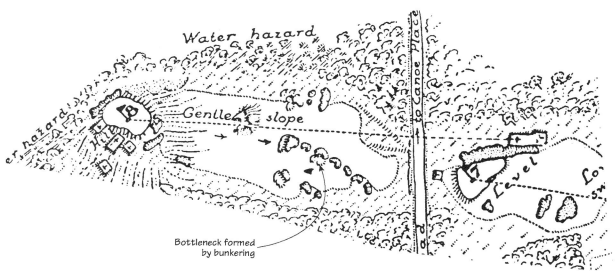

FIGURE 5-88
C. B. Macdonald used the angled cross-bunker concept to tempt play down the left while creating a bottleneck on the right at the eighth hole at the National Golf Links, Southampton, New York. (Copyright © by Erwin Raisz. Reprinted with permission by Raisz Landform Maps, 800-277-0047.)

CLASSIC GOLF HOLE DESIGN

Other early versions of bottleneck holes include Old Tom Morris's third at Muirfield (Figure 5-87), Tom Dunn's ninth at Meyrick Park, and C. B. Macdonald's eighth at the National Golf Links (Figure 5-88). The last was created by bunkers skillfully sited to form a narrow neck that complicated the tee shot. In one period of Robert Trent Jones's illustrious career, he appeared to narrow all his landing areas with formidable hazards placed so that the farther one hit the ball, the more accurate that person was required to be. A still later version of this type of design is the fourth hole on the Canyon Course at La Paloma Golf Club in Arizona. Designed by Jack Nicklaus and Scott Miller, this par-4 is wide at the 150-yard mark and then narrows in front of the green, a modern interpretation of a classic design.

Valley Holes

Valleys can be ideal sites for golf holes, and therefore it is only natural that many holes have been played in them from the earliest days of golf and across the entire history of golf architecture. Among the earliest "valley holes" was the fourth (Ginger Beer) on the Old Course

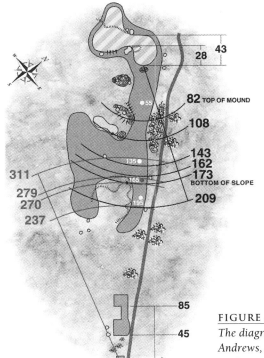

FIGURE 5-89

The diagram doesn't show the terrain on the fourth hole of the Old Course at St. Andrews, Scotland, but you are definitely playing through a valley. (Copyright © DuCam Marketing (UK) Ltd.)

(Figure 5-89). Lyle and Ferrier have issued the following description of that grand hole: "In a sense Gingerbeer can be likened to a valley running between the higher ground to the left and the wall of Gorse on the right. But it is not exactly a quiet pastoral valley. Several ridges enter from the left."

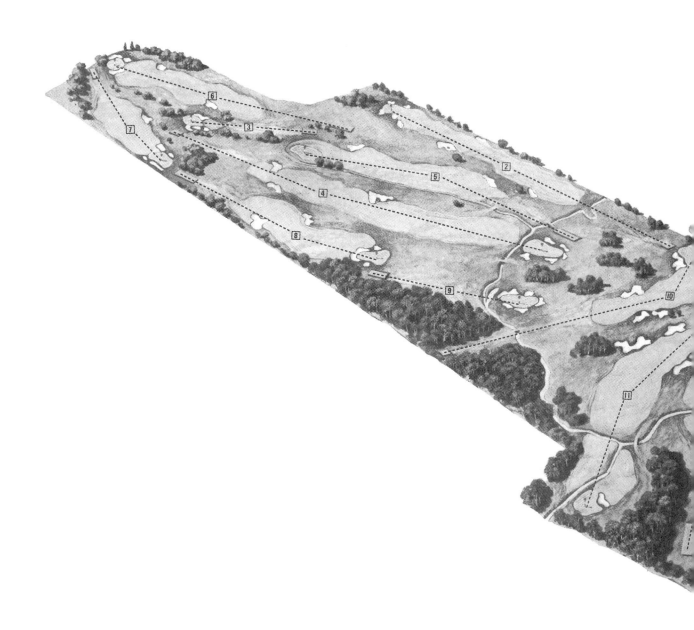

Other early valley holes included the 1st and 17th on the Old Tom Morris version of Dornoch (no longer exists); the original Royal Birkdale (1889), which featured pronounced but shallow valleys; and Royal County Down, which has several. Rye Golf Club in England, H. S. Colt's first creation, sported a pronounced valley on the 15th.

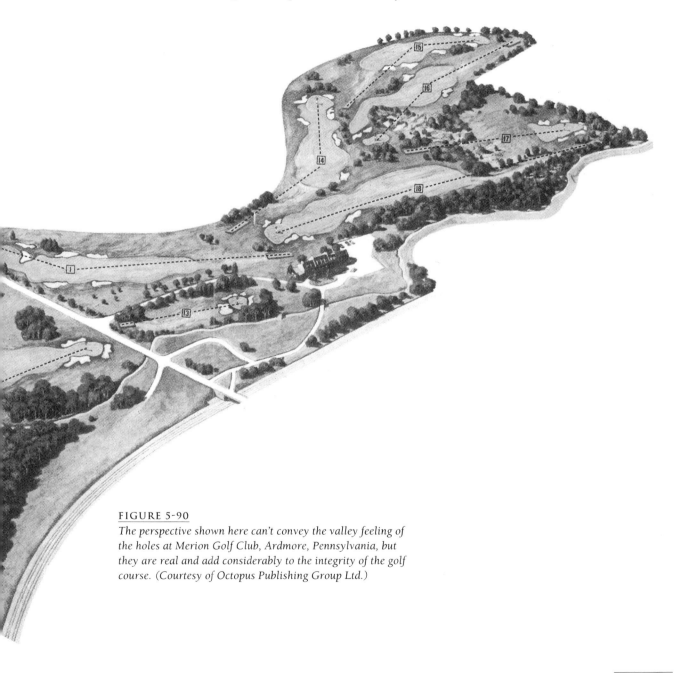

FIGURE 5-90
The perspective shown here can't convey the valley feeling of the holes at Merion Golf Club, Ardmore, Pennsylvania, but they are real and add considerably to the integrity of the golf course. (Courtesy of Octopus Publishing Group Ltd.)

Likewise, Tom Dunn's version of Saunton features a third hole that was appropriately named "Valley." In the United States, James Tufts and Dr. Leroy Culver included two valley holes on their version of Pinehurst No. 1, opened in 1898. Merion, designed by Hugh Wilson, opened in 1912 with three valley holes (Figure 5-90). *The World Atlas of Golf* offered the following brief documentation of each of those holes: "#9, a green in a small valley...#11, a drive into a valley...#16, plays through a valley."

The influential trio of Macdonald, Raynor, and Banks created many a valley hole, beginning with their work on the National Golf Links. They later replicated the valley design on other courses, frequently making it a par-4 and placing it first in the routing. Generally, the shot came from an elevated tee onto a lower elevation, resulting in a quick getaway for golfers. (The word "valley" was used in its broadest sense, as many holes bearing this name simply had an elevated tee rather than an enclosed valley fairway.)

FIGURE 5-91
This photograph, taken from the authors' book Golf Course Design, *shows hole 12 from the left of the tee looking through a natural valley to the green at La Purisima Golf Course, near Santa Barbara, California.*

FIGURE 5-92
A valley flows naturally through La Purisima Golf Course, near Santa Barbara, California. This shot, also of hole 12, looks across the green back to the tee. There's plenty of sitting room for spectators.

CLASSIC GOLF HOLE DESIGN

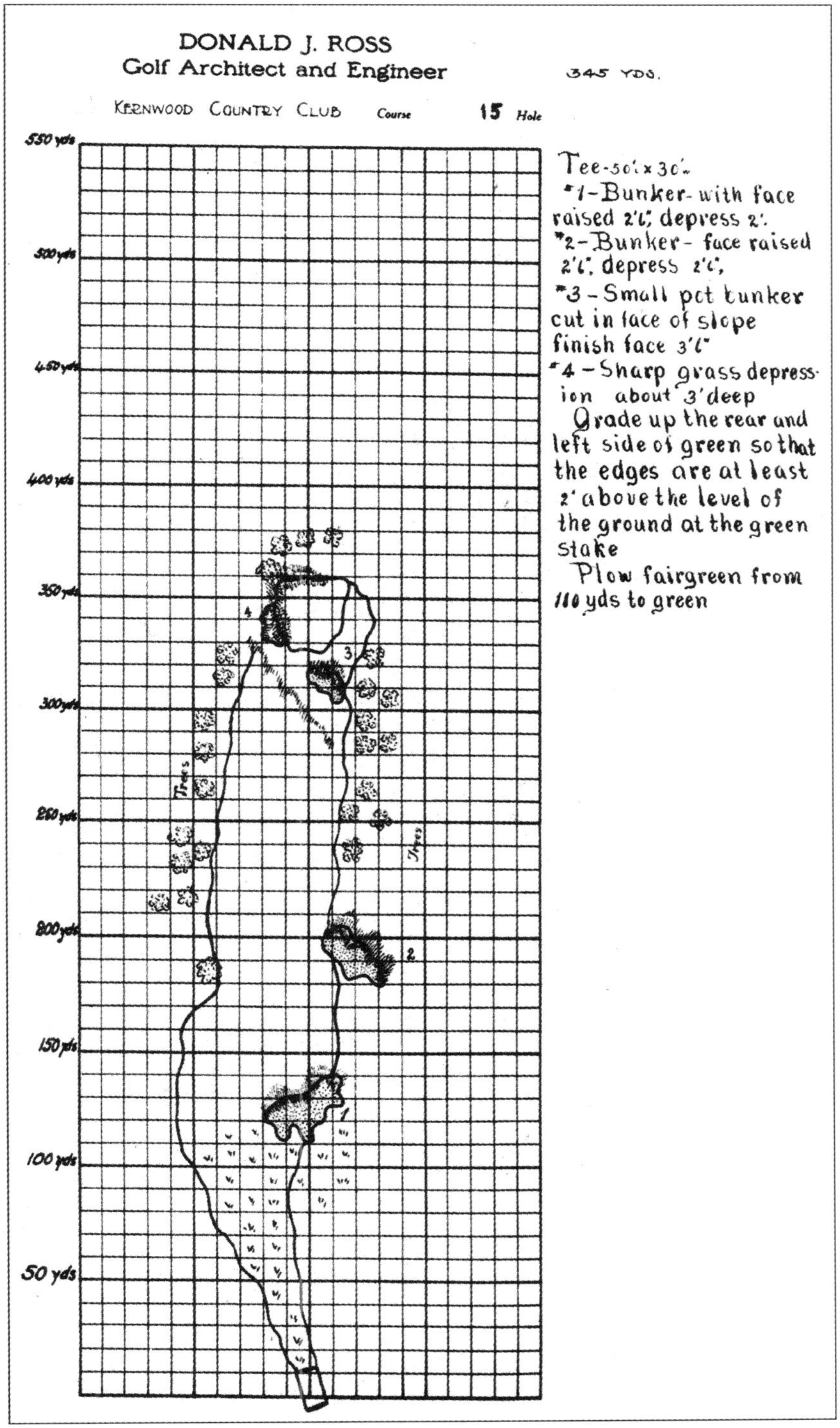
DONALD J. ROSS
Golf Architect and Engineer
345 YDS.
KERNWOOD COUNTRY CLUB Course 15 Hole
550 yds
500 yds
450 yds
400 yds
350 yds
300 yds
250 yds
200 yds
150 yds
100 yds
50 yds
Trees
Trees
Tee-50' x 30'
#1-Bunker- with face raised 2'6" depress 2'.
#2-Bunker- face raised 2'6". depress 2'6".
#3-Small pot bunker cut in face of slope finish face 3'6"
#4-Sharp grass depression about 3' deep
Grade up the rear and left side of green so that the edges are at least 2' above the level of the ground at the green stake
Plow fairgreen from 110 yds to green

FIGURE 5-93

At Kernwood Country Club, Salem, Massachusetts, Donald Ross, the grandmaster, was practicing strategic design as early as 1914.

Valley holes are popular among architects, because a valley is conducive to golf. In fact, entire courses have been designed with valley holes in mind, perhaps most obviously at La Purisima in California, opened in 1986 and designed by Graves and Pascuzzo. This layout features a number of holes in confined valleys, with steep sides that provide wonderful sites for spectators (Figures 5-91 and 5-92).

Compulsory Carries

Finally, there are compulsory carries that do not provide alternate routes. (Note that water sometimes requires the compulsory carry, as do wetlands, long grass, other vegetation, and sand.) They are the epitome of penal design—the type of design that predominated until the Roaring Twenties. Yet the Old Course had become strategic by the middle of the 19th century, when Allan Robertson first, and then Tom Morris, widened the fairways. This allowed golfers to play a safer but longer route that did not require carrying the fearsome hazard, although an extra stroke might be needed. Thus, the stage was set for strategic design and the partial but not absolute demise of penal design. The grandmaster Donald Ross was an early proponent of strategic design (Figure 5-93).

6

SPECIFIC FEATURES OF CLASSIC GOLF HOLES

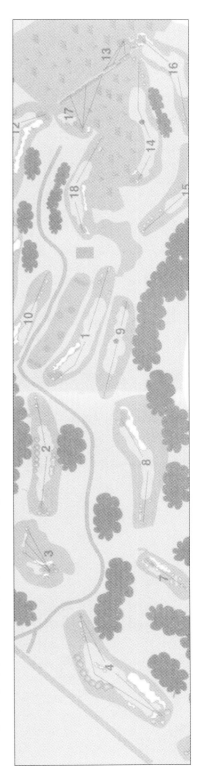

Unique or individual features of golf holes have attracted sufficient attention to make them almost classics in their own right, even when the hole itself cannot be considered one. Prominent features that make a hole include greens, tees, and mounds; bunkers; and ponds (see Figure 3-11, page 54).

Greens, Tees, and Mounds

Legendary course architect A. W. Tillinghast once compared the golf green to the human face, observing that no two are the same. "Sometimes in the passing crowd our eyes rest for a moment on a strange face, so strong, finely chiseled and so filled with character that although it is gone in a second our fleeting glance has indelibly stamped the features upon our memory," he wrote. Continuing on this same theme, Tillinghast also wrote, "A putting green has features like a human face. The character of the putting green and approaches mark the quality of a course to a greater extent than anything else."

For better or for worse, more often the latter, the shapes of greens change due to mowing practices. Often, the architect provides intensely interesting pin placements in the corners, only to see them disappear sooner or later. Still, many different original green designs persist through faithful maintenance by the course superintendent. But shapes are not the only green features that can change over time.

NAMING HOLES

Holes at all the championship courses in Scotland and on many other layouts have been given names. Some result from events that happened over centuries, others from a single event, and still others from a feature, natural or artificial. Architect Tillinghast was one exponent in North America of naming his holes. He believed in providing a name based on his own and others' experiences in a season or more of play. The amazing Canadian golf architect Stan Thompson sometimes selected names even before putting pencil to paper. His names were based on how he envisioned the hole would play or look, although the hole was still entirely in his mind. Yet he was truly prophetic, because many of his names exist today—70 or more years since the holes were named.

With exceptions galore, greens are commonly classified by their elevations in relation to the fairway. We have raised, level, and depressed greens (Figures 6-1 through 6-3). (The well-known "Punch Bowl" [Figure 6-4] is an example of the last, while the "Plateau green" [Figure 6-5], whether natural or manufactured, is the opposite.) Level and raised greens are commonplace, but, as noted earlier, the elevation of a green can rise because of constant topdressing (see Figure 3-7, page 49).

FIGURE 6-1

The 14th green at Orinda Country Club, Orinda, California, is an excellent example of a raised or plateau green. Shortcomings such as not blending into its site are eased by the relevance of a historical design concept.

FIGURE 6-2

The 18th green at St. Andrews, Scotland, is flattish with no visible edge. Part of the Valley of Sin appears at the right edge of the photo.

FIGURE 6-3
A depressed or sunken green could not be sited in many soils because of drainage problems. Yet it is possible on the deep, sandy Scottish soils, as on this hole at St. Andrews.

FIGURE 6-4
This picture is representative of Punch Bowl greens set in hollows below the wind.

FIGURE 6-5
This green at Tamarack Country Club, Greenwich, Connecticut, is an example of the raised or plateau green that appears in hundreds of courses worldwide. That it blends into surroundings was not a factor in the popular design concept.

SPECIFIC FEATURES OF CLASSIC GOLF HOLES

Several Distinguishing Features of Greens

Greens can vary widely in their shapes, depending on surface contouring, geometric design, and size. Other variations include double greens, steeply contoured greens, and greens that fall away.

SURFACE CONTOURING

All-important in green design, surface contouring is used to create a variety of unique shapes. Some greens are humpback, others are inverted saucers, others are dishes, and still others are punch bowls. A green at Woking Golf Club, England, described by Bernard Darwin as divided into two compartments by "a range of mountains," was no doubt a hogback, while Donald Steel offers an unforgettable description of a beautifully contoured green at Saunton, England. He calls the green "a saddle, rejecting all imperfect attempts to mount it like an angry horse." In the United States, the fourth hole at Spyglass (designed by Robert Trent Jones) features a putting surface designed to emulate the rolling swells seen in the adjoining Monterey Bay, and it is a perfect example of the use of surface contouring to distinguish a green. (Note that putting surfaces can be flatish, tilted, contoured, terraced, or a combination.)

GEOMETRIC DESIGN

Geometric shapes have long been a dominant factor in the creation of greens. For example, prior to World War I, greens were often square shaped, just as the early sand greens had been. Donald Ross, Tom Bendelow, the Foulis brothers, C. B. Macdonald, Seth Raynor, and Charles Banks were among the golf architects who intentionally designed square greens. (In other cases, square-shaped greens resulted from mowing with traditional lawn mowers before greens mowers came on the scene.) Continuing on the geometric theme, Stanley Thompson designed a triangular green at Jasper Park Golf Course in the Canadian Rockies, and a fan-shaped putting surface existed at Seaton Carew in England before Alister Mackenzie revised that course in 1925. Another example of a unique green shape can be seen on the 11th hole at Divi Bahamas, designed by golf architect Joe Lee. Its putting surface is elongated, with the longest dimension an extension of the centerline of the hole. Conversely, the greens at Tillinghast's Winged Foot have long been called Africa or pear shaped.

Innumerable other shapes have arisen, because there is no limit to the imagination and creativity of golf course architects (Figures 6-6 and 6-7). Robert Trent Jones, Jr., planned a green in Egypt in the shape of a pyramid and one in Texas in the shape of that state, while the first green at Hayden Lake in Idaho is shaped like the state in which it is located (Figure 6-8). In recent years, putting surfaces have tended to become flatter and less steeply contoured as green speeds have increased.

FIGURE 6-6
This small Scottish green has a geometric shape between a trapezoid and a triangle. The course is located along the roadside on the Isle of Skye, Scotland.

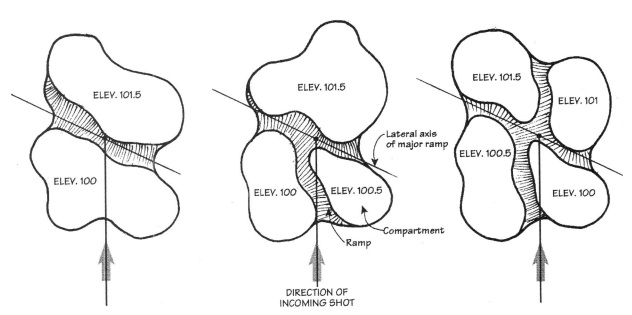

FIGURE 6-7
Compartmental greens, although sometimes geometric in appearance, add intense interest for approaching golfers.

SPECIFIC FEATURES OF CLASSIC GOLF HOLES

159

FIGURE 6-8

You can see the outline of the state of Idaho if you look carefully on the first hole at Hayden Lake Country Club, Hayden Lake, Idaho. The sign on the adjacent tree points this out.

GREEN SIZE

The size of the green is ranked among the most prominent features of a golf course. Donald Ross popularized the "Postage Stamp" green, with surface areas of some 1500 to 3000 square feet (Figures 6-9A and 6-9B), although he often provided much larger greens. For example, Ross's 13th at Franklin Hill Country Club near Detroit is a short 300-yard hole containing a well-known 2000-square-foot Postage Stamp

FIGURE 6-9A
A very small green, the Postage Stamp or eighth green at Royal Troon Golf Club, Ayrshire, Scotland, is famous for both its playability and its name. (Copyright © DuCam Marketing (UK) Ltd.)

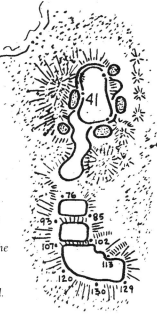

FIGURE 6-9B
Except for the tees, hole 5 at the Tribute Golf Club, The Colony, Texas, is a close adaptation of the Postage Stamp at Royal Troon Golf Club, Ayrshire, Scotland, with even the bunkers replicated. (Lew Graphics, Inc. © 2000.)

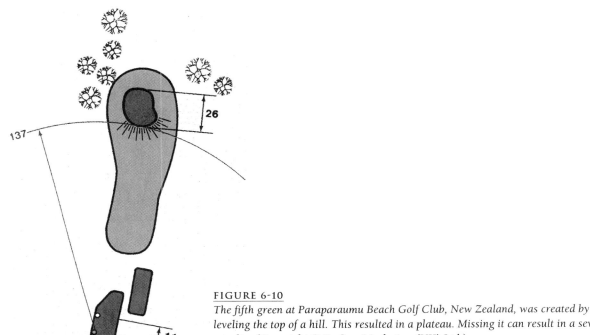

FIGURE 6-10
The fifth green at Paraparaumu Beach Golf Club, New Zealand, was created by leveling the top of a hill. This resulted in a plateau. Missing it can result in a severe penalty. (Copyright © DuCam Marketing (UK) Ltd.)

green. Other architects followed the practice of planning small putting surfaces to add challenge and character (Figures 6-10 and 6-11A through C). The 310-yard par-4 eighth at Pine Valley (Figure 6-12) by George Crump plays left to a small green less than 3000 square feet in area. Another, even smaller green was added in 1987 on the right of the hole to lessen wear on the original. A. W. Tillinghast, who may have played a role in the original Crump plans for the left green at Pine Valley, adapted it to several of his own layouts, notably the 15th at Fenway Golf Club in Westchester County, New York. Historian Jim Finegan dubs the original, "the graveyard of high hopes." Architect William Robinson was also intrigued by the interest of this short Pine Valley hole and its small green. He used a similar design at Hickory Ridge Country Club in Amherst, Massachusetts, where a stream also comes into play (Figure 6-13).

Early in the Depression, Bobby Tyre Jones and Alister Mackenzie produced mammoth greens at Augusta National. However, it wasn't until after the Depression and World War II that such maintenance extravagances gained popularity in the mid-1950s. Then, each year seemed to bring ever-larger greens, culminating in Geoffrey Cornish's 28,000-square-foot monster on the fifth hole at International Golf Club in Bolton, Massachusetts (Figure 6-14). At the time of its cre-

SPECIFIC FEATURES OF CLASSIC GOLF HOLES

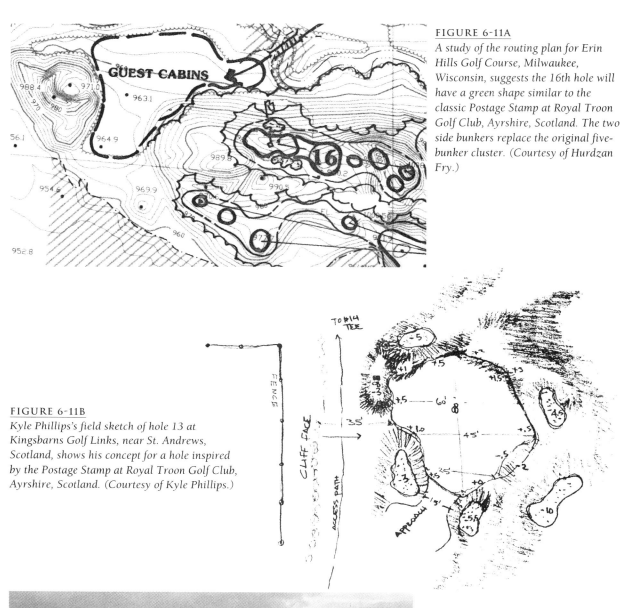

FIGURE 6-11A

A study of the routing plan for Erin Hills Golf Course, Milwaukee, Wisconsin, suggests the 16th hole will have a green shape similar to the classic Postage Stamp at Royal Troon Golf Club, Ayrshire, Scotland. The two side bunkers replace the original five-bunker cluster. (Courtesy of Hurdzan Fry.)

FIGURE 6-11B

Kyle Phillips's field sketch of hole 13 at Kingsbarns Golf Links, near St. Andrews, Scotland, shows his concept for a hole inspired by the Postage Stamp at Royal Troon Golf Club, Ayrshire, Scotland. (Courtesy of Kyle Phillips.)

FIGURE 6-11C

The completed 13th hole at Kingsbarns Golf Links, Scotland, is close to the concepts shown in the field sketch. (Courtesy of Iain Lowe Photography.)

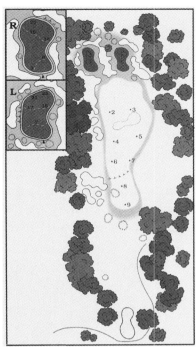

FIGURE 6-12

George Crump designed two small greens on the eighth hole at Pine Valley Golf Club, Pine Valley, New Jersey. The right green was added to reduce wear on the left green.

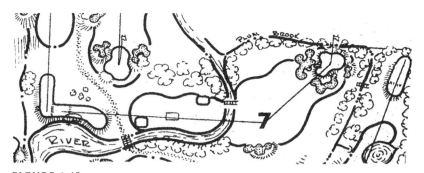

FIGURE 6-13

The seventh green at Hickory Ridge Country Club, Amherst, Massachusetts, is around 2500 square feet. It is an adaptation of the eighth hole at Pine Valley Golf Club, Pine Valley, New Jersey (see Figure 6-12). Playing with the prevailing wind, the golfer can carry the green from the white tee but never hold it.

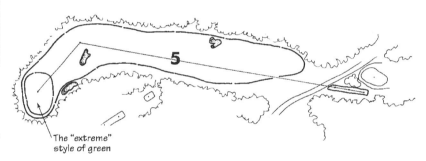

FIGURE 6-14

Hole 5 at the International Golf Club, Bolton, Massachusetts, has a massive green, more than half an acre in size. This very long hole ends with a severely contoured green, with the potential for extremely long putts.

ation, it was the world's largest single green, exceeding in area any of the Biarritz holes. Yet it does not approach the size of several of the huge double greens on the Old Course.

Later, R. M. Graves joined greens at Arrowhead Country Club in California to produce a 12,000-square-foot anomaly, and, still later, Graves's design partner Damian Pascuzzo crafted an intricately contoured 18,000-square-foot green at the Bridges Golf Course in California. For the most part, however, the trend toward ever-larger greens had petered out by the mid-1960s, except when the architect felt the hole called for a large putting surface. Today, most greens are in the range of 4500 to 7000 square feet, a happy medium between the Postage Stamps and mammoth greens of golf's earlier days.

SPECIFIC FEATURES OF CLASSIC GOLF HOLES

Double Greens

From the early days at St. Andrews, holes were played out and back, so that greens served two holes. Several were enlarged greatly around 1848 by the course greenkeeper and accomplished professional Allan Robertson, who was charged by Sir Hugh Playfair, Provost of St. Andrews, with modifying and improving the Old Course. The improvement plan was continued by Robertson's successor, Old Tom Morris, with seven double greens of enormous size finally emerging. All are now several feet higher than at the time of their enlargement as a result of regular topdressings with sand. Today on the Old Course, they are found on holes 2 and 16; 3 and 15; 4 and 14; 5 and 13; 6 and 12; and 8 and 10, together with holes 7 and 11 (Figure 6-15). All are

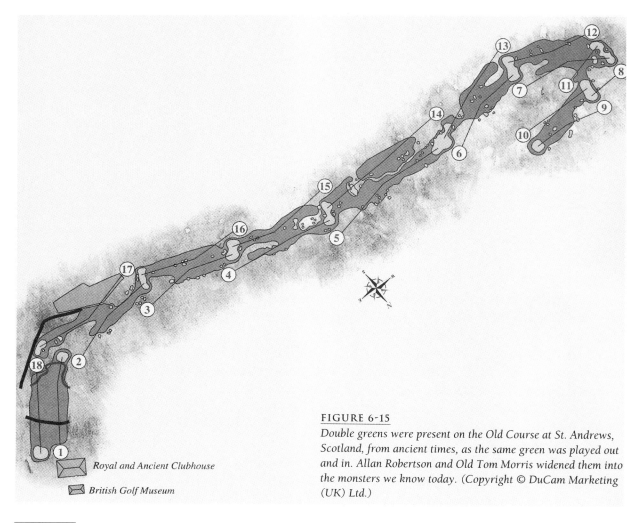

Royal and Ancient Clubhouse

British Golf Museum

FIGURE 6-15

Double greens were present on the Old Course at St. Andrews, Scotland, from ancient times, as the same green was played out and in. Allan Robertson and Old Tom Morris widened them into the monsters we know today. (Copyright © DuCam Marketing (UK) Ltd.)

CLASSIC GOLF HOLE DESIGN

widely known in the world of golf and have inspired the creation of other double greens.

During the 1960s and 1970s, course architects Cornish and W. G. Robinson created scores of double greens. This helped to popularize them in North America. Then the celebrated Jack Nicklaus introduced several on his layouts, including one at Grand Cypress in Florida. Rees Jones followed with a triple green. Despite some popularity, albeit limited, the purpose served by double greens is difficult to see; most likely it is simply to carry on a St. Andrews tradition. Strategy may, on occasion, call for their use if greens need to be set close to each other. However, they seldom conserve space because they must be large for safety's sake.

It is interesting that, with the exception of St. Andrews, few links courses include double greens. (The end of Chapter 2 shows course development at Montrose over several centuries, starting on the malls and streets of the town. It also includes an 1817 drawing entitled "A Reconstruction of the Leith Links." In neither case is there evidence of double greens.) Bernard Darwin described one example at North Berwick as, "A terrible place this double green of Point Garry." That double green served the 1st and 17th holes, but later was changed to two separate putting surfaces. Royal Dornoch seems never to have had a double green, while the 4th and 14th greens at Carnoustie abut each other with play from opposite directions (Figure 6-16). They have been shown as one green on several documents, indicating that at one time they were joined as a double green. At Musselburgh, there is no trace of double greens, but other courses in the British Isles, notably Felixstowe Ferry in England, probably had double greens. None has stood the test of time.

As a twist on the concept of double greens, and not known by the same name, several courses in the United States have two greens per hole, including the eighth at Pine Valley. (The ninth on that famed course also features two greens [Figure 6-17].) Jack Nicklaus's Desert Mountain in Arizona is well known for its use of this feature, with one green on each hole for the proficient and the other for the less accomplished. Harbor Town in South Carolina also includes a hole with two greens. There its purpose is to reduce wear. Several Japanese courses have sported two greens per hole, one for warm- and one for cool-season play. Among these is Yomiuri Country Club in Tokyo, designed by Seichi Inouye, which boasts two greens on each hole.

An interesting adaptation of the two-green concept was done at Quinta Do Gramacho in Portugal. With less than 100 acres available,

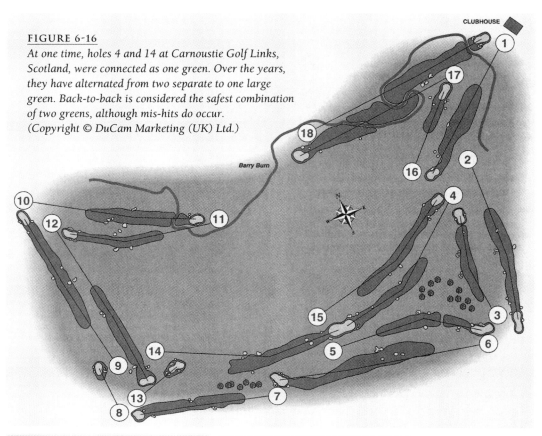

FIGURE 6-16

At one time, holes 4 and 14 at Carnoustie Golf Links, Scotland, were connected as one green. Over the years, they have alternated from two separate to one large green. Back-to-back is considered the safest combination of two greens, although mis-hits do occur. (Copyright © DuCam Marketing (UK) Ltd.)

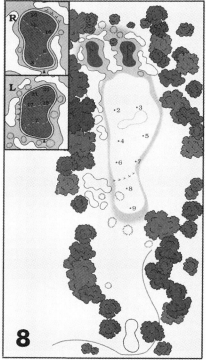

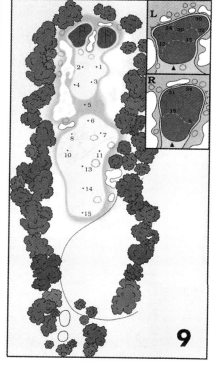

FIGURE 6-17

The presence of consecutive double greens is rare. But Pine Valley Golf Club, Pine Valley, New Jersey, which sports them on the eighth and the ninth holes, is a rare golf course to begin with.

CLASSIC GOLF HOLE DESIGN

the decision was made to create a double-tee, double-green nine-hole golf course. Although this concept has been used before, this is the first time in Europe and in a resort setting (Figure 6-18).

Two adjacent greens can be combined in many ways. Colonie Country Club near Albany, New York, by Cornish has two different examples (Figures 6-19A and 6-19B). At Pawleys Plantation, designed by Jack Nicklaus, holes 13 and 16 share a unique double green (Figures 6-20A through 6-20C).

Despite emulations and adaptations of St. Andrews's famous double greens, use of this feature has never become a true tradition of course design. In practice, double greens sometimes require more space than two separate greens because more area needs to be maintained as putting surface. In addition, the ever-present liability issue is a concern. For these reasons, with the exception of those on the Old Course, it is unlikely that double greens will ever become true classics.

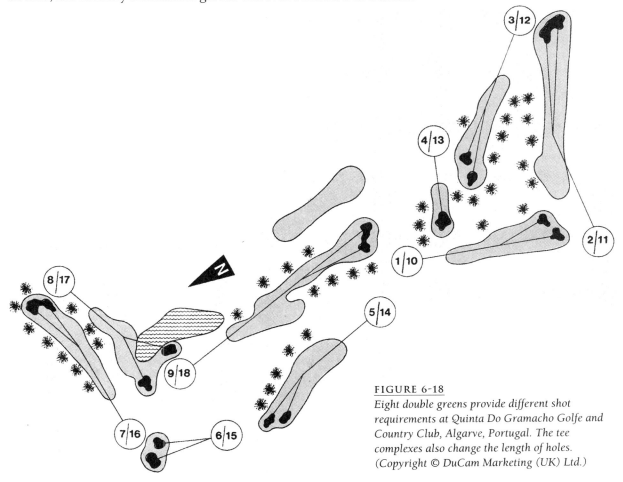

FIGURE 6-18
Eight double greens provide different shot requirements at Quinta Do Gramacho Golfe and Country Club, Algarve, Portugal. The tee complexes also change the length of holes. (Copyright © DuCam Marketing (UK) Ltd.)

FIGURE 6-19A

Greens 5 and 14 are combined at Colonie Country Club, near Albany, New York. They come together at a right angle.

FIGURE 6-19B

Holes 9 and 18 at Colonie Country Club, near Albany, New York, also come together, but they are separated enough to reduce interaction.

Steeply Contoured Greens

Greens featuring severe contours appear in various forms around the world. Perhaps the best-known examples are the "rolling terrors" of Perry Maxwell at Prairie Dunes in Kansas and his precipitous putting surfaces at Crystal Downs in Michigan. Maxwell also installed his famous "Maxwell Rolls" up and down the East Coast during the Depression, including greens at such courses as Augusta National, Pine Valley, Gulph Mills, and the National Golf Links. Yet it was Alister Mackenzie, Maxwell's partner in the last years of the Golden Era and the early years of the Depression, who in 1913 produced the most notorious example of severe green contouring with his 140-yard 18th at Sitwell Park in England. Though many architects continued to create "rolling terrors," many were not accepted. Today, with the Stimpmeter and the demand for ever-increasing green speed, steeply contoured greens have become increasingly rare.

Greens Falling Away

The Redan comes to mind when discussing greens that fall away from the approaching player, but greens in this category exist in many

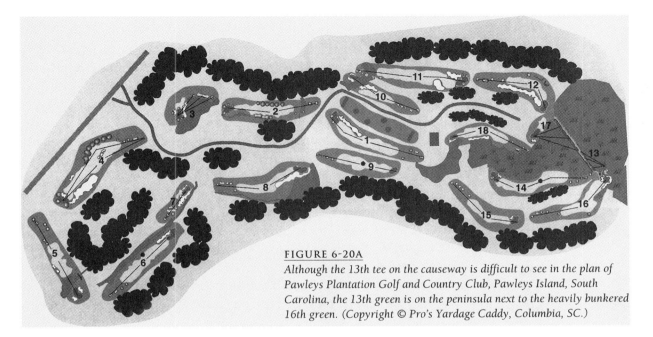

FIGURE 6-20A

Although the 13th tee on the causeway is difficult to see in the plan of Pawleys Plantation Golf and Country Club, Pawleys Island, South Carolina, the 13th green is on the peninsula next to the heavily bunkered 16th green. (Copyright © Pro's Yardage Caddy, Columbia, SC.)

FIGURE 6-20B

The 13th green at Pawleys Plantation Golf and Country Club, Pawleys Island, South Carolina, is in the foreground with the shorter tee area to the right. (Courtesy of Pawleys Plantation Golf and Country Club.)

FIGURE 6-20C

This shows a portion of the 16th green at Pawleys Plantation Golf and Country Club, Pawleys Island, South Carolina, with the 13th green in the background. (Courtesy of Pawleys Plantation Golf and Country Club.)

SPECIFIC FEATURES OF CLASSIC GOLF HOLES

other forms. The double green on the eighth hole at St. Andrews fits this description (Figure 6-21). So does the 13th hole at Royal Melbourne, as revised by Alister Mackenzie. Willie Park installed a green that slopes away on the third hole at Sunningdale in England, and it survived H. S. Colt's subsequent revisions (Figure 6-22). Included also is the first-hole green at Merion East, which was designed by Hugh Wilson following an extensive survey of courses in the British Isles, while Tillinghast's 12th hole at Golden Valley in Minnesota is guarded in the rear by a hazard that provides a severe penalty for those who don't hold a green that slopes away. Kingsbarns in Scotland, designed by Kyle Phillips, is still another version of this concept (Figure 6-23).

Many greens originally designed to fall away have been altered, perhaps because they were not accepted by golfers whose balls did not hold on them (despite what they felt were very well executed shots to the green). We do not consider this feature a classic in itself, although it is a major feature of the Redan, "the classic of classics."

Figures 6-24 and 6-25 indicate the innumerable shapes, elevations, and grades of the world's greens (also see Figure 6-7). All owe something to the early greens of Scotland, especially those placed in hollows to protect them from the wind and those placed on plateaus to add interest.

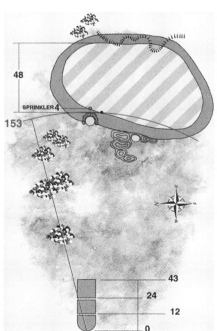

FIGURE 6-21
The Short, the eighth hole at the Old Course at St. Andrews, Scotland, does fall away from the shot, but does not have the horseshoe or thumbprint ridge that was characteristic of C. B. Macdonald, Seth Raynor, or Charles Banks's Shorts. (Copyright © DuCam Marketing (UK) Ltd.)

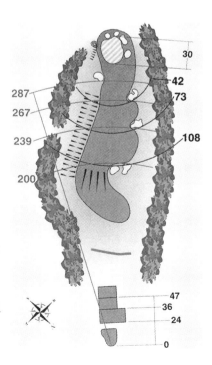

FIGURE 6-22
Even squeamish golfers accept this tough green target that falls away on a short par-4 at the third hole at Sunningdale Golf Club, Berkshire, England. (Copyright © DuCam Marketing (UK) Ltd.)

CLASSIC GOLF HOLE DESIGN

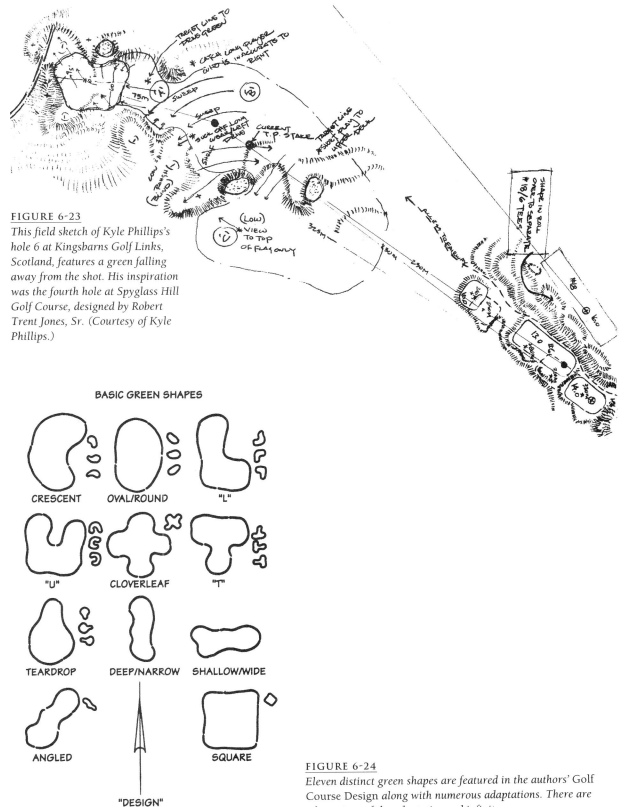

FIGURE 6-23
This field sketch of Kyle Phillips's hole 6 at Kingsbarns Golf Links, Scotland, features a green falling away from the shot. His inspiration was the fourth hole at Spyglass Hill Golf Course, designed by Robert Trent Jones, Sr. (Courtesy of Kyle Phillips.)

BASIC GREEN SHAPES

CRESCENT   OVAL/ROUND   "L"

"U"   CLOVERLEAF   "T"

TEARDROP   DEEP/NARROW   SHALLOW/WIDE

ANGLED   SQUARE

"DESIGN"
LINE OF FLIGHT

FIGURE 6-24
Eleven distinct green shapes are featured in the authors' Golf Course Design along with numerous adaptations. There are adaptations of the adaptations ad infinitum.

SPECIFIC FEATURES OF CLASSIC GOLF HOLES

FIGURE 6-25

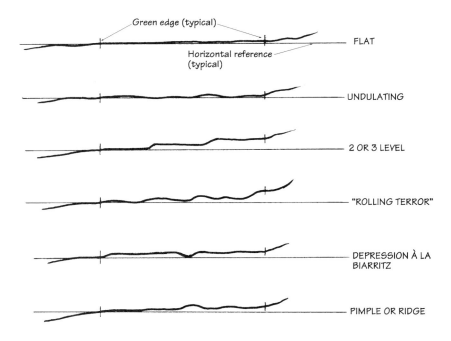

These cross sections of green shapes show six basic styles. Adaptations abound. For example, "Flat" sounds simple but is complicated by invisible slants off to one side, to the front, or to the back. There is a fine dividing line between "Undulating" and "Rolling Terror." Multilevel greens vary by size and shape of the decks and slope and length of the intermediate ramps. "Pimples" and "Ridges" appear periodically in green designs. Greens are also found where the putting surface is divided into compartments of varying levels (see Figure 6-7).

Tees

Until the last quarter of the 19th century, as noted in Chapter 3, teeing areas were a stepchild of course designers; they were given short shrift and did not exist in any meaningful way. Typically, the tee was an area one club-length from the previous hole where players were to tee up with a cone of sand or soil. Unfortunately, the material came directly from that previous hole, often making it ever larger and subsequent putting ever more difficult (see Figure 3-10, page 50). Later, a box filled with sand was placed near the tee area, and by 1874, metal cups were placed in the holes at Crail Golfing Society, a practice soon copied by other clubs. (According to some historians, the term "tee-box" was derived from the term "sand-box.") Improved putting surfaces—not to mention consistent hole sizes—resulted, and tees soon took on a shape of their own (Figure 6-26).

Aleck Bauer in his book *Hazards* comments on the ineptness of course design in the late 19th century. In defense of early designers, we point out that there were some early pioneers who began to consider shape, size, and surface when planning tees. Those designers had few resources and little know-how at their disposal; yet, by utilizing existing terrain, they often created miracles and began the trend toward improved teeing grounds. Indeed, until the last decades of the 20th century, with the exception of a few years in the Roaring

FIGURE 6-26
A typical tee in Great Britain, like this hole, is square or rectangular in shape.

Twenties, the majority of designers were not provided adequate funds, and the "billiard table" tee surfaces we know today were almost unheard of until laser equipment was introduced for leveling and grading in the 1990s (before then, some superintendents achieved smoothness by constant topdressing).

Many tees created in the 1920s and on the landmark courses that preceded them were rectangular in shape. A. W. Tillinghast was one course designer who, during the 1920s, pioneered the concept of larger teeing areas and shapes other than rectangles. Following World War II, Robert Trent Jones demonstrated that long and large tee areas were essential if turf was to be maintained year-round and if flexibility was to be adequate. Separate tees had been provided for women since at least World War I, but often these were of low quality and sited with little thought for the women's game. The concept of multiple tees on a hole goes far back in history, but it was Pete and Alice Dye who made them popular in the United States. Around that same time, in the early 1970s, Lawrence Packard helped start a trend to make free-form tees with his work at Innisbrook Country Club in Florida an outstanding example (Figure 6-27). Nevertheless, rectangular tees remain the most popular and are likely to remain so for the foreseeable future (Figure 6-28). In a way, they are classic.

Mounds

Mounding on golf courses around the world is an attempt to emulate the varied landforms of the Scottish links and the drumlins, eskers,

FIGURE 6-27
Tees can also be free-form, as shown on this hole at Innisbrook Country Club, Tarpon Springs, Florida.

FIGURE 6-28
The Graves and Pascuzzo tees at the Institute Golf Club, Morgan Hill, California, are all rectangular. They don't really blend with the surrounding hillsides but have historical value.

and kames on the higher inland terrain of the British Isles (Figure 6-29). Mounds can play an important role in the architecture of a course, a fact not lost on early Scottish professionals, who introduced the landforms of their native land to other countries. In the beginning, this most often took the form of what are now called "Chocolate Drops," "Dolomites," or "Moguls," three terms we consider to be synonymous (see Figures 4-22 and 4-23, page 75). In addition to helping to capture the style of the links, these mounds were needed for functional reasons, including depth perception, playing interest, and preventing balls from rolling into impossible situations.

Carnoustie in Scotland has mounds in abundance, many triangular and linear in contrast to round chocolate drops. Most of the mounding on this course can be seen near Barry Burn, as it passes

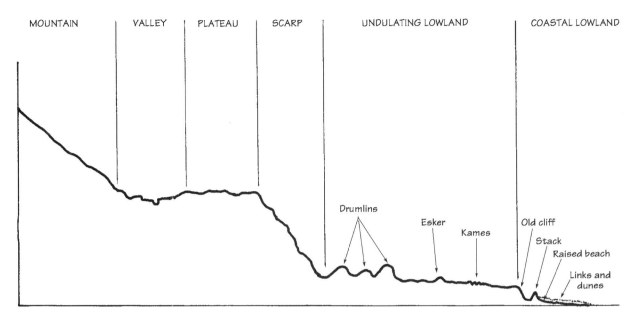

MOUNTAIN   VALLEY   PLATEAU   SCARP   UNDULATING LOWLAND   COASTAL LOWLAND

Drumlins

Esker

Kames

Old cliff

Stack

Raised beach

Links and dunes

through the home holes. Amazingly, all of these triangular mounds are natural. Far from Carnoustie, Foster Golf Links in the state of Washington, built in 1925, included similar mounds (Figure 6-30). Indeed, its ninth green was once completely surrounded by four triangular mounds. All were removed because they proved difficult to maintain.

At Hayden Lake Country Club in Idaho, we find triangular cross-section mounds along the back of the 18th green (Figure 6-31), simi-

FIGURE 6-29
The varying landforms that provide part of the basis for the classification of golf course sites are illustrated in this diagram.

FIGURE 6-30
The designer of this green at Foster Golf Links, Tikwila, Washington, was influenced by golf courses being built in the eastern states in the Roaring Twenties. Similar mounds are still in play at Tamarack Country Club, Greenwich, Connecticut (see Figure 6-32). (Courtesy of the Aliment Family.)

FIGURE 6-31
This triangular-shaped mound at Hayden Lake Country Club, Hayden Lake, Idaho, is still in play today.

FIGURE 6-32
The 11th green, known as the "Punch Bowl," at Tamarack Country Club, Greenwich, Connecticut, is a good example of Charles Banks's dedicated work. Tamarack boasts many classic holes.

lar to those that abound on older New England courses (Figure 6-32). Most can be traced to designers who hailed from Scotland. While many golfers consider these to be hazards, it should be noted that skilled golfers use them to their advantage to deflect balls on certain shots. On Seth Raynor and Charles Banks courses, a large round mound is often found in a bunker. It is named "Chocolate Drop" (see Figures 4-22 and 4-23, page 75). Similarly, golf architect Tom Bendelow placed small, densely vegetated mounds in his bunkers. They were dubbed "Dragon's Teeth" (Figure 6-33). Except for annual burning, Dragon's Teeth were not maintained and therefore proved to

FIGURE 6-33
Referred to as Chocolate Drops in this 1910 photo of the College Arms Golf Club, near Deland, Florida, these sharper mounds were often called Dragon's Teeth.

be far greater problems than those provided by manicured islands found in more modern bunkers (Figure 6-34).

Another offshoot of Chocolate Drops was the "Mae West" mound, so named for the well-endowed movie star. One example is in front of the 12th green at Bel-Air Country Club. "Mae Wests" were quite popular throughout the Golden Years. At Jasper Park in the

FIGURE 6-34
Both bunker clusters by Graves and Pascuzzo are similar in character but dissimilar in location and environment. Photograph A shows Paradise Valley Golf Course, Fairfield, California, in a hilly portion of the Sacramento Valley. Photograph B shows the Sea Ranch Golf Links located near Gualala along the northern California coast.

Canadian Rockies, architect Stanley Thompson installed one set that was so realistic that Sir Henry Thornton, then president of the Canadian National Railroad, which owned the course, ordered Thompson to remove them. As this example shows, the profession of course architecture has not been immune to excesses, and it is not surprising that the "Mae West" mounds led to phallic symbol mounds. Some still exist today, but fortunately they are not recognized as such by club officials and golfers.

Members of private clubs and officials at daily-fee courses appreciate the efforts of the early Scottish designers to bring the contours of their homeland to the New World. But that was before the days of universal irrigation, when skilled golfers used mounds to deflect balls and advance them toward the green. Yet mounds remain an intrinsic part of course design.

Bunkers

Over the centuries, descriptive names were given to features on the ancient links. Perhaps no feature was more feted than the bunker, and as time went on, these features and their names became hallowed. Course architect Desmond Muirhead has even suggested that names of features at St. Andrews possess deeply symbolic or even religious meaning.

Bunker Names

Nevertheless, it is possible to trace the origins of the names of dozens of bunkers on the Old Course to more contemporary and mundane events. Examples that have become classics or near classics include:

- **Cartgate.** This bunker lies close to the Cartgate holes—going out 3rd and coming home 15th (Figures 6-35 and 6-36). The name comes from the fact that at one time a gate was present on an ancient road to the Eden River.
- **Ginger Beer.** The fourth hole on the Old Course owes its name to David Anderson, who as recently as the last decades of the 19th century operated a stall where he sold ginger beer (Figure 6-37). The stall was located behind the green, close to the bunker now called Ginger Beer.
- **Short.** The eighth hole is known as "short" because the bunker is considerably short of the green (see Figure 6-21). Despite its

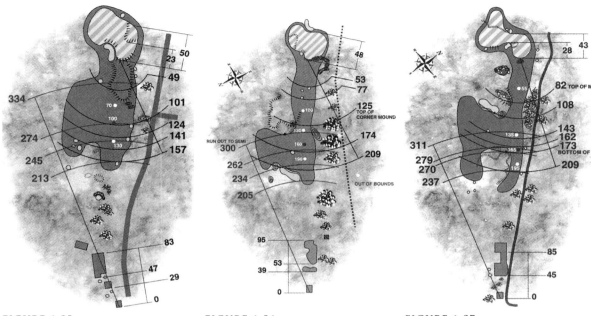

FIGURE 6-35

The cartgate and ancient road once near the third hole on the Old Course at St. Andrews, Scotland, have long since disappeared. (Copyright © DuCam Marketing (UK) Ltd.)

FIGURE 6-36

Cartgate-In, versus Cartgate-Out for hole 3, is the name for the 15th hole on the Old Course at St. Andrews, Scotland. (Copyright © DuCam Marketing (UK) Ltd.

FIGURE 6-37

Hole 4 on the Old Course at St. Andrews, Scotland, is named Ginger Beer. Though once sold nearby, no ginger beer is available here today to soothe the golfer's nerves, just plenty of golf. (Copyright © DuCam Marketing (UK) Ltd.)

name, the hole is now a few yards longer than the Eden (High-In), the 11th.

- **Hole O'Cross.** The bunker with this name comes into play on the 13th (Figure 6-38), but not on the 5th, the other hole that bears the name. Still, both holes owe their names to a cross that once stood nearby. That fact has contributed to the speculation that there is religious significance to bunker names on the Old Course.

- **Road.** This is the deep and terrifying pot bunker set to the left of the 17th green (Figure 6-39), which has played a role in many major championships. The name comes from the road behind and to the right of the green. Yet the hole was probably called "Road" before the bunker took on that name.

Other bunkers on the Old Course are now recognized by their names throughout the world of golf. These include, but are not limited to, Hell, Coffin, Grave, Principal's Nose, Wig, Lion's Mouth, and Mrs. Kruger. Each has a fascinating history. Tournament golfer Sandy

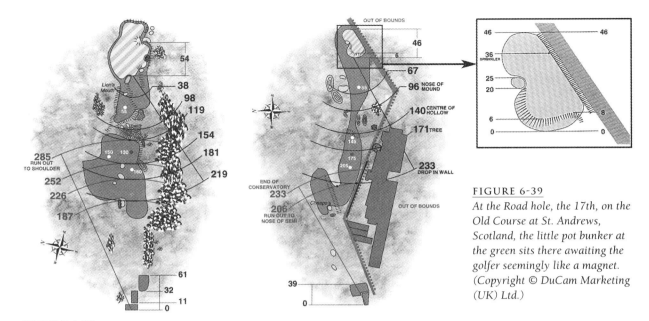

FIGURE 6-38

Hole O'Cross–In is the 13th hole on the Old Course at St. Andrews, Scotland. It takes its name from a cross that was once positioned there. (Copyright © DuCam Marketing (UK) Ltd.)

FIGURE 6-39

At the Road hole, the 17th, on the Old Course at St. Andrews, Scotland, the little pot bunker at the green sits there awaiting the golfer seemingly like a magnet. (Copyright © DuCam Marketing (UK) Ltd.)

Lyle, in collaboration with Bob Ferrier, has provided the basis for the names of all the holes on Scottish championship courses. Not to be out-done, golf architects Ault, Clark & Associates of Maryland named a greenside bunker cluster at Magnolia Creek Golf Links after investors in the course; the three bunkers are named "Hartmen's" (Figure 6-40).

FIGURE 6-40

Three bunkers left of the first green at Magnolia Creek Golf Links, League City, Texas, are called "Hartmen's" in honor of Becky, Mike, and Ed Hartman, who were major investors in the course. (Courtesy of Ault, Clark & Associates, Ltd.)

CLASSIC GOLF HOLE DESIGN

Some bunkers have been named for less happy reasons. "Willie Campbell's Grave," the 16th hole at Prestwick, received its name when Campbell, who was leading the pack in the 1887 Open, put his ball into that bunker (Figure 6-41). Taking several strokes to recover, he lost to Willie Park, Jr. Some say, perhaps incorrectly, that his disappointment contributed to his decision to move to the New World permanently. There he became the first professional at the Country Club near Boston and soon became a pioneer in planning municipal golf courses in America—facilities that became significant in accommodating a tidal wave of people who were taking up the game. American golf, therefore, owes a lot to "Willie Campbell's Grave." Moreover, his wife Georgina became America's first woman professional golfer.

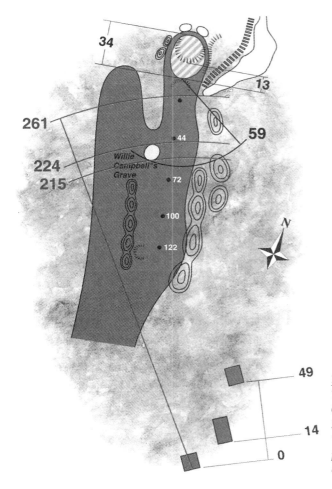

FIGURE 6-41

Taking several strokes to recover from this bunker, Willie Campbell subsequently lost the Open at Prestwick Golf Club, Prestwick, Scotland. Ever since, this bunker has been called "Willie Campbell's Grave." Some say this led to Campbell's permanent emigration to America, where he pioneered early course design. (Copyright © DuCam Marketing (UK) Ltd.)

Classifying Bunkers by Design or Placement

Aside from their individual names, bunkers can be classified by design type or character. Broad categories include sand and grass bunkers. Other descriptive classifications include the following.

CROSS, LATERAL, DIAGONAL, AND RANDOM BUNKERS

Most cross bunkers are penal, although some force the golfer to decide whether to attempt the carry or to play short and safe. In those cases, they are strategic. Yet strategic bunkers are most often sited laterally along the sides of the holes, so that if a golfer dares one and succeeds, a premium results. Random bunkers sited without measurement from the tee are often found on the links. Placed regardless of strategy, they still come into play. Diagonal bunkers placed on an angle to the shot often provide a premium for those who dare the longest carry and succeed. They are therefore strategic.

POT BUNKERS

FIGURE 6-42

These pot bunkers show sod stabilization of the bank and the use of conventional grass cover. Many pot bunkers are holes in the ground with no earthen works around them. Bunker shots spray sand, and, over time, add embankments.

These abound on the world's golf courses, and many are nameless. In some locales, pot bunkers are referred to as pit bunkers, a name that aptly describes them because they are truly holes in the ground (Figure 6-42).

CLASSIC GOLF HOLE DESIGN

TRENCH OR STRIP BUNKERS

These are less common than they were in earlier times, although they remain in existence as the "Church Pews" at Oakmont or as "safe-in" bunkers placed alongside fairways to prevent balls from rolling down cliffs, into deep woods, or into some similar "goal."

FACE BUNKERS

Face bunkers (Figures 6-43 and 6-44) have faces of sand visible to the oncoming golfer.

SOD-FACED BUNKERS

These bunkers have sod as contrasted to sand faces (Figure 6-45).

CRATER OR MOON BUNKERS

These bunkers resemble large shell holes. The "Soup Bowl" bunker on the 18th at Rye Golf Club in England is one example (Figure 6-46). Its steep edge projects above the sloping sand surface to provide

FIGURE 6-43
Two examples of face bunkers include A, an ominous-looking, very steep, clearly visible bunker, its location lost in our files with the memory lingering on. Another bunker, B, located at the Golf Club at Quail Lodge, Carmel Valley, California, shows its face to incoming golfers but in a much more subdued way.

FIGURE 6-44
Robert Trent Jones, Sr., created this impressive greenside bunker on the 16th at Metedeconk National Golf Club, Jackson, New Jersey. It is part face bunker and part grassed bank with Alister Mackenzie–style lace edges. (Photo by Roger Rulewich.)

FIGURE 6-45
The bank of this bunker in Scotland is reveted by sod laid like bricks.

FIGURE 6-46
The Soup Bowl bunker on the 18th hole at Rye Golf Club, Deal, England, is big and steep, with raised timber baffling around its perimeter. It certainly provides a severe penalty for golfers reaching it. (Courtesy of Grant Books.)

FIGURE 6-47
This bunker in Ireland has caught a golfer's ball and left him with a difficult shot. Anything landing near this unkempt bunker gravitates to the bottom.

the effect of a giant soup bowl. Bernard Darwin, in *Golf Courses of the British Isles,* described it as a "pit of desolation looming vast and uncarryable." Later, the American golf course architect Robert Bruce Harris was famous for his bunkers and their moon shapes.

GATHERING BUNKERS

Gathering bunkers (Figure 6-47) are located at the bottom of a depression. They arose on early links from numerous recoveries of balls that rolled into hollows. This "magnet" touch still surrounds many bunkers on links courses, and it tends to nurse balls, even those landing many feet from it, into the hazard.

SAHARA BUNKERS

These bunkers are so immense that they dominate the hole. Two examples are the famed Sahara at Royal St. George's (Figure 6-48) and Hell's Half Acre at Pine Valley (Figure 6-49). (Not incidentally, the area of the latter totals nearly 2 acres.) Still another famous Sahara is found on the 17th at Prestwick (Figure 6-50).

OAKMONT DITCHES

These are truly trench bunkers, but they are grassed. First installed at famed Oakmont to divert running water from coursing over holes,

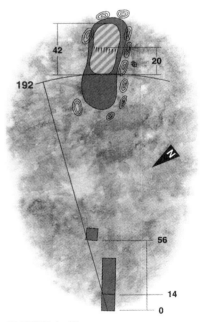

FIGURE 6-48
The space between tee and green on hole 3, called the "Sahara," at Royal St. George's Golf Club, Sandwich, England, is not a well-defined bunker; it is a vast wasteland of sand and grass banks. (Copyright © DuCam Marketing (UK) Ltd.)

FIGURE 6-49
A shot across the vast sandy waste of Hell's Half Acre bunker at Pine Valley Golf Club, Pine Valley, New Jersey, is terrifying. (Courtesy of Treewolf Productions.)

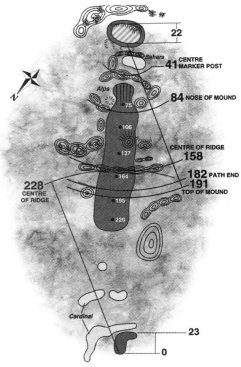

FIGURE 6-50
The Alps hole, the 17th, at Prestwick Golf Club, Prestwick, Scotland, also features a Sahara bunker hidden from the golfer. (Copyright © DuCam Marketing (UK) Ltd.)

they are played as hazards and have become notorious. Replications at other courses have not always been successful.

BUNKER PLACEMENT

Some well-known bunkers are distinguished not by their size or shape but by their positioning. The bunker in the middle of the green on the sixth at Riviera Country Club, designed by Thomas and Bell, is one example. Another is a similarly placed bunker on the short seventh at Woking Golf Club in England. There have been others, but most have disappeared.

A less invasive placement of a bunker involves a hazard protruding into one side of the green (Figure 6-51). As with a bunker situated entirely in the putting surface, a protruding bunker can make it impossible to putt straight for the pin (Figure 6-52). Accomplished golfers have been known to chip over these protrud-

CLASSIC GOLF HOLE DESIGN

FIGURE 6-51
This bunker at Port Ludlow Golf Course, Port Ludlow, Washington, projects into green 9 on the tide nine and can present problems depending on ball and pin location.

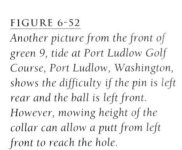

FIGURE 6-52
Another picture from the front of green 9, tide at Port Ludlow Golf Course, Port Ludlow, Washington, shows the difficulty if the pin is left rear and the ball is left front. However, mowing height of the collar can allow a putt from left front to reach the hole.

ing bunkers even if their balls lie on the putting surface. Less talented golfers have tried to do the same and have severely damaged the turf. In some instances, the green has been contoured in a manner that allows golfers to putt around the hazard, leading some to call the bunker placement "gimmicky." Therefore, most courses with bunkers in the green or invading it have called in architects to eliminate or modify them (Figure 6-53).

SPECIFIC FEATURES OF CLASSIC GOLF HOLES

FIGURE 6-53

The Duel hole at San Francisco Golf and Country Club, California, is so called because it is the site where a judge and a senator settled a dispute with firearms. The tee shot is from a high ridge to a green with an angled bunker cutting deep into the right side. Pin placement and shot placement can cause impossible putts.

Bunkerless Holes

Because sand and golf have a mystical link and sand accents a golf hole, we hesitate to consider bunkerless holes as classics, but examples exist of such holes and need to be included. Bunkerless holes are the exception rather than the rule. Yet we found more than a hundred. Most famously, the 18th on the Old Course is bunkerless, probably due to the presence of Swilcan Burn and the Valley of Sin (Figures 6-54A and 6-54B). Ashdown Forest Golf Course in England takes this one step farther with an entire course devoid of bunkers. In the words of Bernard Darwin in *Golf Courses of the British Isles,* there is "not a single hideous rampart on the course or so much even as a pot bunker."

Daniel Wexler, in his informative *Missing Links,* mentions several dozen holes on six former golf courses that were bunkerless. One of them, the original Country Club of Ithaca in the Finger Lakes area of New York, designed by Tillinghast and revised by Robert Trent Jones, had some 12 bunkerless holes. Although it is often claimed that the long sixth hole at famed Canterbury near Cleveland is bunkerless, there are several small greenside bunkers.

CLASSIC GOLF HOLE DESIGN

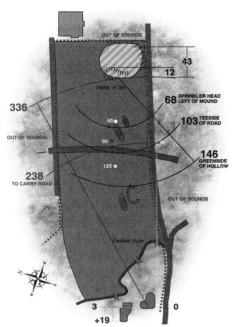

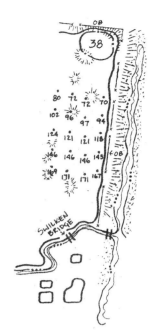

FIGURE 6-54A

This seemingly innocent hole, the 18th on the Old Course at St. Andrews, Scotland, has settled many tournaments. Successfully navigating the Valley of Sin, located left front of the green and mowed at green height, requires prodigious putting or chipping skill to get near the hole. (Copyright © DuCam Marketing (UK) Ltd.)

FIGURE 6-54B

The 18th hole at Tribute Golf Club, The Colony, Texas, replicates the 18th at the Old Course at St. Andrews, Scotland, but without a road crossing.

The World Atlas of Golf includes some 30 golf courses featuring two to five bunkerless holes. The 14th at Royal Dornoch had none (Figure 6-55), while, also in Scotland, Gullane's second hole has none. The first hole at Royal Liverpool is bunkerless (Figure 6-56), but it has an interior out-of-bounds on the right. Other bunkerless holes of note include the 10th at Royal Troon (Figure 6-57A) and the 10th at Christchurch Golf Club in New Zealand. The latest play booklet for Christchurch shows two greenside bunkers (Figure 6-57B). Because of the mystical link between sand and golf, we continue to wonder if any bunkerless hole can be a classic.

Sleepered Bulkheaded Bunkers

Sleepered bulkheaded bunkers (Figure 6-58) appeared on the links of Scotland when early greenkeepers found it necessary to stabilize the pits of sand and to reduce sand movement during periods of high wind. Some are "crater" or "moon" bunkers as described above. They are eye-catchers, particularly when a golfer sees one for the first time, and most of all if his or her ball hits against the wooden wall. Early Scottish designers installed them in North America, but they became unpopular when golfers "beaned" themselves by hitting balls against bulkheads that had not been installed at the correct angle. Then, in the 1960s, golf architects Pete and Alice Dye reintroduced them fol-

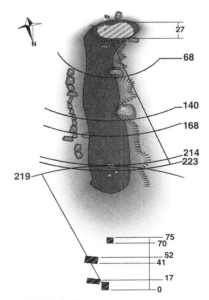

FIGURE 6-55

What complicates the 14th at Royal Dornoch, Dornoch, Scotland, are the mounds, vegetation, and wind in abundance. (Copyright © DuCam Marketing (UK) Ltd.)

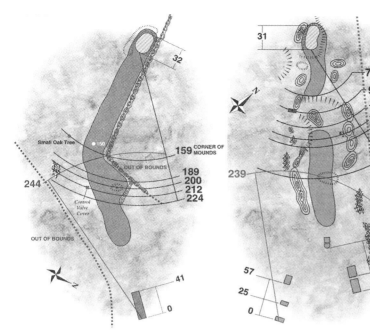

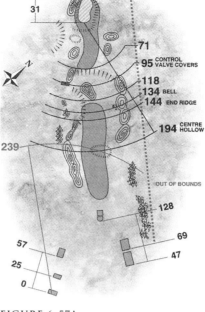

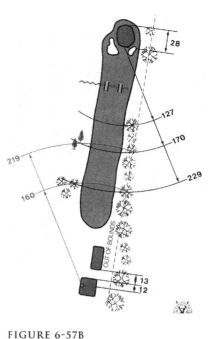

FIGURE 6-56
Without a bunker, a tight out-of-bounds along the right side of hole 1 at Royal Liverpool Golf Club, Hoylake, England, provides adequate trouble for an opening hole. (Copyright © DuCam Marketing (UK) Ltd.)

FIGURE 6-57A
The 10th hole, called "Sandhills," at Royal Troon Golf Club, Ayrshire, Scotland, creates enough havoc without need of a bunker. (Copyright © DuCam Marketing (UK) Ltd.)

FIGURE 6-57B
Though the 10th hole at Christchurch Golf Course in New Zealand is reported not to have bunkers, the latest yardage booklet shows that it has two. (Copyright © DuCam Marketing (UK) Ltd.)

FIGURE 6-58
The Cardinal bunker on the third hole at Prestwick Golf Club, Prestwick, Scotland, is famous on its own. The bulkheads are there to stabilize the grassy hillocks.

CLASSIC GOLF HOLE DESIGN

lowing their historic visit to Scotland. The Dye bulkheads were installed at the correct angle to protect players from ricochet shots. Unfortunately, many who copied the Dyes failed to realize the importance of the angle. (Again, the litigious nature of society may have contributed to this bunker's demise.)

Aleck Bauer describes many sleepered bunkers, including the 15th at Gullane and holes 4 and 15 at Westward Ho! (Royal North Devon). Donald Steel calls the former "the black boarded bunker." Other examples were seen on holes 4, 9, and 18 at Royal West Norfolk at Brancaster, England.

Spectacles Bunkers

Spectacles bunkers are a configuration of two moon-shaped, side-by-side bunkers aligned perpendicular to the approach to the green. The result is that the bunkers look like a pair of eyes to the approaching golfer. They were once fairly common on American courses, with Macdonald, Raynor, and Banks featuring them. Tamarack, a venerable Charles Banks layout in Greenwich, Connecticut, had spectacles on its third hole, the Eden. Although this club is exceptionally protective of its classic holes, it chose not to restore its "Spectacles" during a recent major restoration. This may be because, in America, Spectacles that are not revetted or stacked with sod tend to evolve into caves from which recoveries are impossible.

When referring to "Spectacles," the most renowned example is the 14th at Carnoustie Golf Links, in Scotland, because the bunkers seem to stare at the approaching golfer (Figure 6-59). The 10th hole at Carnoustie, known as "South America," has, on occasion, been called "Spectacles" (Figure 6-60), but the name belongs to the 14th. Another example of spectacles-shaped bunkers occurs at Western Gailes Golf Club (Figure 6-61). Despite their somewhat common adaptation, we do not look on Spectacles as classic.

Trees and Course Furnishings

Trees have been planted in abundance on golf holes. No one can deny that they are impressive and that they can add to playing interest and the savanna preference of our species. Their shadows changing from dawn to dusk provide changing scenes by the hour. But when overdone or planted in the wrong positions, trees contribute to many

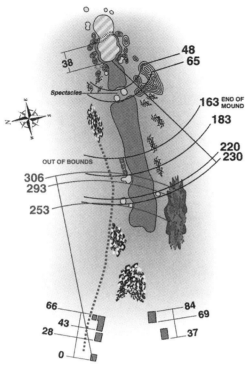

FIGURE 6-59

The diagram shows how the Spectacles bunkers on the 14th hole at Carnoustie Golf Links, Scotland, fit into this fairly short par-5. Besides the potential to confuse the distance from them to the green, these two ocular orifices tend to stare you into a sense of doom, like a goggle-eyed monster lying in wait. (Copyright © DuCam Marketing (UK) Ltd.)

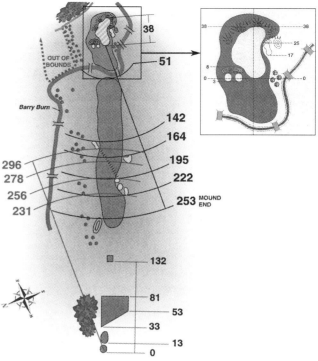

FIGURE 6-60

Bunkers on South America, the 10th hole at Carnoustie Golf Links, Scotland, are offset to the left of the green. They still remind us of eyeglasses, although they occupy a less traditional location. (Copyright © DuCam Marketing (UK) Ltd.)

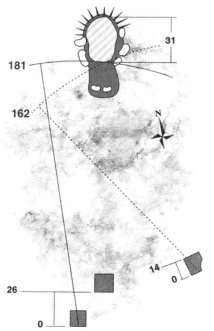

FIGURE 6-61

The Spectacles-like bunkers on the 15 hole at Western Gailes Golf Club, Ayrshire, Scotland, distort the distance between them and the green with that same goggle-eyed effect. (Copyright © DuCam Marketing (UK) Ltd.)

CLASSIC GOLF HOLE DESIGN

FIGURE 6-62
Golfers are thoroughly used to seeing trees as part of the golfing picture. This 1988 aerial photograph of St. Andrews, Scotland, shows the total golf complex but not one tree until you get well inland. Any wonder the early designers couldn't imagine a tree as part of their pictures? (Copyright © DuCam Marketing (UK) Ltd.)

turfgrass problems, block views from hole to hole, mar breathtaking vistas, and compromise playing interest and strategy (Figure 6-62).

Mowing patterns also enhance playing interest and aesthetics, while the creation of wild, unrefined areas around the course has become a major feature of contemporary golf holes.

Contemporary course designers are also enhancing their compositions by using what were once considered mundane features, including bridges of both stone and wood, bulkheads on pond and stream banks, waterscapes, and, that most ordinary feature of all, the golf cart path. In the hands of many talented artists, these features may be considered part of their "paints." Yet some say that using them "gilds the lily."

When designing bridges, contemporary golf architects seek to replicate the old stone bridge at St. Andrews (Figure 6-63). That is the focus point or Mecca where course designers from around the world seek the roots of their art form. That bridge is the classic of golf course bridges and has been widely replicated (Figure 6-64).

FIGURE 6-63
Here is the famous bridge at St. Andrews, Scotland, that one must traverse as part of the quintessential golfing experience for designer or player.

FIGURE 6-64
This is another version of the bridge, just as functional, at Port Ludlow Golf Course, Port Ludlow, Washington, but lacking in centuries of history behind it.

CLASSIC GOLF HOLE DESIGN

7

THE CLASSIC
GOLF HOLES

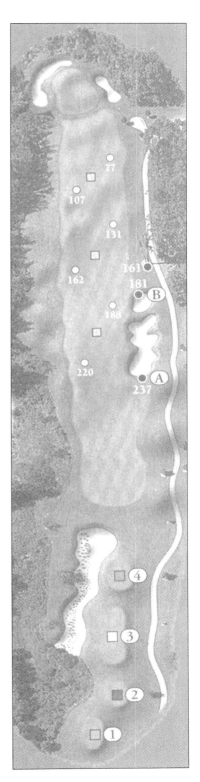

Impressive golf holes emerged from the drawing boards of architects throughout the entire 20th century, but it wasn't until the two decades leading up to the millennium that the most impressive holes were produced. On the links, nature had provided ready-made, dramatic compositions from which the game evolved. During the waning years of the 20th century, a dynamic, creative group of architect artists produced masterpieces marked by integrity, great imagination, and grand ingenuity. Yet these masterpieces all reflect in some ways the principles of famous ancient holes that were once referred to as "classics."

When describing classics, we are not necessarily including all the spectacular holes that abound on the world's golf courses. Sometimes these holes (classics or otherwise) owe their fame, in part at least, to their striking surroundings, for example, the Devil's Cauldron at Banff Springs in the Canadian Rockies, designed by architect Stanley Thompson, or the 16th at Cypress Point on the Monterey Peninsula in California, designed by architect Alister Mackenzie. Those holes are also indebted to their architects for capturing the grandeur in their compositions. On the other hand, many golf holes in less striking surroundings are also famous and owe their magic almost entirely to the talent of those who created them.

To some extent, large or small, in grand or mundane landscapes, each golf hole owes something to the holes that came before it. We call those that have had the greatest impact on the art form "classic." To help define "classic," in the sense we use it, we formulated three criteria:

- A hole that has had a pervasive influence on course design due to the principles that it embodies
- A hole that has stood the test of time
- A hole that has subsequently been adapted, and repeatedly so

A list of holes once put forward as classics is given in Table 7-1. Not all meet the three requirements listed above.

TABLE 7-1
Holes Considered to Be Classics

Hole Name	Original
Alps	The 17th, Prestwick Golf Club, Scotland.
Biarritz	The 3rd or 12th, Golf de Biarritz, Biarritz, France. The hole no longer exists.
Cape	The 14th, National Golf Links of America on Long Island, although the 5th at the Mid Ocean Club in Bermuda that opened 13 years later is probably a better known "Cape."
Cardinal	The 3rd at Prestwick.
Dell	The 6th at Lahinch Golf Club, Ireland.
Eden (High-Out)	The 7th, the Old Course at St. Andrews, Scotland.
Eden (High-In)	The 11th, the Old Course at St. Andrews.
Gibraltar	A hole at Seacroft Golf Club and the 8th at Moortown Golf Club, both in England.
Hell's Half Acre	The 7th, Pine Valley Golf Club, Pine Valley, New Jersey.
Island Green	The 9th at Ponte Vedra Golf Club, Ponte Vedra, Florida. (Several less well known "islands" preceded it. Today, the "Dye Island" on several of architect Pete Dye's courses are the best known.)
Long	The 14th, the Old Course at St. Andrews.
Maiden	The 6th, Royal St. George's Golf Club, England.
Perfection	The 14th, North Berwick Golf Club, Scotland.
Postage Stamp	The 8th, Royal Troon Golf Club, Scotland.
Punch Bowl	The 4th, Royal Cinque Ports Golf Club, England, and the 9th at Royal Liverpool Golf Club, Hoylake, England.
Redan and Reverse Redan	The 15th, North Berwick.
Reef	Said to be a Tillinghast original, it may have been preceded by the 3rd at MacGregor Links, Saratoga Springs, New York, by architect Devereux Emmet.
Road	The 17th, the Old Course at St. Andrews.
Sahara	The 3rd, Royal St. George's Golf Club.
Short	The 5th, National Golf Links. (The 8th on the Old Course is called "short" but appears not to be the model for innumerable Shorts.)

CLASSIC GOLF HOLE DESIGN

At the low end of this list of possible classics is ***Perfection, the 14th at North Berwick***. It is now a 376-yard par-4 with a blind second shot to a green adjoining a beach (Figure 7-1A). Golf has been played at North Berwick since the 16th century. Over centuries, the 14th evolved into a par-3 and was mentioned in the early literature of golf. As a par-3, it influenced early Scottish designers as early as the third quarter of the 19th century (Figure 7-1B). It emerged in its contemporary form as a par-4 during the tenure of David Strath, greenkeeper and professional at North Berwick from 1876 to 1878, before his

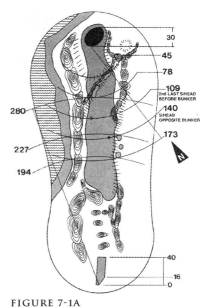

FIGURE 7-1A

Perfection, the 14th hole at North Berwick Golf Club, Scotland, must have been a super hole as a par-3 to create such intense interest. For unknown reasons it was changed to a less interesting par-4. (Copyright © DuCam Marketing (UK) Ltd.)

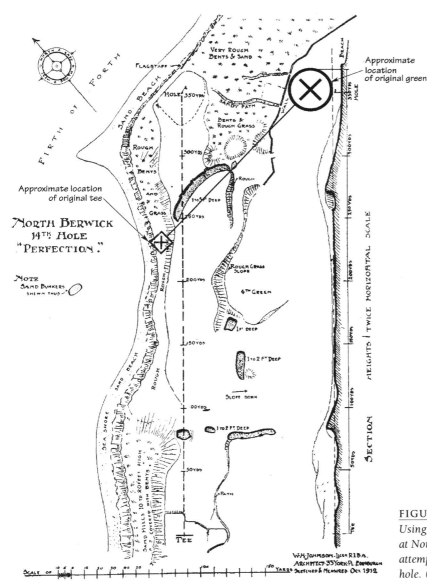

FIGURE 7-1B

Using a diagram of the existing Perfection at North Berwick Golf Club, Scotland, we attempt to re-create the alignment of the old hole. (Courtesy of Grant Books.)

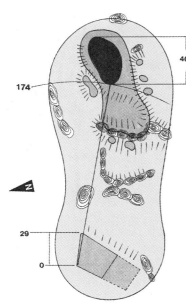

40

174

29

0

FIGURE 7-2

The Redan, the 15th hole at North Berwick Golf Club, Scotland, is one of the most adapted and replicated holes in golf. This diagram shows the original. (Copyright © DuCam Marketing (UK) Ltd.)

untimely death en route to Australia in 1879. Converted to a par-4, Perfection became a nebulous classic at best.

On the other hand, the **Redan, the 15th at North Berwick,** is, by our definition, without a doubt a classic (Figure 7-2). (This hole is also a Strath creation, with modifications by professional Bernard Sayers.) C. B. Macdonald adapted the Redan for his National Golf Links. Some, including Sayers, say he improved it.

Macdonald chose not to adapt Perfection for the National Golf Links, though he borrowed its first shot and created a composite hole with green and bunker guards like the 15th at Muirfield, as the latter hole existed in the early years of the 20th century. Apparently, Macdonald did not admire Perfection enough to use it in its entirety at National, where a major objective was to adapt the best British golf holes. Nevertheless, we think that the original Perfection, the par-3, would have made our list as a runaway.

Gibraltar, a renowned hole at *Seacroft Golf Club* in Lincolnshire, England, by Tom Dunn (1892), was long regarded as a classic. The original, as Bernard Darwin described its second shot, "played over a range of sandy mountains." A similar hole, the *eighth at Moortown* by Alister Mackenzie (1909), features a Plateau green and is described in *The World Atlas of Golf* as a "superb hole built on a foundation of rock" (Figure 7-3). Many Gibraltars, however, have no relation to Seacroft or Moortown. For example, one hole at Banff was so named by its architect Stanley Thompson because of the resemblance of a mountain in the background to the Rock of Gibraltar. On the other hand, the *15th at Timber Point Golf Club* (which no longer exists [NLE]) (Figure 7-4), designed by Colt and Alison in 1927 with an elevated green, was considered a replica of Mackenzie's Gibraltar at

FIGURE 7-3

One might expect the Gibraltar at Moortown Golf Club, Leeds, England, designed by Alister Mackenzie, to be more imposing.

CLASSIC GOLF HOLE DESIGN

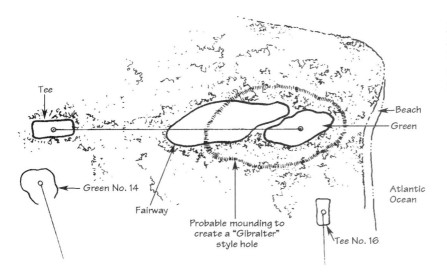

FIGURE 7-4
Reportedly, the Gibraltar at the 15th hole at Timber Point Golf Club, Great River, New York, was no more imposing than the original.

Moortown. We conclude that the various Gibraltars lack an overriding theme or design feature and, therefore, are not truly classics.

The famous *Postage Stamp, the eighth at Royal Troon* (see Figure 6-9A, page 160), measures only 123 yards, but calls for a full wood, depending on the wind. Due to its unique and severe and ever-changing microclimate, Royal Troon's eighth has seldom, if ever, been authentically replicated, but the principle of a short hole playing into a variable wind has asserted itself often. For example, the *seventh at Pebble Beach* (Figure 7-5), with a larger green but approximately the same yardage, also has winds that determine club selection. *Papoose*

FIGURE 7-5
This early 1920s photo shows the site of hole 7 at Pebble Beach Golf Links, Pebble Beach, California, before it was finalized by Chandler Egan.

THE CLASSIC GOLF HOLES

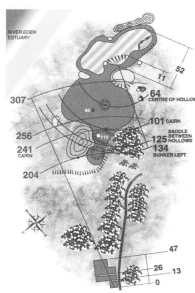

RIVER EDEN
ESTUARY

307

256
241
CAIRN

204

11
52
64
CENTRE OF HOLLOW
80
101 CAIRN
SADDLE
BETWEEN
HOLLOWS
110
125
134 BUNKER LEFT

47
26 13
0

FIGURE 7-6

The Eden, called the "High-Out," on the Old Course at St. Andrews, Scotland, never achieved the fame of the other Eden, called the "High-In." (Copyright © DuCam Marketing (UK) Ltd.)

at Banff Springs, measuring 138 yards, can call for a wood off the tee if the wind is gusting down the bordering Bow River. Adding to the challenge is the fact that wind velocity cannot be determined from the sheltered tee. (Edward, Prince of Wales, is reputed to have taken eight shots on this short hole because he disregarded the advice of his caddy, who had walked ahead to ascertain wind speed.)

In addition to the wind factor, Royal Troon's smallish green size has also been imitated on par-4s, notably on the 315-yard par-4 *eighth at Pine Valley* in New Jersey (see Figure 6-12, page 163). One interesting replication of the hole at Pine Valley is the *15th at Fenway Golf Club*, a 300-yard hole on this Tillinghast course in Westchester County, New York. Hickory Ridge in Amherst, Massachusetts (see Figure 6-13, page 163), has a similar short par-4, with a stream adding interest. The tiny green, measuring 2000 square feet, has been reached once from the middle tee when the wind was favorable—a rare feat—and by its coarchitect William G. Robinson, who knew he must wait for a favorable wind gust.

Royal Troon's Postage Stamp green has been emulated on both par-3s and par-4s, but its orientation must be considered in relation to a strong prevailing wind. We do not include it as a true classic.

Likewise, the *Eden or High-Out, the seventh at St. Andrews* (Figure 7-6), has also been replicated, but because its principles have not been widely used, it also fails to live up to our definition of a classic. Nor do we consider the *Reef* (Figure 7-7) a classic. It was popularized by Tillinghast, even though it may not have been one of his originals. Few Reef holes still exist, perhaps because longer ball

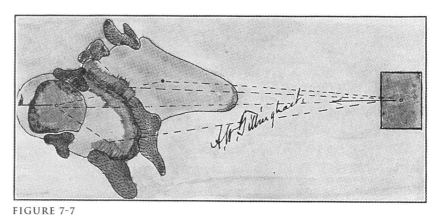

FIGURE 7-7

Although architect A. W. Tillinghast defined the Reef as a ridge hazard, still other adaptations occurred. The diagram shows a simulated Reef Tillinghast designed in 1926.

CLASSIC GOLF HOLE DESIGN

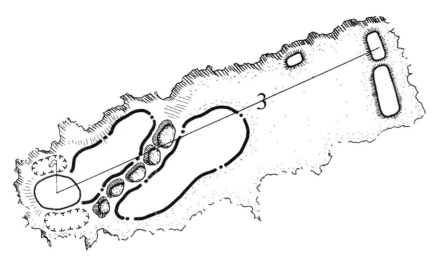

FIGURE 7-8
At MacGregor Links, near Saratoga, New York, the Reef or ridge of bunkers on the third hole crosses the fairway at a reduced angle to the centerline.

flights allow golfers to go for the green without worrying about bunkers stretching across the hole on a diagonal (Figure 7-8).

The *Sahara, the third at Royal St. George's* in England (see Figures 4-12, page 69, and 6-48, page 185), was long considered a classic, but due to a 1975 elevation of the green, this hole, although improved, can no longer be called classic. Similarly, the *Maiden, the sixth at Royal St. George's* (see Figure 5-67, page 137), has been modified heavily, with its original characteristics removed. These modifications eliminate it from our list of classics.

Hell's Half Acre, the eighth hole at Pine Valley, with its fearsome 2-acre bunker, is notorious in the world of golf. Indeed, the huge bunker on the 17th at Baltusrol may have been connected to it, because Baltusrol's architect A. W. Tillinghast consulted with Pine Valley's architect George Crump on several occasions. Yet it also does not quite fit our definition of a classic golf hole.

THE TRUE CLASSICS

From the earlier list we have now eliminated Eden (High-Out), Gibraltar, Hell's Half Acre, Maiden, Perfection, Postage Stamp, Reef, and Sahara. This leaves a baker's dozen as our true classics.

ALPS

Hole 17, Prestwick Golf Course
Scotland, par-4, 391 yards (see Figure 5-63, page 136)

This hole was likely designed by Old Tom Morris, who lived from 1821 to 1908 and served as Prestwick's greenkeeper and professional from 1852 to 1865. James Braid may have revised it in 1914 and 1930 when he planned major changes and added four holes there. Both the green and the cross bunker that fronts it are invisible. Yet C. B. Macdonald and H. J. Whigham wrote, "The popularity of the Alps is proof that not all blind holes are bad."

There are numerous adaptations of the Alps. They include many par-4s and several par-3s, but the latter are often Dells.

Hole 3, National Golf Links
Southampton, New York

Playing from 360 to 420 yards (see Figure 4-7, pages 66–67), this hole by C. B. Macdonald opened in 1911. It is worth noting that many feel Macdonald's Alps surpassed the original. At the National, the best line of play is to the right, whereas at Prestwick the left is preferable.

Hole 6, Tamarack Country Club
Greenwich, Connecticut

This 298- to 387-yard hole (Figure 7-9) by Charles Banks opened in 1929. Banks achieved the Alps effect by siting the green on the crest of an

FIGURE 7-9
At Tamarack Country Club in Greenwich, Connecticut, the embankment levels off about 100 yards short of the green on the sixth hole, thereby hiding the view into the green. Though not the same method as used at the Alps at Prestwick Golf Club, Scotland, it's still effective. (Courtesy of Aqua Agronomic Solutions, Inc.)

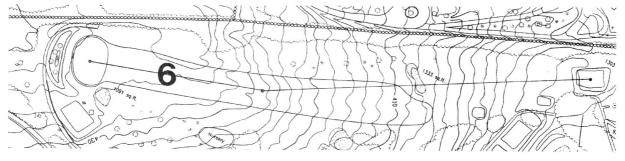

CLASSIC GOLF HOLE DESIGN

uphill slope, where it is invisible to approaching golfers. Some say there was once a hidden bunker across the entire front of the putting surface. If so, it replicated the hidden bunker on the original, which was short of the green.

Hole 2, The Links (NLE)
Roslyn, New York, 388 yards (Figure 7-10)

C. B. Macdonald and Seth Raynor designed this hole as a greatly modified version of the original; still, it embodies its principles.

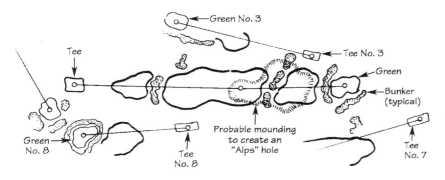

FIGURE 7-10
The hidden green effect on the Alps at the Links, Roslyn, New York, is accomplished by cross bunkers and mounding.

Hole 5, Oakland Golf Club (NLE)
Bayside, New York, 300 to 360 yards (Figure 7-11)

This hole was created by Raynor in a 1914 revision of the club, originally designed by Tom Bendelow. Playing just 300 to 360 yards, this hole is described by Wexler as an Alps on a smaller scale.

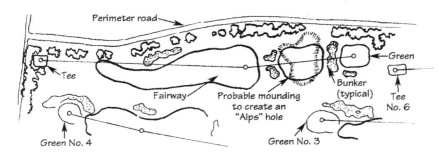

FIGURE 7-11
Mounding concealed the green at Oakland Golf Club, Bayside, New York, from the approaching golfer, thus providing the Alps effect.

All the holes above are par-4s, but the principles have been adapted to par-3s. Two examples are:

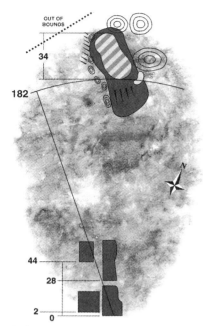

FIGURE 7-12
Sandy dunes occur in the vast green space between tee and green on the 11th hole at Royal Liverpool Golf Club, Hoylake, England. (Copyright © DuCam Marketing (UK) Ltd.)

Hole 11, Royal Liverpool Golf Club
Hoylake, England, 142 to 193 yards (Figure 7-12)

Robert Chambers, Jr., and George Morris built this challenging par-3 in 1869. The green is described in The World Atlas of Golf *as an oblong oasis in the dunes, with the sandy dunes creating the Alps effect.*

Hole 2 South, Magnolia Creek Golf Links
League City, Texas, 324-yard par-4

Designed by Ault, Clark & Associates, this is a bona fide Alps replication (Figures 7-13A and B).

The following is a par-5 Alps:

Hole 6, Black Creek Country Club
Chattanooga, Tennessee

Designed by Brian Silva, this is a modern 552-yard par-5 Alps that features a grass embankment and bunker hiding the green (Figure 7-14).

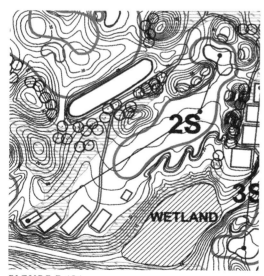

FIGURE 7-13A
The large hill projecting toward the green effectively conceals at least half of the green on hole 2 south at Magnolia Creek Golf Links, League City, Texas. (Courtesy of Ault, Clark & Associates, Ltd.)

FIGURE 7-13B
This attractive sketch by Ault, Clark associate Anthony Cusat shows how the Alps hole was planned at Magnolia Creek Golf Links, League City, Texas. (Courtesy of Ault, Clark & Associates, Ltd.)

FIGURE 7-14
A modern Alps was designed by Brian Silva for Black Creek Country Club, near Chattanooga, Tennessee. The grass embankment and bunker hide the green. A target on a pole is provided for direction. (Photo courtesy of Scott Wicker.)

BIARRITZ

Hole 3, Golf de Biarritz
France

At one time this hole was played as 12, but it no longer exists. Designed by Willie and Tom Dunn, the hole attracted wide attention and was a par-3 when it opened for play in 1888. It was played from the top of a cliff across a ravine to a large green divided by a swale (Figure 7-15A). Oddly, Willie Dunn did not adapt it on any of his courses in America, nor did his brother, Tom, use it in his later work in the British Isles.

Yet Macdonald and his protégés used its principles repeatedly. According to Wexler, their holes were "often in the 220-yard range with a geometrically precise green." The huge raised putting surface and its adaptations were divided by a swale measuring 4 feet or deeper. Long, narrow bunkers sited at the bottom of steeply sloping sides guarded both sides. Cross bunkers or other hazards—often on a diagonal—were sited between tee and green to simulate the forced carry across the chasm on the original (Figure 7-15B). In many adaptations, the putting surface is cupped on both the front and the back sections and at some courses even in the deep swale.

Unfortunately, during periods of economic downturn, when clubs' maintenance budgets were lowered, the front section was often maintained as fairway. That compromises one principle of the Biarritz: that it seems to provide a bland shot to a huge green, requiring the golfer on the tee to fight off the feeling that "there is nothing but length to this hole."

FIGURE 7-15A

This diagram simulates, to the best of our research, the original Biarritz hole at Golf de Biarritz, France. One wonders why Willie and Tom Dunn created this configuration on the green surface.

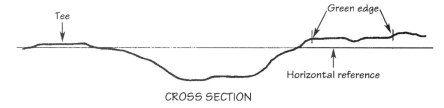

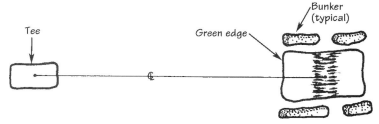

FIGURE 7-15B

This generalized diagram shows how C. B. Macdonald and his protégés adapted the Biarritz on the many courses they designed.

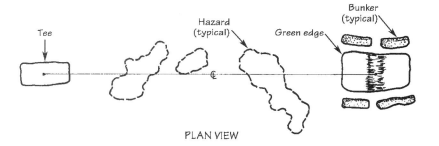

That is not true. The old saying, "If you are tired of the Biarritz, you are tired of golf itself," constantly reasserts itself despite the blandness of the view from the tee.

Adaptations of the Biarritz, almost all (Black Creek is by Brian Silva and Cottonwoods is by Hale Irwin) by Macdonald and his protégés, include:

Hole 9, Yale University Golf Course
New Haven, Connecticut
by C. B. Macdonald and Seth Raynor, opened 1926 (Figure 7-16)

This hole requires a carry across water.

FIGURE 7-16
It seems that the deep swale across the green on the ninth hole, the Biarritz, at Yale University Golf Course, New Haven, Connecticut, was not mowed at green height at one period.

Hole 8, Whippoorwill Golf Club
Armonk, New York
by Charles Banks, opened 1929

From the course's opening, the front section of this hole has been maintained as fairway.

Hole 12, Tamarack Country Club
Greenwich, Connecticut
by Charles Banks, opened 1929 (Figure 7-17)

This hole is sometimes referred to as the signature hole on this layout. It epitomizes the exceptionally protective efforts of the club to retain Banks's style and objectives.

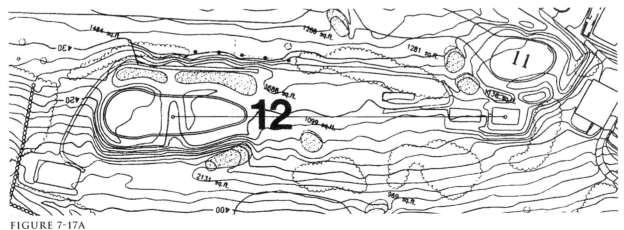

FIGURE 7-17A
The management at Tamarack Country Club, Greenwich, Connecticut, has maintained its Biarritz, the 12th hole, in vintage condition. (Courtesy of Aqua Agronomic Solutions, Inc.)

FIGURE 7-17B

As seen from the side, the long, narrow bunkers of the Biarritz at Tamarack Country Club, Greenwich, Connecticut, are an integral part of the original.

FIGURE 7-17C

Here is the swale on the Biarritz at Tamarack Country Club, Greenwich, Connecticut, in all its glory. In some designs, the cup is located in the swale.

**Hole 18, Tucker's Point Golf Club
Tuckers Town, Bermuda
by Charles Banks, opened 1932 (Figure 7-18).**

**Hole 13, Mid Ocean Club
Tuckers Town, Bermuda
by C. B. Macdonald, opened 1924.**

**Hole 17, Black Creek Country Club
Chattanooga, Tennessee
by Brian Silva, opened 2000 (see Figure 4-5, page 63)**

This is a fine replica of Seth Raynor's Biarritz at the nearby Lookout Mountain Club.

FIGURE 7-18

There's lots of sand and an interesting chip and/or putt situation on the Biarritz green, the 18th, at Tucker's Point Golf Club, Tuckers Town, Bermuda.

CLASSIC GOLF HOLE DESIGN

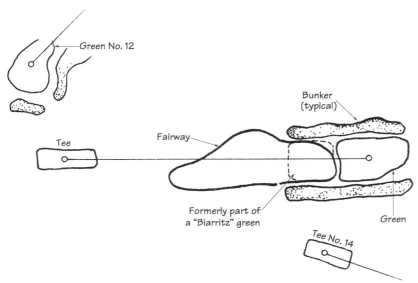

FIGURE 7-19
The front portion of this Biarritz, the 13th hole of the Oneck Course (which no longer exists) at Westhampton Country Club, Westhampton, New York, was maintained as fairway—the fate of many a Biarritz in periods when maintenance budgets are low.

Hole 13, Oneck Course (NLE), Westhampton Country Club
Westhampton, New York
by Charles Banks, opened 1929 (Figure 7-19)

According to Wexler, this was the "standard brute" and into the wind. Westhampton's original 18 by Seth Raynor still has its Biarritz in play.

Hole 3, The Links (NLE)
Roslyn, New York
by C. B. Macdonald with Seth Raynor, opened 1919

The elevated green was surrounded by a huge horseshoe bunker. According to Wexler, a very difficult long-iron approach was called for.

Hole 6, Shinnecock Hills Golf Club (NLE)
Southampton, New York
revised by C. B. Macdonald and Seth Raynor (Figure 7-20),
and reopened in 1916

Hole 14, Oakland Golf Club (NLE)
Bayside, New York
revised by Seth Raynor in 1914

Hole 8, Lido Golf Club (NLE)
Lido Beach, New York
by C. B. Macdonald and Seth Raynor, opened 1917 (Figure 7-21)

With natural hazards, the symbolic bunkers were not needed to catch the essence of the original Biarritz. It has been said, however, that Lido's Biarritz was the finest replication ever of that classic.

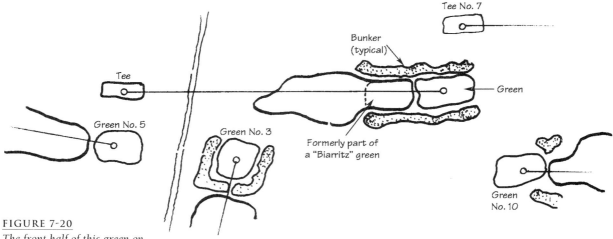

FIGURE 7-20

The front half of this green on hole 6 at Shinnecock Hills Golf Club, Southampton, New York, was maintained as fairway during low-budget periods.

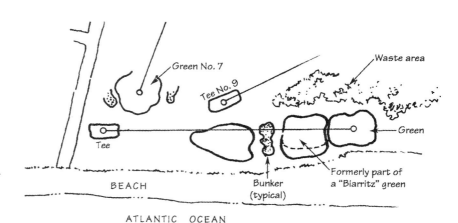

FIGURE 7-21

At Lido Golf Club (which no longer exists), Lido Beach, New York, the usual long, linear bunkers of the Biarritz are missing on hole 8.

Hole 5, Fishers Island Golf Club
Fishers Island, New York
by Seth Raynor, opened 1917 (Figure 7-22)

While hole 14 at Cottonwoods Golf Club, Tunica, Mississippi, by Hale Irwin Golf Design, opened 1998, appears to be a Biarritz, it's not. The tee shot is from the right and the deep swale is aligned with the line of flight (Figure 7-23).

FIGURE 7-22
The fifth hole at Fishers Island Golf Club, Fishers Island, New York, is another Biarritz, but we can't tell whether the officials left it in its original state or pulled the fangs.

FIGURE 7-23
The 14th green at Cottonwoods Golf Club, Tunica, Mississippi, is adjacent to a Biarritz-style swale. However, the swale is located off the green. (Courtesy of Stan Gentry—Hale Irwin Golf Design.)

CAPE

Hole 14, National Golf Links
Southampton, New York
355-yard par-4, by C. B. Macdonald, opened 1912
and
Hole 5, Tucker's Point Golf Club
Tuckers Town, Bermuda
425-yard par-4, by C. B. Macdonald, opened 1924

The 14th at the National is truly a C. B. Macdonald original, though there are earlier Capes on British courses, notably the first at Machrihanish in Scotland (Figure 7-24). This Scottish example involves a "bite-off" from the tee. However, the green is not perched precariously above water as on the 14th (a dogleg right) at the National Golf Links (see Figure 4-7, pages 66–67) or the renowned 5th (a dogleg left) at the Mid Ocean Club (Figure 7-25).

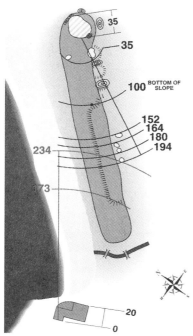

FIGURE 7-24
Hole 1 at Machrihanish Golf Club,
Scotland, is a mild Cape hole. Not
much is asked of the golfer to get the
tee shot to the fairway. The carry over
water is minimal and the green is
located well inland. (Copyright ©
DuCam Marketing (UK) Ltd.)

FIGURE 7-25
The fifth hole at Mid Ocean Club, Tuckers Town, Bermuda, has the classic bite-off tee
shot with the second to a green where you dare not miss left.

Adaptations of the Cape include:

**Hole 2, Tucker's Point Golf Club
Tuckers Town, Bermuda
by Charles Banks, opened around 1932 (Figure 7-26)**

A "bite-off" tee shot is followed by an approach across water to a green
sited at the water's edge.

**Hole 6, Griffith Park Municipal Golf Course
Los Angeles, California
by George Thomas, opened around 1926**

The golfer has to determine how much of the embankment to carry on this
dogleg left.

FIGURE 7-26

As much a carry requirement, the
bite-off aspect is still part of the
golfer's dilemma to solve on the
second hole at Tucker's Point Golf
Club, Tuckers Town, Bermuda.

Hole 2, La Cumbre Country Club
Santa Barbara, California
by George C. Thomas and William Park Bell,
reopened around 1920

Reaching the green required a long carry over a lake; an alternate safer route allowed shorter golfers to get home in three.

Hole 3, La Cumbre Country Club
Santa Barbara, California

Measuring 328 yards if played by the dogleg, this hole requires a 285-yard carry into the wind if played directly toward the green.

Hole 7, Avon Country Club
Avon, Connecticut
by Geoffrey S. Cornish and William G. Robinson, opened 1966
(see Figure 5-47, page 130)

A prevailing head wind makes the direct shot to the green almost impossible, yet with a light or favorable wind it has been carried, notably by Robinson on opening day.

Hole 12, The Classic at Madden's
Brainerd, Minnesota
361-yard par-4, by Scott Hoffman (Figure 7-27)
opened 1997, with similarities to the hole at Avon

The green has never been carried.

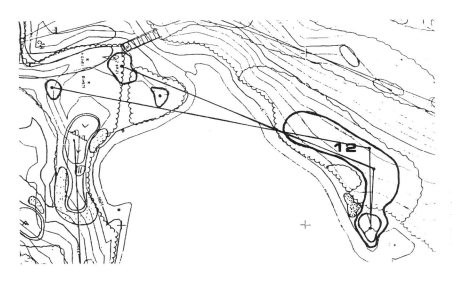

FIGURE 7-27
Hole 12 at the Classic, at Madden's, Brainerd, Minnesota, was designed by Scott Hoffman as a bite-off or Cape with a carry off the tee.

THE CLASSIC GOLF HOLES

Hole 4, Laguna Blanca
Santa Barbara, California
by George C. Thomas and William P. Bell, opened in the 1920s

This hole offers a dogleg left with an impossible carry from tee to green, but it affords a premium for those who play close to the lake on their tee shots.

Hole 8, Los Angeles Country Club, North Course
Los Angeles, California
by George C. Thomas, opened 1927 (Figure 7-28)

The tee shot determines the length and type of approach on this par-5 Cape.

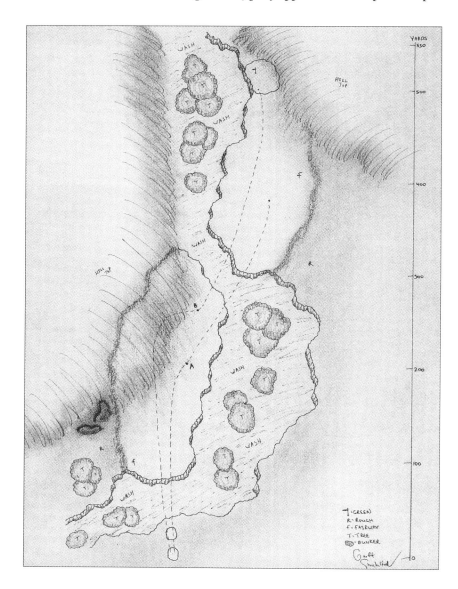

FIGURE 7-28
The tee shot is critical to reaching the green in two on the eighth hole of George C. Thomas's North Course at Los Angeles Country Club, Los Angeles, California. (Drawing by Geoff Shackelford.)

CLASSIC GOLF HOLE DESIGN

Hole 7, Riviera Country Club
Pacific Palisades, California
by George C. Thomas with William P. Bell, opened 1927
(Figure 7-29)

This is a Cape to the right.

Hole 13, Riviera Country Club
Pacific Palisades, California
by George C. Thomas with William P. Bell, opened 1927
(Figure 7-30)

This is a true Cape because the wash creates a bite-off from the tee.

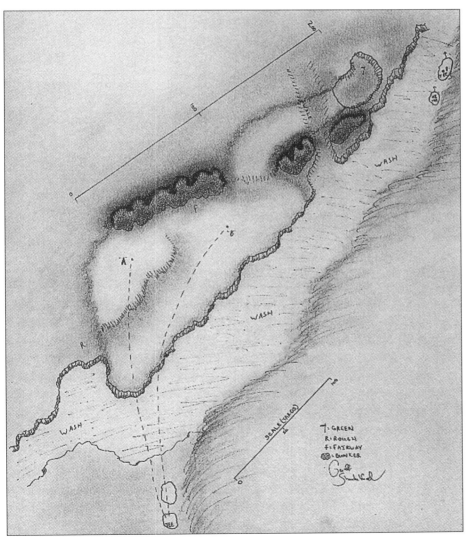

FIGURE 7-29
The seventh hole at the Riviera Country Club, Pacific Palisades, California, is a Cape to the right across a wash. A precarious bite-off is required to reach the green in two. (Drawing by Geoff Shackelford.)

**Hole 17, Bel-Air Country Club
Los Angeles, California
by George C. Thomas with William P. Bell and Jack Neville
opened 1927 (Figure 7-31)**

A long drive provides plenty of room to avoid the wash.

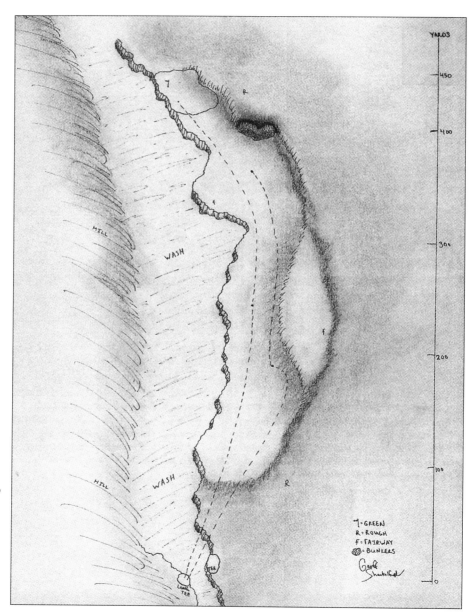

FIGURE 7-30
The wash creates a bite-off from the tee and a true Cape to the left of the 13th hole at Riviera Country Club, Pacific Palisades, California. The closer one plays to the wash, the shorter the distance to the green. (Drawing by Geoff Shackelford.)

Hole 18, Pebble Beach Golf Links
Pebble Beach, California
by Jack Neville, Douglas Grant, and Chandler Egan
opened in 1918 and revised in 1928 (Figure 7-32)

It could be argued that this par-5 is not a true Cape because the green is not perched precariously above the Pacific Ocean; still, the water is not far from the green.

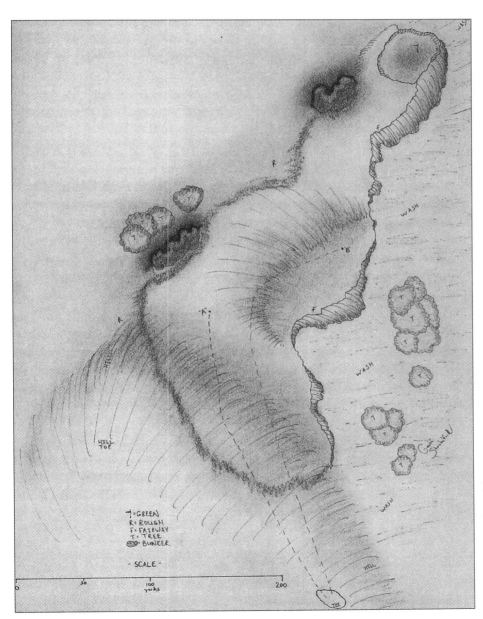

7 = GREEN
R = ROUGH
F = FAIRWAY
T = TREE
⬤ = BUNKER

- SCALE -

FIGURE 7-31
The long 17th at Bel-Air Country Club, Los Angeles, California, provides plenty of room to avoid the wash. The steep downhill fairway helps on a 460-yard par-4. (Drawing by Geoff Shackelford.)

FIGURE 7-32
One of golf's most widely recognized holes, the 540-yard 18th at Pebble Beach stretches alongside the rocky shore of Carmel Bay, producing a vision of intimidation rarely equaled among golf's great finishing holes. (Photograph copyright Joann Dost. Pebble Beach, Pebble Beach Golf Links, The Lone Cypress, Spanish Bay Golf Links and Spyglass Hill Golf Course, their courses, and individual hole designs are trademarks, service marks and trade dress of Pebble Beach Company, used under license by Joann Dost Golf Editions, LLC.)

Hole 18, Cherry Hills Country Club
Denver, Colorado
by William Flynn, opened 1923 (Figure 7-33)

The green on this hole also lacks water immediately on one side of it that defines a true Cape, but the rest of the hole certainly fits the style.

Hole 5, Knoll Country Club
Parsippany, New Jersey
by Charles Banks, opened 1929 (Figure 7-34)

This hole is another of the few par-5 Capes; the bite-off for the tee shot is present, while the green is perched above a deep bunker.

Hole 14, Wentworth by the Sea
Portsmouth, New Hampshire
by Geoffrey Cornish, opened 1965 (Figure 7-35)

This hole is notorious because its bite-off follows an approach to the green that slopes away Redan fashion, but it is protected on the left by the Atlantic Ocean.

FIGURE 7-33
Golf architect William Flynn was not a fan of water holes. On his Cape on the finishing hole at Cherry Hills Country Club, Denver, Colorado, the elevated green is a considerable distance from the water. (Courtesy USGA. All rights reserved.)

CLASSIC GOLF HOLE DESIGN

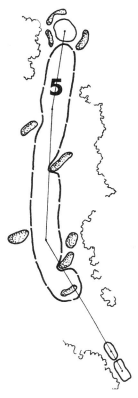

FIGURE 7-34
Even at 525 yards, hole 5 at Knoll Country Club, Parsippany, New Jersey, may be played as a two-shot Cape by today's proficient golfers.

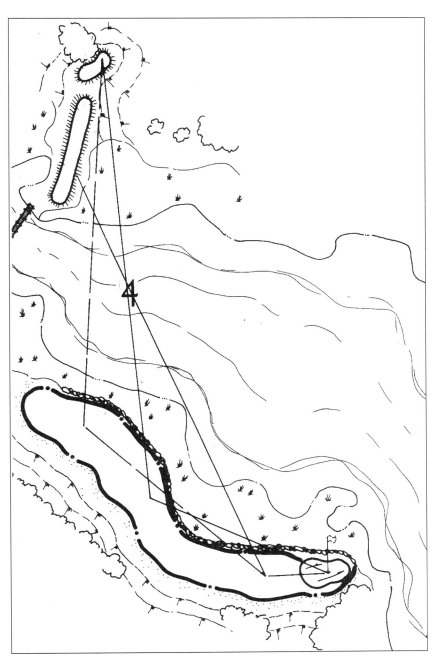

FIGURE 7-35
This notorious 380-yard 14th hole (now No. 4) at Wentworth by the Sea Golf Club, Portsmouth, New Hampshire, has a Cape bite-off followed by an approach to a green that slopes away Redan fashion. The Atlantic Ocean is a formidable water feature all along the left side.

THE CLASSIC GOLF HOLES

Hole 9, Wakefield Golf Club
Raleigh, North Carolina
by Stan Gentry, opened in the 1950s (Figure 7-36)

This Cape is distinguished by wide, spreading tees, and it's all water to carry from the tips.

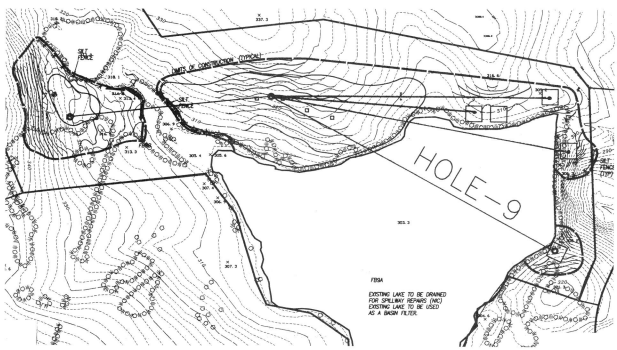

FIGURE 7-36A

This grading study of hole 9 at Wakefield Golf Club, Raleigh, North Carolina, illustrates a Cape, particularly from the long tee. (Courtesy of Stan Gentry—Hale Irwin Golf Design.)

FIGURE 7-36B

This shot of the ninth hole at Wakefield Golf Club, Raleigh, North Carolina, shows the back tee and a full carry to the landing area. (Courtesy of Stan Gentry—Hale Irwin Golf Design.)

Hole 3, Pawleys Plantation
Pawleys Island, South Carolina
by Jack Nicklaus (Figure 7-37)

Nicklaus capped off this beautiful Cape with a Redan touch—the angled green and the sandy waste.

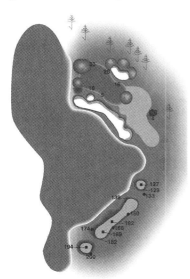

FIGURE 7-37

Jack Nicklaus designed a beautiful 194-yard Cape at hole 3 at Pawleys Plantation Golf and Country Club, Pawleys Island, South Carolina. It's all water and sand to reach the green. (Drawing copyright Pro's Yardage Caddy, Columbia, SC; photo courtesy of Pawleys Plantation Golf and Country Club.)

CARDINAL

Hole 3, Prestwick Golf Club
Prestwick, Scotland (see Figure 5-51, page 132)

This 482-yard par-5 is named after its prominent bunker, the "Cardinal," and ranks among the earliest of double doglegs. Its present form likely dates back to Old Tom Morris's tenure as greenkeeper and professional at Prestwick (1852–1865) and to modifications by his successor, Charles Hunter. Later revisions to the course and hole were made by James Braid in 1918 and 1930. Double doglegs are not uncommon; many arose as an architect's original and were perhaps not derived from Prestwick's classic third hole. As with many famous features from the early days of course architecture, no one knows for sure.

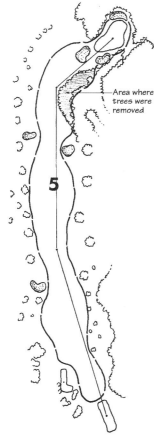

FIGURE 7-38

By removing trees, architect C. E. Robinson made it possible for the golfer to reach the green on the second shot on hole 5 at St. Charles Country Club South, Winnipeg, Manitoba.

Adaptations of the Cardinal include:

Hole 5, St. Charles Country Club, South Course
Winnipeg, Canada
by Donald Ross, opened 1920 (Figure 7-38)

This hole was played as Ross intended for decades, before greater distances achieved by golfers led to a short, wasted second shot to get around the second bend. Golf architect C. E. "Robbie" Robinson corrected this scenario by removing trees at the second corner so that long and courageous hitters could cut the corner on their second shot if they decided to go for the green. This is dangerous, but, if successful, the golfer is amply rewarded.

Hole 18, Cranberry Valley Golf Club
Cape Cod, Massachusetts
by Cornish and Robinson, opened 1975
(see Figure 5-53, page 133)

At 430 to 530 yards, this finishing hole has enjoyed acceptance since opening day. The golfer is rewarded by a long drive. Indeed, an exceptionally long drive may permit an attempt at the green on the second. More often, golfers are content with a second shot sufficiently long enough to allow a pitch to the green on the third.

Hole 15, Paako Ridge, Sandia Park, New Mexico
by Ken Dye, opened 2000 (see Figure 5-54, page 133)

This par-5 double dogleg is 492 to 640 yards.

Hole 5, Osage National Golf Club
Lake of the Ozarks, Missouri
by Ed Seay and Arnold Palmer, opened June 1997(Figure 7-39)

The golfer can drive either right or left on this 455- to 588-yard par-5.

DELL

Hole 6, Lahinch Golf Club
County Clare, Ireland
by Old Tom Morris, opened 1893 (see Figure 5-68, page 138)

The original 156-yard par-3 Dell was notorious and was replicated worldwide, but as play increased and society became more litigious, most have been modified to eliminate blindness. The television program Candid Camera *once created a unique and humorous situation involving a foursome arriving at a blind Dell green only to find all four balls in the cup.*

Because of its blindness, few, if any, attempts are now made to replicate the Dell, though modifications have resulted in a safer hole. As noted earlier, golf architect Steve Durkee succeeded by creating an opening between the mounds on the 12th on his nine-hole addition at the venerable Dorset Field Club in Vermont (see Figure 5-70, page 138). The green is visible from a portion of the tee. As a result, the golfer can first see if the "coast is clear" before taking his or her shot from a portion of the tee where the green is not visible. Incidentally, the Dorset Field Club did not name its modified hole "the Dell."

Kildonan Golf Course in Winnipeg, Canada, opened in 1921 with a par-3 playing like a Dell but over a railroad track, with the green visible through a tunnel. (We assume the designer was probably unaware of the Dell in Ireland.) Hackett observes that the celebrated comedian Bob Hope, in one of his earliest rounds of golf, topped his ball on this hole and it rolled through the tunnel onto the green and into the cup for that avid golfer's first hole-in-one.

Over a dozen other Dells were found during our research, mostly in Scotland, Ireland, and England. *Hole 2 at Hawk Creek* in Oregon was one of the few examples noted in the United States. Four Dell replicas are:

Hole 3, Burnham and Berrow Golf Course
Somerset, England
by C.H. Alison in 1947 but dating back decades before that
(see Figure 5-69, page 138)

The large mound placed in front of the green creates the Dell effect on this 329- to 376-yard par-4.

Hole 4, Tenby Golf Club
Tenby, Wales
by C. K. Cotton, opened 1948

This 439-yard par-4 offers a delightfully pleasant Dell.

Hole 16, "The Links"
Seascale, England
by Willie Campbell, opened in 1892

The green on this 473-yard par-4 is well hidden from sight as well as from the wind.

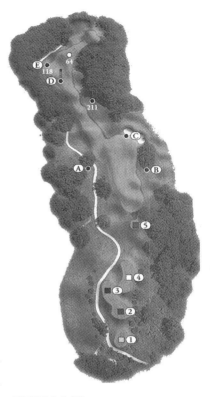

FIGURE 7-39
On this par-5 hole 5 at Osage National Golf Club, Lake of the Ozarks, Missouri, first you dogleg to the left. Then you dogleg to the right. Sounds like a barn dance, but it creates an interesting hole. (Holes by Holeview Yardage Book Co.)

Hole 14, "The Whins"
Cruden Bay, Scotland
by Fowler and Simpson, opened 1926

The approach shot on this 372-yard par-4 is challenging.

EDEN (HIGH-IN)

Hole 11, the Old Course at St. Andrews (Figure 7-40)

Muirhead and Anderson describe the 176-yard par-3 Eden as "a hole of renown." They add that "On a still day pros would hit a seven iron from the tee. But depending on the wind, they could use anything from a driver to a nine iron." A weakness of the hole has been described, though the authors have never witnessed it: that a topped ball can reach the green if the ground is hard despite the presence of Hill and Strath bunkers.

Many replications, particularly those by Macdonald, Raynor, and Banks, have a huge bunker or a grass hollow behind the green to symbolize the shoreline and beach of the Eden River. Adaptations include:

Hole 3, Tamarack Country Club
Greenwich, Connecticut
by Charles Banks, opened 1929 (Figure 7-41)

Two (originally one) huge and deep bunkers, one behind and one left of the green, symbolize the Eden River. Two bunkers (originally three) obviate the possibility of a topped ball reaching the green, as on the classic.

FIGURE 7-40
The original Eden is hole 11 on the Old Course at St. Andrews, Scotland. (Courtesy of Dave Gordon, ASGCA.)

CLASSIC GOLF HOLE DESIGN

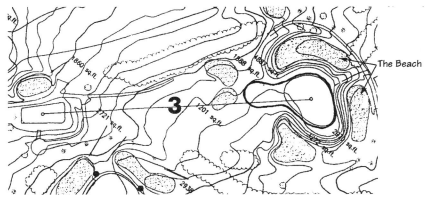

FIGURE 7-41
An integral part of the Eden (High-In) on the Old Course at St. Andrews, Scotland, is the Eden River beach behind the green. It lies waiting for shots that carry over the green. In this drawing, bunkers simulate the beach at Tamarack Country Club, Greenwich, Connecticut. (Courtesy of Aqua Agronomic Solutions, Inc.)

Hole 17, Oneck Course (NLE) of Westhampton Country Club
Westhampton, New York
by Charles Banks, opened 1929

The complete course is shown in Figure 4-32, page 83. Though Moriches Bay was well back behind the green, Banks added a huge bunker rear and right of the green to further simulate the Eden River of the original.

Hole 16, The Links Club (NLE)
Roslyn, New York
by C. B. Macdonald with Seth Raynor, opened 1919

The entire course appears in Figure 4-30, page 81. The Eden River was emulated here by a huge bunker. Both Hill and Strath bunkers were present.

Hole 11, Shinnecock Hills Golf Club (NLE)
Southampton, New York
revised by C. B. Macdonald and Seth Raynor in 1916

A bunker behind the green emulated the Eden River. Hill and Strath bunkers were present.

Hole 2, Maidstone Club, East Course (NLE)
by Willie Park with an addition by Seth Raynor, revised in the late 1920s (Figure 7-42)

As at Shinnecock, a bunker behind the green emulated the Eden River. Hill and Strath bunkers were present but wide apart.

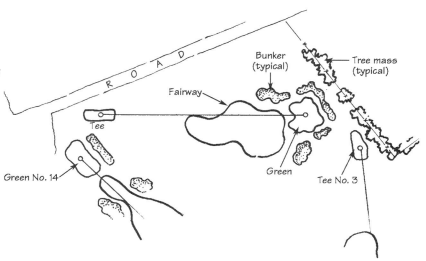

FIGURE 7-42

Again no Eden River with beach on hole 2 at Maidstone Club, East Course, East Hampton, New York (which no longer exists), but bunkers replace it. Because the beach is not visible on the tee of the original Eden, its absence doesn't affect the visual picture.

Hole 18, Garden City Golf Club
Garden City, New York
by Dev Emmet, opened 1899
revised by Walter Travis from 1909 to 1920

This was an early example of replication in North America, although Macdonald and Raynor had introduced the practice before Travis.

Hole 5, Meadow Club
Fairfax, California
by Alister Mackenzie and Robert Hunter, opened 1927 and restored by Michael DeVries in 2000 (Figure 7-43)

This hole is an effective replication of the Eden but not a copy. The hollow behind the green replicates the Eden River. An important restoration pro-

FIGURE 7-43

This adaptation of the Eden, hole 5 at the Meadow Club, Fairfax, California, tries to stay close to the original despite different site and environmental conditions.

CLASSIC GOLF HOLE DESIGN

ject is currently under way at the Meadow Club in Fairfax, California, by golf course architect Mike DeVries. The before photo of the Eden (Figure 7-44A) is of interest to one of the authors because the bunker shapes resulted from restoration work believed to be done about the same time as the back tee was added. Bunker locations were not changed, but more appropriate shapes were created. The after photo (Figure 7-44B) demonstrates replication of the feathery edge so prevalent in Mackenzie's work.

FIGURE 7-44A
The hole characteristics were close to the original Eden on the fifth hole at the Meadow Club, Fairfax, California, but in need of more work. (Courtesy of Mike DeVries, DeVries Designs, Inc.)

FIGURE 7-44B
Hole 5 at the Meadow Club, Fairfax, California, was restored by course architect Mike DeVries. By restoring the bunkers, DeVries created an excellent replica of the Eden (High-In). (Courtesy of Mike DeVries, DeVries Designs, Inc.)

Hole 4, Augusta National Golf Club (NLE)
Augusta, Georgia
by Alister Mackenzie, opened 1933 (Figure 7-45)

This hole was once an Eden, but it is now barely recognizable after many modifications.

Hole 5, Saucon Valley Country Club
Bethlehem, Pennsylvania
revised by William F. Gordon, opened 1951

In late 1951, Gordon, a prominent golf course architect from Pennsylvania, undertook the design of the first nine at Saucon Valley Country Club with the intention of making hole 5 a reproduction of the Eden at St.

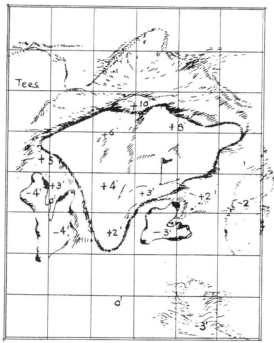

FIGURE 7-45
There is a resemblance in this Alister Mackenzie sketch to the latest yardage booklet rendition of the fourth hole at Augusta National Golf Club, Augusta, Georgia. Neither is close to the original Eden. (Courtesy of USGA. All rights reserved.)

Andrews. Gordon's son David, another prominent course architect, kindly gave the authors a fascinating package of correspondence and photographs covering his father's investigation and gathering of information on the Eden from an engineer located in St. Andrews.

Prior to receiving the data from Scotland, Bill Gordon worked out a rough sketch for the dozer operator to make a start (Figure 7-46). Then the Gordons studied many pictures of the hole sent from Scotland by a local engineer (Figures 7-47 through 7-50). Next, Dave Gordon made a drawing of the hole based on his interpretation of the data (Figure 7-51). The finished product is a fine adaptation of this often-replicated classic (Figure 7-52). Gordon wrote the Scots that he appreciated their efforts and was well pleased with the final results. (The authors hope to use this valuable documentation of how a classic hole was created to start a museum of golf course architecture.)

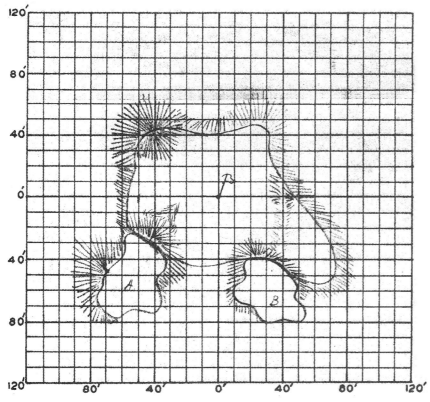

FIGURE 7-46
This was golf architect William Gordon's sketchy idea at the start of his construction process of an Eden at Saucon Valley Country Club, Bethlehem, Pennsylvania. It was amazingly close to the original at the Old Course at St. Andrews, Scotland. (Courtesy of Dave Gordon, ASGCA.)

FIGURE 7-47

There are two unnamed bunkers on the east side of the fairway on the 11th hole at the Old Course at St. Andrews, Scotland. Note the shallow mouths and the tufted bank on the south side and the marram and sea lime grasses surrounding these hazards. (Courtesy of Dave Gordon, ASGCA.)

FIGURE 7-48

The view across the Hill bunker to the Cockle bunker on the 11th hole at the Old Course at St. Andrews, Scotland, shows the sand blown by the prevailing wind and the marram and sea lime grasses surrounding the bunkers. Note that both bunkers have shallow mouths on the right. (Courtesy of Dave Gordon, ASGCA.)

FIGURE 7-49

The view of the Strath bunker looking toward the 11th hole on the Old Course at St. Andrews, Scotland, shows the sloping shoulder of the bunker rising toward the hole and the tufted bank and the marram and sea lime grasses surrounding it. (Courtesy of Dave Gordon, ASGCA.)

FIGURE 7-50

This view of the Cockle or Shell bunker on the 11th hole at the Old Course at St. Andrews, Scotland, shows that soft sand has been blown onto the east bank by the prevailing wind. Note that the banking of this bunker is sown with marram grass. (Courtesy of Dave Gordon, ASGCA.)

CLASSIC GOLF HOLE DESIGN

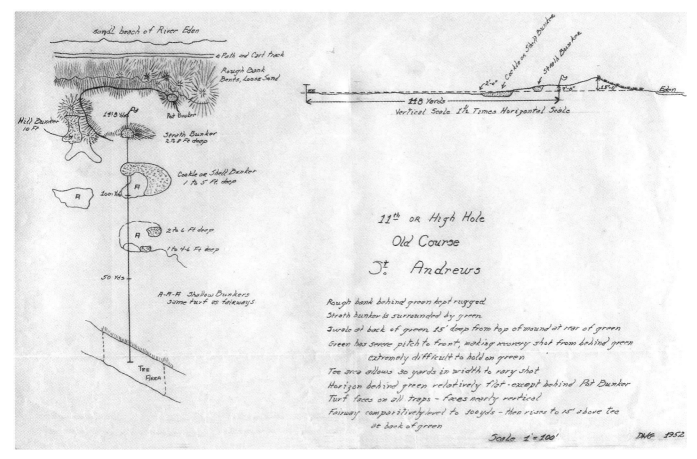

sand beach of River Eden

Path and Cart track

*Rough Bank
Bents, Loose Sand*

*Hill Bunker
10 Ft*

14:8 Yds

Pot Bunker

*Strath Bunker
2½ 8 Ft deep*

*Cockle or Shell Bunker
1 to 5 Ft deep*

100 Yds

2 to 6 Ft deep

1 to 4 6 Ft deep

50 Yds

*A-A-A Shallow Bunkers
some turf as fairways*

*Tee
Area*

118 Yards
Vertical Scale 1½ Times Horizontal Scale

Cockle or Shell Bunker

Strath Bunker

2'-0"

4'-0"

15'-0"

Eden

11ᵗʰ or High Hole
Old Course
St. Andrews

Rough bank behind green kept rugged
Strath bunker is surrounded by green
Swale at back of green 15' deep from top of mound at rear of green
Green has severe pitch to front, making recovery shot from behind green
extremely difficult to hold on green
Tee area allows 30 yards in width to vary shot
Horizon behind green relatively flat - except behind Pot Bunker
Turf faces on all traps - faces nearly vertical
Fairway comparitively level to 100 yds - then rises to 15' above tee
at back of green

Scale 1" = 100'

DWG 1952

FIGURE 7-51
*This drawing illustrates the
original Eden at the Old Course
at St. Andrews, Scotland, as
portrayed by an on-site engineer
and interpreted by golf architect
David Gordon. (Courtesy of
Dave Gordon, ASGCA.)*

FIGURE 7-52
*The finished replication of the Eden,
hole 5, at Saucon Valley Country
Club, Bethlehem, Pennsylvania, is a
fine adaptation of one of the most
replicated classics. (Courtesy of
Dave Gordon, ASGCA.)*

No doubt the extensive publicity received by the Tournament Players Club (TPC) courses has led Island Greens to become classics. Eminent architect Pete Dye is undoubtedly the pioneer of Island Greens in the modern age, but many were present long before Dye installed his first Island Green on the Stadium Course of the TPC at Sawgrass, Florida, opened in 1983. Ron Whitten, *Golf Digest*'s architectural editor and historian, outlined the evolution of Island Greens in *The Architects of Golf*. His story starts with the **ninth at Ponte Vedra**, designed by golf architect Herbert Strong and opened in 1932. Yet others preceded it, notably Hugh Wilson's **12th at Cobb's Creek Golf Course**, Philadelphia, Pennsylvania, opened in 1917. It has also been claimed that there was an Island Green on the version of Baltusrol in Springfield, New Jersey, that came before A. W. Tillinghast's famous layout.

Some well-known renditions include:

Hole 9, Ponte Vedra Golf Club
Ponte Vedra Beach, Florida
by Herbert Strong, opened 1932 (Figure 7-53)

Although opened in the depths of the Depression, this hole became renowned. An Island Green in addition to being a par-3 finishing hole makes this one an original.

FIGURE 7-53
A par-3 finishing hole (9 or 18) is not common. Having an Island Green in addition is truly unique, as shown on hole 9 at Ponte Vedra Golf Club, Ponte Vedra Beach, Florida. (Courtesy of Ron Whitten.)

Hole 16, Golden Horseshoe Golf Club, Gold Course
Williamsburg, Virginia
by Robert Trent Jones, opened 1964 (Figure 7-54)

Though the island may appear to be a peninsula at first glance, a closer look reveals the bridge.

Hole 18, Mission Hills Country Club, Old Course
Rancho Mirage, California
by Desmond Muirhead, opened 1970 (Figure 7-55)

The green's design slopes to the water versus artificial bulkheading.

FIGURE 7-54
From this angle, the island on the 16th hole at Golden Horseshoe Golf Club, Williamsburg, Virginia, looks like a peninsula. Part of the green is bulkheaded and part slopes to the water. (Courtesy of Ron Whitten.)

FIGURE 7-55
Desmond Muirhead created a beautiful relationship of shapes and spaces on the finishing hole at Mission Hills Country Club, Rancho Mirage, California. He also designed Aberdeen (see Figure 7-60). (Courtesy of Ron Whitten.)

Hole 17, Tournament Players Club (TPC) at Sawgrass, Stadium Course Ponte Vedra Beach, Florida by Pete Dye, opened 1983 (Figure 7-56)

Although comparatively new, this Island Green received wide publicity that stimulated the creation of numerous others.

Hole 17, Professional Golf Association (PGA) West, Stadium Course La Quinta, California by Pete Dye, opened 1986 (Figure 7-57)

Almost a duplicate of hole 17 at TPC at Sawgrass, the green has a stone (rip-rap) bulkhead.

FIGURE 7-56

Bulkheads at the island's edge define the green's boundaries on the 17th at Tournament Players Club at Sawgrass, Ponte Vedra Beach, Florida. There is no room for error. The golfer is either on the green or in the hazard. (Courtesy of Ron Whitten.)

FIGURE 7-57

On hole 17 at PGA West, Stadium Course, La Quinta, California, Pete Dye used rip-rap at the green edge in contrast to a wooden bulkhead or Desmond Muirhead's grassy slopes. (Courtesy of Ron Whitten.)

FIGURE 7-58
No two-way traffic problems to deal with on the 533-yard 13th hole at Tournament Players Club at The Woodlands, Houston, Texas, designed by Bernard von Hagge and Bruce Devlin. Bulkheads again form the island. (Courtesy of Ron Whitten.)

FIGURE 7-59
For this unique double Island Green, holes 7 and 15 of the Cochise Course of the Golf Club at Desert Mountain, Scottsdale, Arizona, Jack Nicklaus used a combination of grassy slopes and rock features. (Courtesy of Ron Whitten.)

Hole 13, Tournament Players Club at The Woodlands
Houston, Texas
by Bernard von Hagge and Bruce Devlin, opened in 1982

Provides an exceptionally interesting Island Green because the hole is a par-5 (Figure 7-58)

Holes 7 and 15, Golf Club at Desert Mountain, Cochise Course
Scottsdale, Arizona
by Jack Nicklaus, opened 1987 (Figure 7-59)

This green has the distinction of being the first double Island Green.

Hole 8, Aberdeen Golf and Country Club
Boynton Beach, Florida
opened in 1987 (Figure 7-60)
Hole 7, Stone Harbor Golf Club
Cape May, New Jersey, opened 1987

Both designed by Desmond Muirhead, they provide interesting Island Greens. Called "Clashing Jaws," greens are built alongside floating bunkers. Found too unforgiving, both were eventually remodeled.

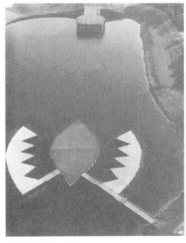

FIGURE 7-60
Hole 8 at 149 yards, called "Clashing Jaws," at Aberdeen Golf and Country Club, Boynton Beach, Florida, was designed by Desmond Muirhead. Apparently too tough for too many golfers, it was remodeled to be more user-friendly—proof again that golf is very much a mental game. (Courtesy of Ron Whitten.)

Hole 14, Coeur d'Alene Resort Golf Club
Coeur d'Alene, Idaho
by Scott Miller, opened 1991 (Figure 7-61)

Given its location, its scale, and its ability to be moved, this is said to be the ultimate in Island Greens.

Hole 14, Pine Valley Golf Club
Pine Valley, New Jersey
by George Crump with H. S. Colt, opened 1922 (Figure 7-62)

Though the tee is elevated, the shot must be very accurate to reach the green circled by sand as well as water.

FIGURE 7-61

The 14th hole at Coeur d'Alene Resort Golf Club, Coeur d'Alene, Idaho, features the ultimate in Island Greens—one that floats. Both alignment and distance can vary. (Courtesy of Ron Whitten.)

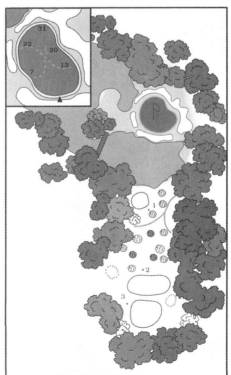

FIGURE 7-62

On hole 14 at Pine Valley Golf Club, Pine Valley, New Jersey, the rear tee is elevated, but the shot through trees requires extreme accuracy to a well-guarded green.

Hole 9, Shackamaxon Golf and Country Club
Scotch Plains, New Jersey
by A. W. Tillinghast, opened 1917 (Figures 7-63A and 7-63B)

Though the setting may seem idyllic, Tillinghast introduced a unique hazard: a rough grass mound on the green, an island on an island.

FIGURE 7-63A
The ninth hole at Shackamaxon Golf and Country Club, Scotch Plains, New Jersey, is truly a beautiful setting, but the green can be ominous for the golfer. (Courtesy of Treewolf Productions.)

FIGURE 7-63B
Not shown in Part A is an island on an island on the ninth hole at Shackamaxon Golf and Country Club, Scotch Plains, New Jersey. There is a rough, grassy mound somewhat like the bunker in the middle of the sixth green at Riviera Country Club, Pacific Palisades, California. (Courtesy of Treewolf Productions.)

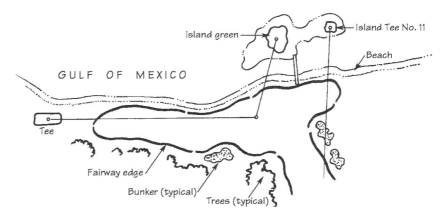

FIGURE 7-64

The Island Green on the 10th hole at
Key West Golf Course, Key West,
Florida, was an impressive sight with
the adjacent tee 11. Unfortunately, it
did not survive Depression and war.

Hole 10, Key West Golf Course (NLE)
Key West, Florida
by William Langford, opened 1925 (Figure 7-64)

*This hole, on a course that fell victim to the Depression, was widely
known in the world of golf.*

Hole 17, Cherry Hills Country Club
Denver, Colorado
by William Flynn, opened 1923 (see Figure 5-16, page 107)

*A par-5 to an Island Green requires careful placement of the tee shot for
the second to be successful or to let the golfer consider going for the green
on the second shot.*

Hole 10, Brooklake Country Club
Florham Park, New Jersey
by Geoffrey Cornish, Brian Silva, and Mark Mungeam
opened 1987 (Figure 7-65)

*Although the hole was originally planned as a Cape, the green evolved
into a virtual island during construction.*

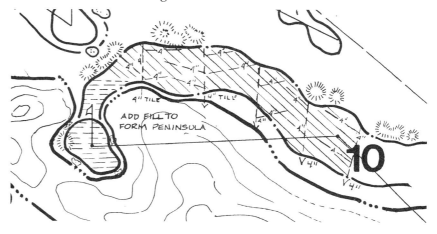

FIGURE 7-65
*This peninsula hole, the 10th, at
Brooklake Country Club, Florham
Park, New Jersey, designed by
Cornish, Silva and Mungeam came
close to being an island. The shot
requirement is the same.*

Hole 18, Mission Hills Country Club, Tournament Course
Rancho Mirage, California
by Desmond Muirhead, opened 1970

Muirhead's rendering (Figure 7-66) captures the beauty of this 646-yard par-5 finishing hole topped off with an Island Green.

Hole 9, Fair Oaks Golf Park
Fairfax, Virginia
by Ault, Clark & Associates, opened 1992 (Figure 7-67)

An Island Green on this par-3 hole provides an unexpected experience.

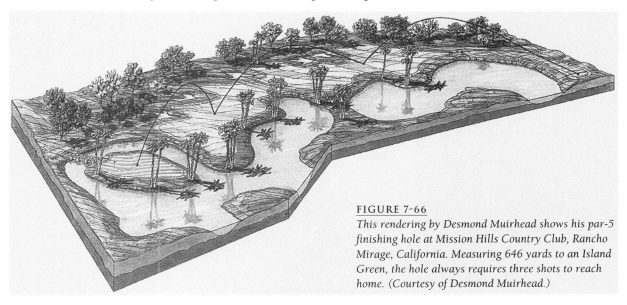

FIGURE 7-66
This rendering by Desmond Muirhead shows his par-5 finishing hole at Mission Hills Country Club, Rancho Mirage, California. Measuring 646 yards to an Island Green, the hole always requires three shots to reach home. (Courtesy of Desmond Muirhead.)

FIGURE 7-67
Hole 9 at Fair Oaks Golf Park, Fairfax, Virginia, designed by Ault, Clark & Associates, has an Island Green on a par-3 course, where you don't normally expect to have that experience. (Courtesy of Ault, Clark & Associates, Ltd.)

Hole 14, the Old Course at St. Andrews (Figure 7-68)

The form of this 567-yard par-5 Long hole evolved over centuries. Several very different routes are now provided from tee to green. Obviously, not all golf holes dubbed Long are replicas or are even related to the 14th at St. Andrews; their names simply arise from their length.

Replications and other classic Longs include:

Hole 17, Lido Golf Club (NLE)
Lido Beach, New York
by C. B. Macdonald and Seth Raynor, opened 1917
(see Figure 4-29, page 81)

Not only were the length and routing of the original borrowed when designing this hole, but also the Hell bunker was simulated and another bunker replicated the Beardies.

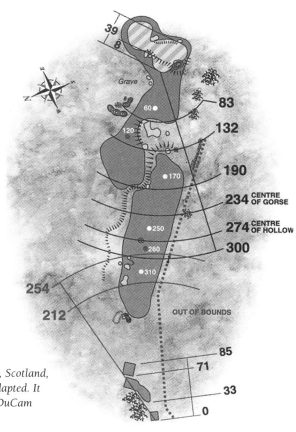

FIGURE 7-68

Hole 14 on the Old Course at St. Andrews, Scotland, is the classic Long that has been widely adapted. It was a long hole in its day. (Copyright © DuCam Marketing (UK) Ltd.)

CLASSIC GOLF HOLE DESIGN

Hole 17, Baltusrol Golf Club
Springfield, New Jersey
by A. W. Tillinghast, 623 yards, opened 1922

Though not related to the classic, the Long at Baltusrol has itself become a renowned hole, with only a handful of golfers getting home on their second shots. It also includes a Hell's Half Acre bunker.

Hole 14, Baltimore Country Club, Five Farms East Course
Timonium, Maryland
by A. W. Tillinghast, opened 1926 (Figure 7-69)

This is another Tillinghast Long at 600 yards that also contains a Hell's Half Acre.

Hole 5, International Golf Club
Bolton, Massachusetts
by Geoffrey S. Cornish, opened 1958 (see Figure 6-14, page 163)

The architect was instructed to create a par-5 hole where no golfer could reach home on the second. Accordingly, he produced a monster from the back tee. Before the course officially opened, however, touring professional Paul Harney reached home on his second by cutting across a forest. Forty-five years later, this is now impossible because the trees have matured. The putting surface has an area of over half an acre.

Hole 9, National Golf Links of America
Southampton, New York
by C. B. Macdonald, opened 1913 (see Figure 4-7, pages 66–67)

Not intended as a pure replication of the Long hole on the Old Course, this hole is better described as a composite.

FIGURE 7-69
At 600 yards, hole 14 on the Five Farms East Course at Baltimore Country Club, Timonium, Maryland, is truly a three-shot hole with a Hell's Half Acre bunker coming into play on the second shot. It was long in 1926. (Courtesy of Baltimore Country Club.)

THE CLASSIC GOLF HOLES

Hole 17, Black Mountain Country Club
Black Mountain, North Carolina, revised by Ross Taylor

According to British architect Donald Steel, this is the longest hole in the world, although he adds that in 1927 the sixth hole at Prescott Country Club in Arkansas measured 838 yards. A course in Japan now sports an even longer hole.

Hole 17, Boca Raton Resort Golf Club (NLE)
Boca Raton, Florida
by William Flynn, opened 1928 (Figure 7-70)

This hole, once widely known as "long," bore little relationship to the Long on the Old Course.

Hole 6, Center Valley Club
Center Valley, Pennsylvania
by Cornish, Silva and Mungeam, opened 1992 (Figure 7-71)

Percy Clifford, a course architect and winner of six Mexican Amateurs and three Mexican Open Championships, once explained to Cornish how to re-create the Long with all its mystique. Cornish took advantage of Clifford's insights when planning this hole.

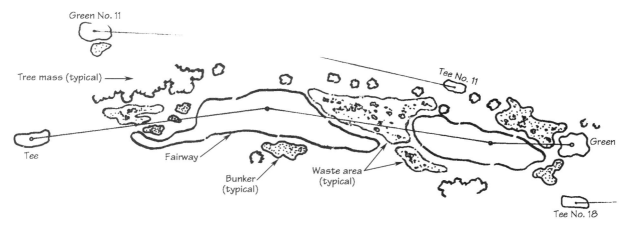

FIGURE 7-70
Though 570 yards, hole 17 on the South Course at Boca Raton Resort Golf Club, Boca Raton, Florida (which no longer exists), did not resemble the original Long on the Old Course at St. Andrews, Scotland. It did provide many hazards to deal with.

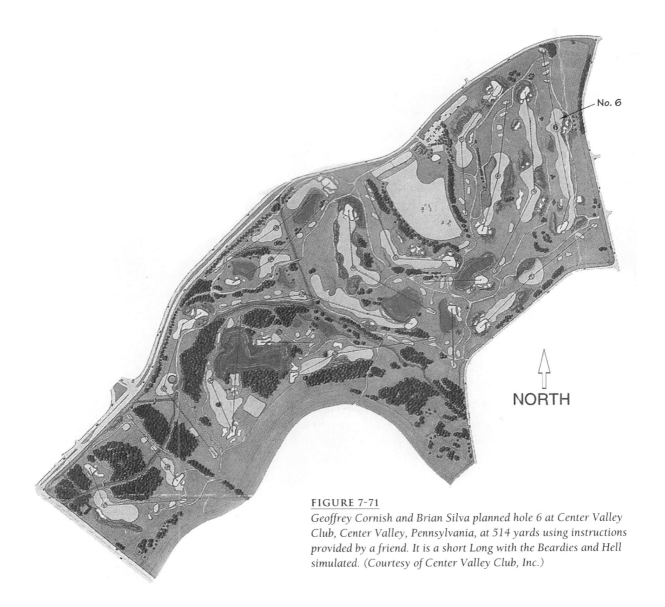

NORTH

FIGURE 7-71
Geoffrey Cornish and Brian Silva planned hole 6 at Center Valley Club, Center Valley, Pennsylvania, at 514 yards using instructions provided by a friend. It is a short Long with the Beardies and Hell simulated. (Courtesy of Center Valley Club, Inc.)

PUNCH BOWL

Any hole that includes a depressed green with mounds or banks on three or four sides is probably a Punch Bowl. One of the best known and an early example is at Royal Liverpool Golf Club, Hoylake, England, but numerous natural sites, similar to those of existing Punch Bowls, were selected by early Scottish designers to protect their greens from the desiccating winds of the Scottish coasts. Not surprisingly, numerous Punch Bowls are found on linksland. Perhaps most

THE CLASSIC GOLF HOLES

in the United States worthy of the honor of being called classic are those designed by C. B. Macdonald and his protégés. Some are carved into hillsides and are therefore above fairway level. That type of Punch Bowl has also been referred to as a "Rocking Chair."

Not all architects are fond of the Punch Bowl concept. A. W. Tillinghast wrote despairingly when he called them sunken greens. "I consider a severely bowled green as utterly unsuited to the pitched iron, and particularly the mashie shot," he once opined. Yet he also allowed that "Very long shots from the brassie or cleek, shots which make their way to a green after striking the fairway in front, may be regarded as sound." And Tillinghast's sunken green on *hole 12 at Shawnee Country Club* was considered to be great.

Three other examples of quality Punch Bowls include:

Hole 11, Tamarack Country Club
Greenwich, Connecticut
by Charles Banks, opened 1929 (Figure 7-72)

This exceptional replication has a putting surface that falls off on the back right. According to golf architect Ronald Forse, this encourages golfers to play a running approach down the left side of the fairway.

Hole 15, Wyantenuck Country Club
Great Barrington, Massachusetts
by Charles Banks, opened around 1930

The green is carved into a hillside, producing a Rocking Chair Punch Bowl.

FIGURE 7-72

The Punch Bowl, hole 11, at Tamarack Country Club, Greenwich, Connecticut, designed by Charles Banks, also features the triangular cross-sectional mounding often seen on the Banks layouts.

CLASSIC GOLF HOLE DESIGN

Hole 15, Sodus Point Heights Golf Course
Sodus Point, New York
by Geoffrey S. Cornish and William G. Robinson, opened 1966

The Punch Bowl or Rocking Chair green on this exceptionally long par-4 provides some safety for those attempting to reach the green on their second shots. Like all Punch Bowls, it holds nearly all shots.

Other Punch Bowls worthy of note are:

Hole 9, Royal Liverpool Golf Club
Hoylake, England
by R. Chambers and George Morris, opened 1869 (Figure 7-73)

On this 310- to 390-yard par-4, the Punch Bowl is formed by a series of mounds.

Hole 3, Aberdovey Golf Club
Aberdovey, Wales
original architect unknown but revised by H. S. Colt, James Braid, and Herbert Fowler on separate occasions (Figure 7-74)

The green on this 126- to 173-yard par-3 is shaped like a basin encircled by small hills.

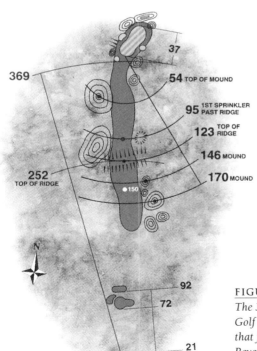

FIGURE 7-73
The 390-yard Punch Bowl, hole 9, at Royal Liverpool Golf Club, Hoylake, England, features a series of mounds that form the bowl. The green angle is reminiscent of a Reverse Redan. (Copyright © DuCam Marketing (UK) Ltd.)

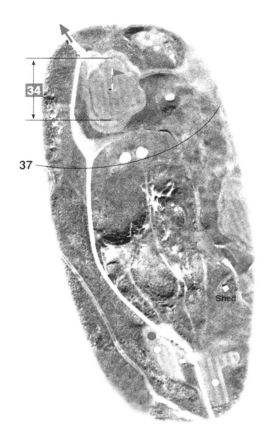

34

37

Shed

FIGURE 7-74

The yardage booklet describes the Punch Bowl, hole 3, at Aberdovey Golf Club, Aberdovey, Wales, as a basin-type green. Bernard Darwin states, "The green is almost entirely circled round with small hills and there is only a very narrow opening through which to play." (Copyright © 2000 Golfair.co.uk.)

Hole 14, Cottonwoods Golf Club
Tunica, Mississippi (Figure 7-75)

Though this Punch Bowl isn't particularly deep, the 480-yard par-4 hole is difficult because it must be played uphill into the wind.

FIGURE 7-75

The Punch Bowl, the 14th hole, at Cottonwoods Golf Club, Tunica, Mississippi, is not deep, but the hole is 480 yards uphill into the wind. The designer, Stan Gentry, felt that the golfer deserved some visibility of the putting surface. (Courtesy of Stan Gentry—Hale Irwin Golf Design.)

FIGURE 7-76

Hole 4, the Punch Bowl, at Plum Lake Golf Club, Sayner, Wisconsin, was over 8 feet deep but due to drainage problems was partially filled, leaving it around 5½ feet deep. The course design has been variously attributed to C. B. Macdonald or his protégés. (Courtesy of Terry Monroe.)

Hole 4, Plum Lake Golf Club
Sayner, Wisconsin, architects and opening date unknown
(Figure 7-76)

This Punch Bowl is exceptionally deep.

REDAN

Hole 15, North Berwick Golf Club
Scotland
designed by David Strath, greenkeeper and professional at North Berwick from 1876 to 1878

His successor, Bernard Sayers, likely modified the 193-yard par-3 hole (see Figures 4-10, page 69, and 7-77A and 7-77B).

According to Webster's, a Redan is a "fort or rampart consisting of two ramparts in the form of a V having its angle toward the enemy and opened at the back." Because the green on the original Redan hole at North Berwick is protected by bunkers in somewhat the same manner, one might assume that this is the reason for its name. Yet it appears that a Scottish veteran of the Crimean War, about to play the hole for the first time, exclaimed, "I would prefer to storm the Redan at Sevastopol again rather than play this hole." His widely publicized exclamation popularized the name. North Berwick's Redan has since become the most widely adapted of all classic golf holes.

FIGURE 7-77A
The woodwork on the original Redan, the 15th hole, at North Berwick Golf Club, Scotland, looks like a fortress rather than a golf hole. Famed Scottish professional Ben Sayers is shown surveying the green from the bulkhead. (Courtesy of Grant Books.)

FIGURE 7-77B
The bulkhead on the Redan, the 15th hole, at North Berwick Golf Club, Scotland, has been replaced by a grassed slope, making it look more like a green than a fortress. Yet it is still tough to storm.

Hole 17, Pebble Beach Golf Links
Pebble Beach, California
by Jack Neville, Douglas Grant, and Chandler Egan, revised 1928 (Figure 7-78)

The daunting bunker on the original Redan is present on the left, but the green does not slope away from the shot. A steep roll in the putting surface provides the difficult putting of a Redan for those who have played to the front of the green and do not dare the terrifying bunker.

Hole 4, National Golf Links of America
Southampton, New York
by Charles Blair Macdonald, opened 1911 (see Figure 4-7)

Some say that Macdonald's Redan surpasses the original in terms of playing interest.

CLASSIC GOLF HOLE DESIGN

FIGURE 7-78
Hole 17 at Pebble Beach Golf Links, Pebble Beach, California, is a reasonable adaptation of the Redan due to the angle between the centerline and the long axis of the green. A roll in the putting surface makes for difficult putting versus the slope-away in the original. (Courtesy of the Bancroft Library, University of California, Berkeley.)

Hole 7, Tamarack Country Club
Greenwich, Connecticut
by Charles Banks, opened 1929 (Figures 7-79A and 7-79B)

The putting surface on this hole does not fall away from the shot as it does on the original. Banks obviously intended to replicate Macdonald's version of the Redan at the National Golf Links rather than the original.

Hole 17, Whippoorwill Club
Armonk, New York
by Charles Banks, opened 1930

Another Banks version of the Redan, this hole is said to be one of the finest replications of the original. Yet the contours of the putting surface differ from the classic.

FIGURE 7-79A
From a distance, the huge sand bunker that controls shot requirements on the seventh hole at Tamarack Country Club, Greenwich, Connecticut, is barely visible, but it's there.

FIGURE 7-79B
A closer look reveals the sand at hole 7 at Tamarack Country Club, Greenwich, Connecticut, ready to wreak havoc on those who reach it.

Hole 4, Somerset Country Club
St. Paul, Minnesota
by Seth Raynor, opened around 1922 (Figure 7-80)

This is a fine replication, but its Redan characteristics have long been compromised by the presence of stately American elms along the left of the hole that preclude playing directly to the left side of the putting surface.

Hole 9, Oneck Course (NLE), Westhampton Country Club
Westhampton, New York
by Charles Banks, opened 1929 (see Figure 4-32, page 83)

The shot to this Redan green was across water to a putting surface that fell away to the back left.

FIGURE 7-80
This aerial photograph of the fourth hole at Somerset Country Club, St. Paul, Minnesota, shows both bunkers. The left creates the Redan. Unlike the original hole, a similar bunker appears on the right side, as did many on 1920s courses. (Courtesy of Jerry M. Murphy, Somerset Country Club.)

CLASSIC GOLF HOLE DESIGN

Hole 14, Shinnecock Hills Golf Club (NLE)
Southampton, New York
by C. B. Macdonald, revised 1916

The C. B. Macdonald revision of the Willie Davis and Willie Dunn course included this hole, often said to be "the finest Redan ever built." The Redan was retained as the seventh by William Flynn when he rebuilt the course.

Hole 2, Somerset Hills Country Club
Bernardsville, New Jersey
by A. W. Tillinghast, opened 1917 (Figure 7-81)

This is another superb adaptation of the original.

Hole 10, Blind Brook Club
Purchase, New York
by Seth Raynor with George Low, opened 1917 (Figure 7-82)

The greenside bunkers are by no means as deep as those found on the original or on many of its adaptations.

Hole 13, The Links (NLE)
Roslyn, New York
by C. B. Macdonald with Seth Raynor, opened 1919

This hole, with its green set at an angle opposite to the tee shot at North Berwick, was once described as the most demanding replica of the Redan.

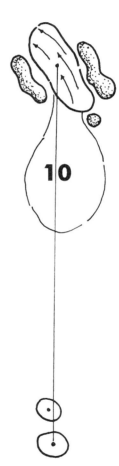

FIGURE 7-81
Angles are changed on the second hole at Somerset Hills Country Club, Bernardsville, New Jersey, but the left bunker sets this A. W. Tillinghast Redan up to be a true Redan. (Courtesy of USGA. All rights reserved.)

FIGURE 7-82
Though the bunkers are not that deep on hole 10 at Blind Brook Club, Purchase, New York, it's still a Redan. Note the green slopes away from the shot, as in the original.

**Hole 4, Riviera Country Club
Pacific Palisades, California
by George C. Thomas and William P. Bell, opened 1927
(Figure 7-83)**

This Redan is played into the prevailing wind.

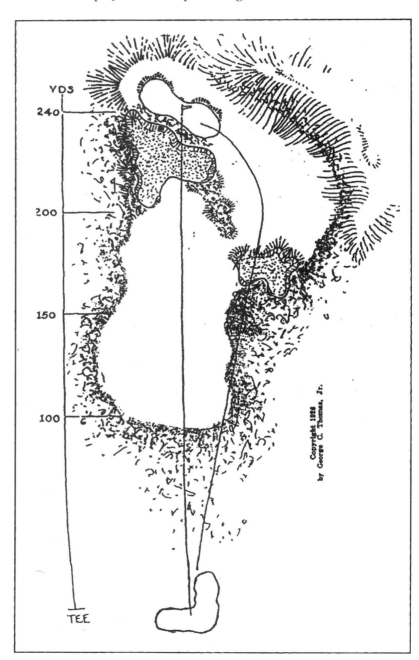

FIGURE 7-83

The angle between the hole centerline and the green axis on the fourth hole at Riviera Country Club, Pacific Palisades, California, is close to that of the original. Riviera's features a more expansive bunker but less difference in elevation between it and the green. (Contributed by Geoff Shackelford.)

Hole 3, La Cumbre Country Club
Santa Barbara, California
by Tom Bendelow in 1918, revised by William P. Bell in 1920
(Figures 7-84A and 7-84B)

This hole qualifies as a Redan because of the shot making required, though the hole is not a replica of the original.

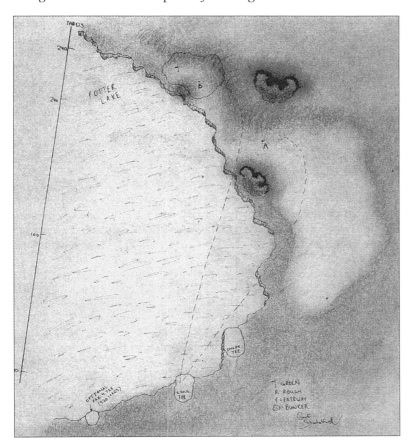

FIGURE 7-84A
Unlike the original Redan, a carry is required over water on hole 3 at La Cumbre Country Club, Santa Barbara, California, but the bunkers are less ominous. This hole is truly a Cape-Redan combination. (Drawing by Geoff Shackelford.)

FIGURE 7-84B
In this photo, the Cape concept over water is more evident than the Redan concept from the tee on hole 3 at La Cumbre Country Club, Santa Barbara, California. A miss to the left may get wet. (Courtesy of Geoff Shackelford.)

Hole 13, Pine Valley Golf Club
Pine Valley, New Jersey
by George C. Crump, opened 1922 (Figure 7-85)

This is a Redan-type green on a par-4 hole.

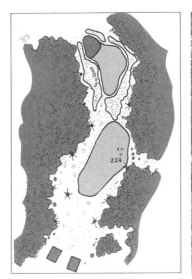

FIGURE 7-85
*The Redan bunker concept is not followed exactly on hole 13 at Pine Valley
Golf Club, Pine Valley, New Jersey, but sand expanses and grassy hills and
valleys present serious problems.*

Hole 11, Widgi Creek Golf Club
Bend, Oregon

*The principles of the Redan on this 118- to 216-yard par-3 hole are
apparent in the plan view, but not obvious from some angles at the tee
(Figure 7-86).*

Hole 7, Stratton Mountain Country Club, Forest Course
Stratton, Vermont
by Cornish and Silva, opened 1983 (Figure 7-87)

*This 114- to 174-yard par-3 hole is a subtle Redan with a curving rather
than a sloping roll.*

Hole 11, Grandover West Course
Greensboro, North Carolina (Figure 7-88)

*Bunker placement and angles make this 145- to 190-yard par-3 hole a
Redan.*

CLASSIC GOLF HOLE DESIGN

FIGURE 7-86

Graves and Pascuzzo used the principles of the Redan on hole 11 at Widgi Creek Golf Club, Bend, Oregon. There is a bunker on the right, and the rolling green provides difficult putting but does not slope away. Water adds another dimension. (Holes by Holeview Yardage Book Co.)

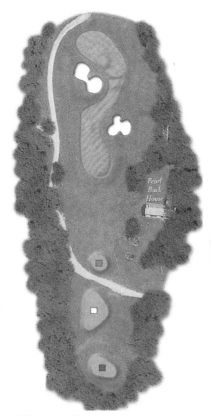

FIGURE 7-87

The Redan design concept is evident on the Forest 7 bunker at Stratton Mountain Country Club, Stratton, Vermont. (Holes by Holeview Yardage Book Co.)

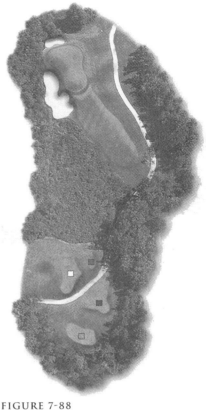

FIGURE 7-88

Bunker placement and angles are correct for a Redan on hole 11 of the West Course at Grandover Golf Club, Greensboro, North Carolina. The green is bulkheaded left and rear, making it vaguely similar to the original Redan (see Figure 7-77A). (Holes by Holeview Yardage Book Co.)

REVERSE REDAN

With the spread of golf architecture to every part of the world, numerous adaptations of the Redan were created. It is not surprising that course designers recognized the interesting possibilities of a "reverse" Redan. But it should be noted that "reverse" Redan refers not to reversing the V shape, but rather to the putting surface falling away left to right with the protecting bunkers altered. A Reverse Redan at **hole 7, Black Creek Country Club** near Chattanooga, Tennessee, by Brian Silva, opened in 2000 (Figure 7-89), clearly demonstrates this concept.

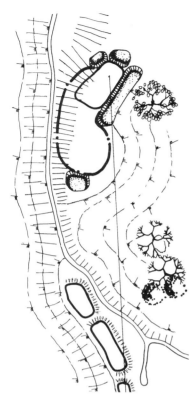

FIGURE 7-89
Brian Silva designed the Reverse Redan on hole 7 at Black Creek Country Club, near Chattanooga, Tennessee, demonstrating adherence to Redan concepts, only in reverse.

Other examples include:

Hole 11, Bayside Golf Links (NLE)
Bayside, New York
by Alister Mackenzie, revised 1932 (Figure 7-90)

The frightening greenside bunker was to the right of the green, with two other bunkers short of it.

Hole 2, Edina Country Club
Edina, Minnesota
by Tom Bendelow, opened in the early 1920s (Figure 7-91)

This hole, which resembles a Reverse Redan, was apparently planned in-house by members and not by architect Bendelow.

Hole 6, Augusta National Golf Club
Augusta, Georgia
by Alister Mackenzie, opened 1933 (see Figure 5-2, page 97)

As on many of the original holes that remain at this famous layout, the features of this Redan are now barely recognizable.

Hole 13, The Links (NLE)
Roslyn, New York
by C. B. Macdonald with Seth Raynor, opened 1919

This hole is exceptionally long for a Redan. Most are in the 175- to 190-yard range.

Hole 11, Los Angeles Country Club, North Course
Los Angeles, California
by George C. Thomas and William P. Bell, opened 1929 (Figure 7-92)

Huge bunkering makes this an effective Reverse Redan.

FIGURE 7-90
Though the bunker shaping was different on hole 11 at Bayside Golf Links, Bayside, New York (which no longer exists), the Reverse Redan concept was present, although without the critical angular relationship of green-to-hole centerline.

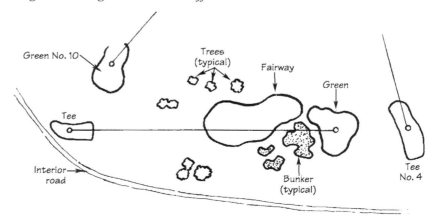

CLASSIC GOLF HOLE DESIGN

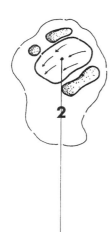

FIGURE 7-92
Massive bunkering on the 11th hole of the North Course at Los Angeles Country Club, Los Angeles, California, displays Thomas's admiration for the "lure, intrigue and importance of the one-shotter."

FIGURE 7-91
The angles as well as the bunker/ green relationship on hole 2 at Edina Country Club, Edina, Minnesota, resemble a Reverse Redan, but the green surface slopes to the front.

Hole 3, Gibson Island Country Club (NLE)
Gibson Island, Maryland
by C. B. Macdonald and Seth Raynor, opened 1922
(see Figure 4-28, page 79)

On this Reverse Redan, the green sloped down from back left to back right. It's worth noting that water came into play here more than on most Redans.

Four additional adaptations of the Reverse Redan show authentically the angular relationship between the hole centerline and the long axis of the green.

Hole 13, Bellerive
St. Louis, Missouri (Figure 7-93)

This 119- to 179-yard par-3 hole is an excellent example of a Reverse Redan.

Hole 13, St. Andrews Golf Club, Fox Hill Course Hastings-on-Hudson, New York (Figure 7-94)

Water adds an unusual feature on this 146- to 209-yard par-3 Reverse Redan.

Hole 2, Stratton Mountain Country Club, Mountain Course Stratton, Vermont (Figure 7-95)

This 114- to 205-yard par-3 hole has the correct angles of an authentic Reverse Redan.

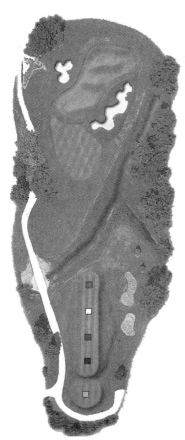

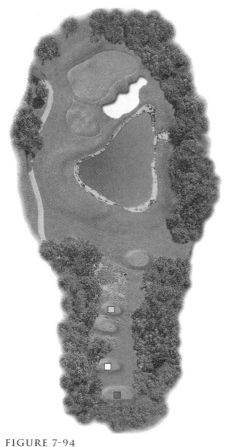

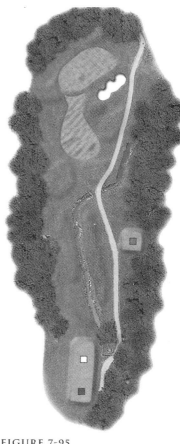

FIGURE 7-93

Hole 13 at Bellerive Country Club, St. Louis, Missouri, is an authentic adaptation of the Reverse Redan, including a terraced green. (Holes by Holeview Yardage Book Co.)

FIGURE 7-94

The green/bunker relationship is authentic, while the water adds to the golfer's thought processes on hole 13 at St. Andrews Golf Club, Hastings-on-Hudson, New York. (Holes by Holeview Yardage Book Co.)

FIGURE 7-95

Hole 2, the Mountain, at Stratton Mountain Country Club, Stratton, Vermont, is an authentic Reverse Redan with a deep bunker to consider on the right. (Holes by Holeview Yardage Book Co.)

CLASSIC GOLF HOLE DESIGN

Hole 8E, Magnolia Creek Golf Links
League City, Texas
by Ault, Clark & Associates (Figure 7-96)

Bunker placement makes this an excellent adaptation of the Reverse Redan.

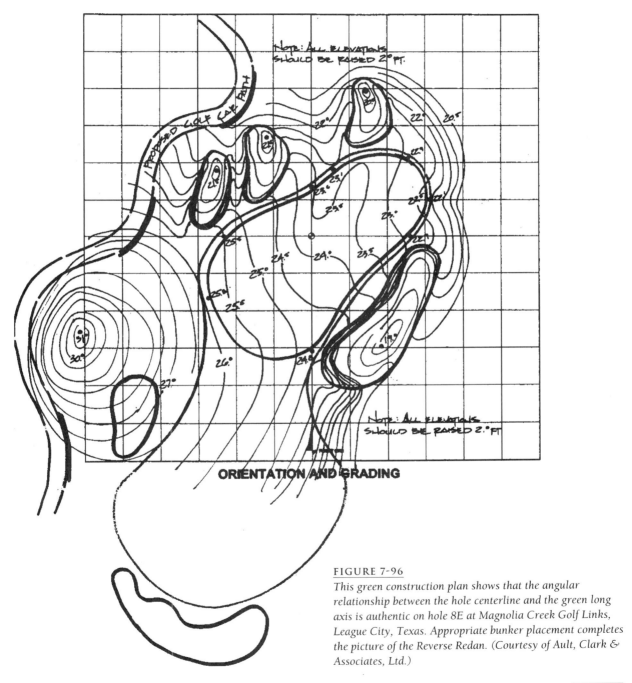

FIGURE 7-96

This green construction plan shows that the angular relationship between the hole centerline and the green long axis is authentic on hole 8E at Magnolia Creek Golf Links, League City, Texas. Appropriate bunker placement completes the picture of the Reverse Redan. (Courtesy of Ault, Clark & Associates, Ltd.)

Hole 17, the Old Course at St. Andrews (see Figure 5-60, page 136)

This 461-yard hole is unquestionably one of the most difficult—and best known—par-4s in golf. It is now framed by a hotel and attendant structures that replaced the stationmaster's house and drying shed. A road right of the green also comes into play. British Amateur Champion (1913) Harold Hilton, who nearly lost the championship on the Road, wrote, "No hole in existence has been the innocent cause of so many opprobrious epithets and language of so lurid a hue as the Road hole."

While none is as famous as the original, other similar holes do exist. To compensate for the lack of buildings, architects have used trees in place of them, making many Roads difficult to recognize from holes that are gentle doglegs around trees. One clue for botanically minded golfers is that the architect often selects a fast-growing species such as poplars or willows to create the effect.

Hole 7, National Golf Links
Southampton, New York
by C. B. Macdonald, opened 1911 (see Figure 4-7, pages 66–67)

Macdonald's version at the National is longer than the original, and he has replaced the structures and garden on the right with "a great expanse of bunkers and mounds" that avoids a frequent out-of-bounds scenario. Finally, and most importantly, he simulated the road on the right with a massive 5-foot-deep bunker.

Hole 11, Blind Brook Club
Purchase, New York
by Seth Raynor with George Low, opened around 1917

This short version of the Road includes a drop-off and trees replacing the hotel. Three greenside bunkers on the right simulate the road. Tall and fast-growing poplars were selected to replace the structures. Nevertheless, the hole is still difficult to recognize as a Road.

Hole 18, Westhampton Country Club, Oneck Course (NLE)
Westhampton, New York
by Charles Banks, opened 1929 (see Figure 4-32, page 83)

On this hole, described by Wexler as a genuine classic, fairway bunkers on the right simulate structures on the Old Course, while a huge bunker right of the green simulates the road. Wexler says that its length was more in keeping with the original Road than were many replications by Macdonald, Raynor, and Banks, which tended to be shorter.

Hole 17, Shinnecock Hills Golf Club (NLE)
Southampton, New York
by C. B. Macdonald and Seth Raynor, revised 1916

A fairway bunker was on the left of this hole, but nothing appeared on the right to simulate the existing or previous structures on the original.

Five additional Roads are included that bear the title "Road" but are not true replications of the Road.

Hole 17 (Road), Grand Cypress Resort
Orlando, Florida
by Jack Nicklaus (Figure 7-97)

This 410- to 485-yard par-5 adaptation of the Road includes the infamous little bunker to the right of the green.

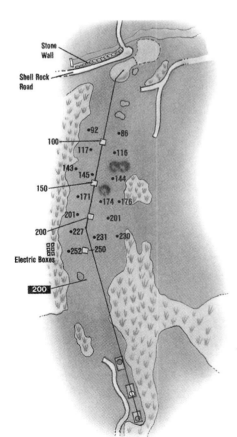

FIGURE 7-97

Jack Nicklaus created an interesting adaptation of the Road on the 17th hole at Grand Cypress Resort, Orlando, Florida. No buildings here, but there are mounds. At the green, there is the road, left side versus right as on the original, while the infamous little bunker is right of the green. (Courtesy of Florida State Golf Association.)

Hole 15 (The Road), Royal Troon Golf Club, Portland Course
Ayrshire, Scotland (Figure 7-98)

While this 432- to 494-yard par-5 is actually a Cape, some consider it a Road.

Hole 2 (Road), Royal Liverpool Golf Club
Hoylake, England (Figure 7-99)

Similar to Figure 7-98, this 334- to 371-yard par-4 features a series of mounds angled across the fairway.

Hole 16 (Dun), Royal Liverpool Golf Club
Hoylake, England (Figure 7-100)

Though this 430- to 532-yard par-5 may be called a Dun, the problems one encounters playing it are that of a Road.

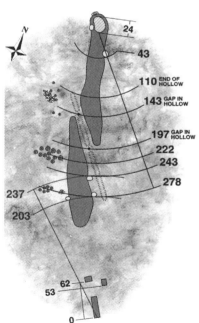

FIGURE 7-98

At hole 15 on the Portland Course at Royal Troon Golf Club, Ayrshire, Scotland, the tee shot angles across a narrow hollow. Perhaps it was an old roadbed? Although a Cape, to some it has some characteristics of a Road. (Copyright © DuCam Marketing (UK) Ltd.)

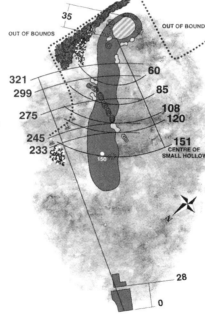

FIGURE 7-99

Similar to the configuration of the Road hole at Royal Troon Golf Club, a series of mounds angles across the fairway versus a hollow on hole 2 at Royal Liverpool Golf Club, Hoylake, England. (Copyright © DuCam Marketing (UK) Ltd.)

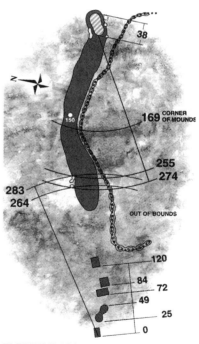

FIGURE 7-100

Although called "Dun" and not Road, hole 16 at Royal Liverpool Golf Club, Hoylake, England, has Road problems to solve. With out-of-bounds along the right side, the golfer must be careful when lining up both the tee shot and the second shot. (Copyright © DuCam Marketing (UK) Ltd.)

CLASSIC GOLF HOLE DESIGN

FIGURE 7-101
Trees and water form the barrier on the left side versus the right on the ninth hole at Somerset Country Club, St. Paul, Minnesota. There's more water to deal with as you approach the green. (Courtesy of Jerry M. Murphy, Somerset Country Club.)

**Hole 9, Somerset Country Club
St. Paul, Minnesota (Figure 7-101)**

This Road includes several water barriers.

SHORT

The *eighth on the Old Course at St. Andrews* carries the title "Short" and measures 195 yards from the new tee (see Figure 4-18, page 70). It is a stretch to say it is an ancestor of Macdonald's Short at the National Golf Links, which measures only 130 yards (see Figure 4-7, pages 66–67). The latter is the true classic, with its distinctly contoured putting surface almost completely surrounded by sand and characterized by a terrace with a U-shaped opening toward the tee. The resulting "horseshoe" demands accurate placement and local knowledge, as each portion of the green can propel the ball right, left, or off the putting surface completely. While many clubs have holes referred to as "Short," this is most often due to their diminutive length and not in reference to the original. The true Short features a squarish green almost completely surrounded by bunkers, with the trademark horseshoe terrace putting surface (Figure 7-102).

FIGURE 7-102

The horseshoe ridge on Shorts created by C. B. Macdonald, Seth Raynor, and Charles Banks is subtle. This diagram shows the general layout of the ridge that is sometimes referred to as the "thumbprint." It requires interesting approach shots and putts.

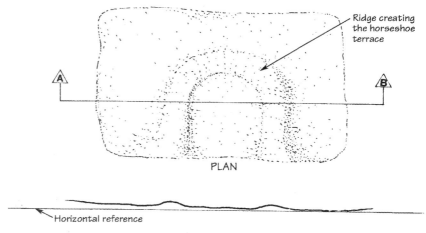

The Shorts listed below mostly include those related to the classic at the National Golf Links, but other renowned Shorts are also included.

Hole 15, Tamarack Country Club
Greenwich, Connecticut
by Charles Banks, opened 1929 (Figure 7-103)

Although the characteristic horseshoe terrace in the putting surface is not clearly visible, it is present. It has been said the terrace was mellowed on purpose by a program of repeated and heavy topdressing before World War II.

Hole 4 (formerly 13), Whippoorwill Club
Armonk, New York
by Charles Banks (Figure 7-104)

The characteristic horseshoe roll is present on this green.

FIGURE 7-103

The horseshoe ridge often tended to disappear, as on hole 15 at Tamarack Country Club, Greenwich, Connecticut, because of heavy topdressing over decades. Many golfers thought the ridge quite unfair. (Courtesy of Aqua Agronomic Solutions, Inc.)

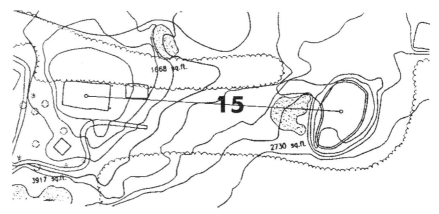

FIGURE 7-104
A Plateau green is part of this Short on hole 4 (formerly hole 13) at Whippoorwill Club, Armonk, New York. (Courtesy of USGA. All rights reserved.)

Hole 5, Yale University Golf Course
New Haven, Connecticut
by C. B. Macdonald and Seth Raynor, opened 1926

Deep bunkers are featured on this Short.

Hole 10, Pine Valley Golf Club
Pine Valley, New Jersey
by George Crump (Figures 7-105A and 7-105B)

The right greenside bunker, described by club historian Jim Finegan as "Satan's anal aperture," has become a widely known feature of this hole, which boasts several notorious hazards. It is not in the Macdonald-Raynor tradition, but is one of the world's greatest Short holes.

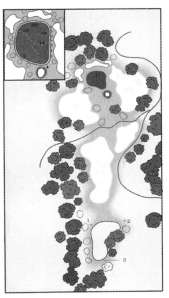

FIGURE 7-105A
This world-renowned Short, hole 10, at Pine Valley Golf Club, Pine Valley, New Jersey, is not similar to C. B. Macdonald–Seth Raynor Shorts except for length. Yet its bunkers provide plenty of challenge. (Courtesy of USGA. All rights reserved.)

FIGURE 7-105B
At only 137 yards, a close look confirms the difficulties that abound on hole 10 at Pine Valley Golf Club, Pine Valley, New Jersey, including the renowned, deep and high-walled bunker described as part of Satan's anatomy.

Hole 3, Westhampton Country Club, Oneck Course (NLE)
Westhampton, New York
by Charles Banks, opened 1929

Hole 17, El Caballero Country Club (NLE)
Tarzana, California
by W. P. Bell and George Thomas, opened 1926 (Figure 7-106)

The severely contoured green, surrounded by bunkers, puts this hole in the category of a "true" Short, although the influence, if any, of Macdonald's Short is not known.

Hole 12, Timber Point Golf Club (NLE)
Great River, New York
by Charles Alison, opened 1927

A once widely known Short, this hole by Alison featured Macdonald's bunker placement, but not the horseshoe terrace on the putting surface.

Hole 10, Meadowbrook Hunt Club (NLE)
Westbury, New York
by Devereux Emmet, opened 1914 (Figure 7-107)

Considering Macdonald's and Emmet's longtime friendship and Emmet's assistance in providing sketches of British holes for Macdonald's National Golf Links, it is reasonable to assume that Macdonald's Short influenced the design or redesign of this hole, although at one time it was an Island Green.

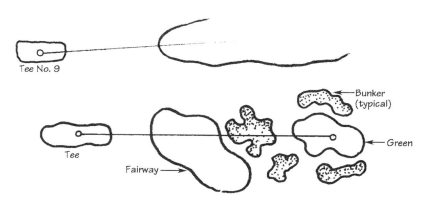

FIGURE 7-106
Heavy bunkering and a short 115 yards qualified the 17th hole at El Caballero Country Club, Tarzana, California (which no longer exists), as an adaptation of the Short.

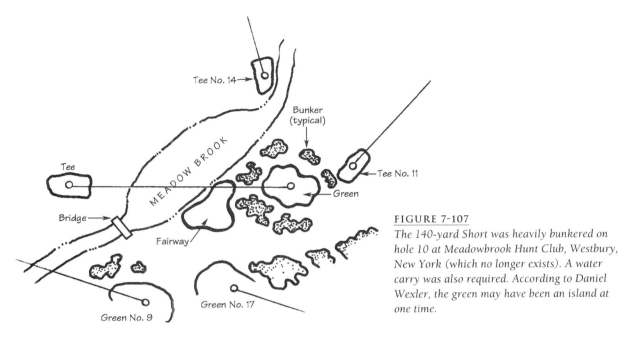

FIGURE 7-107
The 140-yard Short was heavily bunkered on hole 10 at Meadowbrook Hunt Club, Westbury, New York (which no longer exists). A water carry was also required. According to Daniel Wexler, the green may have been an island at one time.

Hole 14, Boca Raton Resort Golf Club, South Course (NLE)
Boca Raton, Florida
by William Flynn, opened 1928

While a connection to Macdonald's Short is tenuous, the bunker placement on this hole bore similarities.

Hole 8, Deepdale Golf Club (NLE)
Great Neck, New York
by C. B. Macdonald and Seth Raynor, opened 1925
(see Figure 4-26, page 77)

This Short lacked the horseshoe-shaped terrace in the putting surface.

Hole 8, Gibson Island Country Club (NLE)
Gibson Island, Maryland
by C. B. Macdonald and Seth Raynor, opened 1922
(see Figure 4-28, page 79)

Here was a typical Macdonald-Raynor Short with a severely contoured green surrounded by sand and with nearby water coming into play.

Hole 14, Lido Golf Club (NLE)
Lido Beach, New York
by C. B. Macdonald and Seth Raynor, opened 1917
(see Figure 4-29, page 81)

With the wind blowing, Wexler reveals, this Short hole required significant finesse even when the wind was blowing at moderate force.

THE CLASSIC GOLF HOLES

Hole 8, The Links (NLE)
Roslyn, New York
by C. B. Macdonald and Seth Raynor, opened 1919

This was a typical Macdonald-Raynor Short, but with a distinctly round green.

Hole 3, Shinnecock Hills Golf Club (NLE)
Southampton, New York
by C. B. Macdonald and Seth Raynor, revised 1916

The green was ringed by sand on this Macdonald-Raynor revision.

FIGURE 7-108
Hole 16 at Longmeadow Country Club, Longmeadow, Massachusetts, is a Donald Ross Short. Except for length, it has little or no resemblance to the classic C. B. Macdonald–Seth Raynor–Charles Banks Short. (Courtesy of USGA. All rights reserved.)

Hole 16, Longmeadow Country Club
Longmeadow, Massachusetts
by Donald Ross, opened 1921 (Figure 7-108)

This Short had little or no connection to those of Macdonald and his protégés because Ross's canvases were most often the land itself.

Hole 3, Wannamoisett Country Club
Rumford, Rhode Island
by Donald Ross, opened 1914 and revised 1926

Bunkered similarly to the Macdonald–Raynor–Banks Short, this green also bears similarities to the sixth at Royal Dornoch.

Hole 3, Inverness Club
Toledo, Ohio
by Donald Ross, revised 1919

Hole 13, Seminole Golf Club
Palm Beach, Florida
by Donald Ross and revised by Brian Silva,
originally opened 1929

Hole 10, Winged Foot Golf Club, West Course
Mamaroneck, New York
by A. W. Tillinghast and revised by George Fazio, opened 1923
(Figure 7-109)

While its architect A. W. Tillinghast stated this hole was the "best par-3 ever built," Ben Hogan is reputed to have said, "It's only a 5-iron into the neighbor's bedroom." It bears little or no connection to the classic Short.

Hole 14, Bayside Golf Links (NLE)
Bayside, New York
by Alister Mackenzie, opened 1923 (Figure 7-110)

While the putting surface did not feature the horseshoe step and the green was protected by bunkers on only two sides (front and back), this hole bears some resemblance to the Macdonald–Raynor–Banks Short.

FIGURE 7-109
Hole 10 on the West Course of Winged Foot Golf Club, Mamaroneck, New York, is certainly not short at 190 yards. It's an excellent par-3.

FIGURE 7-110
Heavy bunkering to the front and right side of hole 14 at Bayside Golf Links, Bayside, New York (which no longer exists), was evident on this Short by Alister Mackenzie.

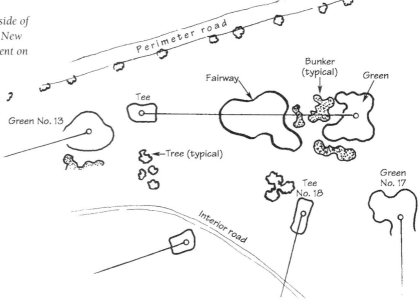

Hole 4, Sharp Park Golf Club (NLE)
Pacifica, California
by Alister Mackenzie, opened 1931 (Figure 7-111)

Except for length, there was little or no resemblance to the Short holes of Macdonald and his protégés.

Hole 2, Oakland Golf Club (NLE)
Bayside, New York
revised by Seth Raynor

Length on this Short hole is the only resemblance to the holes of Macdonald and his protégés.

FIGURE 7-111

Truly short at 120 yards, the fourth hole at Sharp Park Golf Course, Pacifica, California (which no longer exists), had bunkers on both sides that were troublesome.

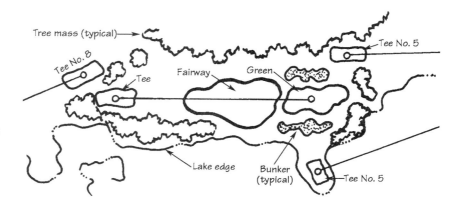

Hole 6, Tailer's Ocean Links (NLE)
Newport, Rhode Island
by Seth Raynor, opened 1920

This hole was a true adaptation of the National's Short.

Hole 18, Sitwell Park Golf Club
England
by Alister Mackenzie, opened 1913 (see Figure 5-39, page 124)

This hole was the original "Rolling Terror," and the concept for it was later used by Mackenzie elsewhere and probably led to the "Maxwell-Rolls" (steeply contoured putting surfaces) commonly employed by golf architect Perry Maxwell, but it is not related to the classic Short.

Hole 15, Cypress Point Golf Club
Pebble Beach, California
by Alister Mackenzie, opened 1928 (Figure 7-112)

Again, this renowned Short is not related to the classic.

<u>FIGURE 7-112</u>
Often overlooked because of the impressive 16th that follows, the 15th at Cypress Point Golf Club, Pebble Beach, California, offers everything you could ask for in a Short hole.

Hole 16 (The Wee Bogie), Gleneagles, King's Course
Perthshire, Scotland
by James Braid and C. K. Hutchison, opened 1919 (Figure 7-113)

Short but demanding, this hole has nine greenside bunkers. (A "wee bogie" is a small imp.)

Hole 15, Blind Brook Club
Purchase, New York
by Seth Raynor and George Low (Figure 7-114)

Here the putting surface exhibits the horseshoe roll. A bunker that once protected the front and right of the putting surface has been replaced with pot bunkers guarding the front only.

Hole 3, Black Creek Country Club
near Chattanooga, Tennessee
by Brian Silva (Figure 7-115)

This hole is heavily bunkered, as is the classic sixth hole at National Golf Links.

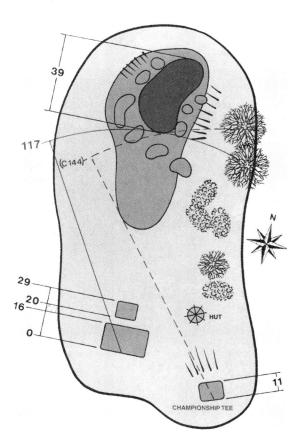

FIGURE 7-113
Hole 16, called "the Wee Bogie," on the King's Course at Gleneagles Golf Club, Perthshire, Scotland, has nine bunkers to give any golfer cause to think carefully. (Copyright © DuCam Marketing (UK) Ltd.)

CLASSIC GOLF HOLE DESIGN

FIGURE 7-114
The basin resulting from the horseshoe ridge can just be seen in this photo of a Raynor green, the 15th hole at Blind Brook Club, Purchase, New York. The ridge has likely been subdued over the years, but it is present.

FIGURE 7-115
This Short at Black Creek Country Club, near Chattanooga, Tennessee, includes massive bunkers typical of Shorts, along with steep banks next to the green. (Photo Courtesy of Scott Wicker.)

EPILOGUE

The game of golf and its playing fields incorporate life's lessons—its struggles as well as its triumphs and failures. In the last half-millennium, as society has flourished, so too has golf, and when society has suffered, the game has suffered. Golf, like society, has survived recessions, depressions, and war. Over the centuries, the game has radiated from Scotland and now inhabits nearly every nation and land on earth. Regardless of growth, however, the game and its playing fields harken back to their roots. Course architects recognize that all golf holes owe something to their predecessors. Sometimes this is barely evident, sometimes it is recognizable but not obviously so, and in some 13 instances it is clearly apparent. We have referred to these as the classics.

Centuries ago, Scots discovered that sandy, unpredictable terrain known as linksland lent itself to exciting and pleasurable golf holes with no modifications required. This now mythical land, and its God-given playing fields, gave rise to the game of golf, and around the middle of the 19th century, following at least 500 years of trial and error, methods were developed for the selection and creation of golf holes. Professional golfers were commissioned to select holes on the links and join them together in circuits. By the end of the 19th century, the art of golf course architecture had taken shape as the heathlands near London were modified for golf. Around the same time, early designers were practicing their craft in the New World.

This new and extraordinary profession was charged not only with creating exciting and challenging layouts, but also with providing a measure of authenticity that would stand the test of time. To achieve this timeless quality, the profession and its practitioners reached back to golf's homeland, transporting the classic holes of Scotland, England, and Ireland to other continents. In some cases, this meant attempting to duplicate holes, but more often it involved an interpretation of the model, borrowing and adapting the principles of the original, if not its exact lines. Before long, new classics arose, and they, in turn, were adapted to other sites. By the end of the 20th century, golfers worldwide enjoyed well over half a million golf holes. Whether classic or modern, each hole is an artistic composition and each can trace its heritage, if not its exact form, back to the very earliest holes in Scotland.

The profound influence of true classic golf holes must never be overlooked. Like those who came before them, ingenious and inventive contemporary course architects look to them for inspiration. They study their principles, adapt their styles, and, in some cases, even copy them. This reliance on the past begs the question: Has every generation of golf architects realized, consciously or subconsciously, that they could do no better than the hand of God that shaped those first golf holes on the coast of Scotland? The simple but profound answer is no, because golf architects are continually driven to keep the game fresh. Vigorous minds have introduced new concepts and dreamt up new holes, while always bowing reverently to the game's traditions. Truly, the adapting or even copying of golf holes, classic and otherwise, is part of the art form of course design. The stability of the game and the credibility of the profession of golf architecture depend on it, just as both also rely on new ideas and imaginative minds.

The impact of the "Classics" is obviously not absolute. Indeed, it is nebulous. Yet it is real and pervasive.

Course architects are trained to recognize classic holes and features when they encounter them, and many golfers can do likewise, although the adaptations, forms, and principles of classics are often vague. Recognition by the golfer of the principles of classic course design can add another dimension to his or her game. We hope that the text and abundant illustrations found in this book will help golfers identify and appreciate the classics of course architecture and their principles. Whether they are complete holes or individual features, their recognition by the golfer adds excitement and intrigue to the royal and ancient game of golf.

All golf holes have some magic. It arises from the game itself, the beauty of the composition and its surroundings, together with the greensward and accent provided by sand, water, and trees. They contribute to a savanna effect reminiscent of the landscape where our species started and spent most of its evolutionary history. In turn, this savanna effect is said to provide all humans with a sense of well-being when they encounter it. Indeed, a golf hole is a savanna on a miniature scale.

Combining more than a century in practice, the authors are aware that the present generation of course architects is exceptionally creative and vigorous. This bodes well for the future of the game and its playing fields. We are sure that the art of course design will remain original and stimulating, with classic holes and features continually appearing and reappearing to add magic to the compositions of future generations.

To further emphasize the pervasive influence of classic holes, a list of their adaptations *concludes this Epilogue*. Some adaptations are obvious; others are subtle; indeed, a few were created by architects who were not thinking of the originals; yet all are real. We realize that a golfer playing a course for the first time derives comfort and satisfaction when encountering a recognizable hole or feature.

We hope our list encourages clubs and courses to restore their classics. It is an ongoing project. The authors welcome additions, deletions, or corrections mailed, faxed, or e-mailed to Robert Muir Graves.

ALPS

Black Creek Country Club, Chattanooga, Tennessee; Hole #: 6; Par: 5; Length: 552; Designer: Brian Silva.

Deepdale Golf Club (NLE), Great Neck, New York; Hole #: 11; Par: 4; Length: 420; Designer: C. B. Macdonald and Seth Raynor.

Gibson Island Country Club (NLE), Gibson Island, Maryland; Hole #: 18; Par: 4; Length: 354; Designer: C. B. Macdonald and Seth Raynor.

Lido Golf Club (NLE), Lido Beach, New York; Hole #: 10; Par: 4; Length: 414; Designer: C. B. Macdonald and Seth Raynor.

Long Cove Golf Club, Hilton Head, South Carolina; Hole #: 5; Par: 4; Length: 317; Designer: Pete Dye.

Magnolia Creek Golf Links, South, League City, Texas; Hole #: 2; Par: 4; Length: 324; Designer: Ault, Clark & Associates.

National Golf Links of America, Southampton, New York; Hole #: 3; Par: 4; Length: 426; Designer: C. B. Macdonald.

Oakland Golf Club (NLE), Bayside, New York; Hole #: 5; Par: 4; Length: 360; Designer: Tom Bendelow, revised by Seth Raynor.

Old Marsh Golf Club, Palm Beach Gardens, Florida; Hole #: 5; Par: 4; Length: 320; Designer: Pete Dye.

Paraparaumu Beach Golf Club, New Zealand; Hole #: 2; Par: 3; Length: 195; Designer: James Watt.

Prestwick Golf Club, Ayrshire, Scotland; Hole #: 17; Par: 4; Length: 391; Designer: Tom Morris.

Royal Liverpool Golf Club, Hoylake, England; Hole #: 11; Par: 3; Length: 200; Designer: Robert Chambers, Jr., and George Morris.

St. Andrews (Old Course), Fife, Scotland; Hole #: 4; Par: 4; Length: 463; Designer: Nature.

Tamarack Country Club, Greenwich, Connecticut; Hole #: 6; Par: 4; Length: 387; Designer: Charles Banks.

The Links (NLE), Roslyn, New York; Hole #: 2; Par: 4; Length: 388; Designer: C. B. Macdonald and Seth Raynor.

BIARRITZ

Black Creek Country Club, Chattanooga, Tennessee; Hole #: 17; Par: 3; Length: 210; Designer: Brian Silva.

Deepdale Golf Club (NLE), Great Neck, New York; Hole #: 12; Par: 3; Length: 220; Designer: C. B. Macdonald and Seth Raynor.

Fishers Island Golf Club, Fishers Island, New York; Hole #: 5; Par: 3; Length: 207; Designer: Seth Raynor.

Gibson Island Country Club (NLE), Gibson Island, Maryland; Hole #: 10; Par: 3; Length: 220; Designer: C. B. Macdonald and Seth Raynor.

Golf de Biarritz (NLE), France; Hole #: 3; Par: 3; Length: 220; Designer: Tom and Willy Dunn.

Lido Golf Club (NLE), Lido Beach, New York; Hole #: 8; Par: 3; Length: 234; Designer: C. B. Macdonald and Seth Raynor.

Mid Ocean Club, Tuckers Town, Bermuda; Hole #: 13; Par: 3; Length: 225; Designer: C. B. Macdonald, Seth Raynor, Charles Banks, and Ralph Barton.

Oakland Golf Club (NLE), Bayside, New York; Hole #: 14; Par: 3; Length: 220; Designer: Tom Bendelow.

CLASSIC GOLF HOLE DESIGN

Shinnecock Hills Golf Club (NLE), Southampton, New York; Hole #: 3; Par: 3; Length: 120; Designer: C. B. Macdonald and Seth Raynor.

Shinnecock Hills Golf Club (White) (NLE), Southampton, New York; Hole #: 6; Par: 3; Length: 200; Designer: William Davis, William Dunn, and C. B. Macdonald.

Tamarack Country Club, Greenwich, Connecticut; Hole #: 12; Par: 3; Length: 200; Designer: Charles Banks.

The Links (NLE), Roslyn, New York; Hole #: 3; Par: 3; Length: 201; Designer: C. B. Macdonald and Seth Raynor.

Westhampton Country Club (Oneck) (NLE), Westhampton, New York; Hole #: 13; Par: 3; Length: 220; Designer: Charles Banks.

Whippoorwill Club, Armonk, New York; Hole #: 8; Par: 3; Length: 226; Designer: Charles Banks.

Yale University Golf Course, New Haven, Connecticut; Hole #: 9; Par: 3; Length: 225; Designer: C. B. Macdonald and Seth Raynor.

CAPE

Augusta National Golf Club, Augusta, Georgia; Hole #: 5; Par: 4; Length: 450; Designer: Alister Mackenzie with Robert Tyre Jones.

Augusta National Golf Club, Augusta, Georgia; Hole #: 13; Par: 5; Length: 485; Designer: Alister Mackenzie with Robert Tyre Jones.

Augusta National Golf Club, Augusta, Georgia; Hole #: 18; Par: 4; Length: 420; Designer: Alister Mackenzie with Robert Tyre Jones.

Avon Country Club, Avon, Connecticut; Hole #: 7; Par: 4; Length: 348; Designer: Geoffrey S. Cornish and William G. Robinson.

Bay Hill Club, Orlando, Florida; Hole #: 6; Par: 5; Length: 558; Designer: Dick Wilson and Joe Lee.

Bel Air Country Club, Los Angeles, California; Hole #: 17; Par: 4; Length: 468; Designer: George C. Thomas and William P. Bell with Jack Neville.

Black Creek Golf Club, Chattanooga, Tennessee; Hole #: 15; Par: 4; Length: 353; Designer: Brian Silva.

Casa de Campo Cajuiles, Dominican Republic; Hole #: 7; Par: 3; Length: 195; Designer: Pete Dye.

Casa de Campo Cajuiles, Dominican Republic; Hole #: 8; Par: 4; Length: 440; Designer: Pete Dye.

Casa de Campo Cajuiles, Dominican Republic; Hole #: 14; Par: 5; Length: 500; Designer: Pete Dye.

Casa de Campo Cajuiles, Dominican Republic; Hole #: 15; Par: 4; Length: 370; Designer: Pete Dye.

Cerromar Beach Golf Club, Dorado Beach, Puerto Rico; Hole #: 5; Par: 4; Length: 397; Designer: Robert Trent Jones, Sr.

Champions Golf Club, Houston, Texas; Hole #: 14; Par: 4; Length: 430; Designer: Ralph Plummer and George Fazio.

Cherry Hills Country Club, Denver, Colorado; Hole #: 18; Par: 4; Length: 465; Designer: William Flynn.

Country Club of North Carolina, Pinehurst, North Carolina; Hole #: 18; Par: 5; Length: 484; Designer: Willard Byrd, Robert Trent Jones, Sr., and Ellis Maples.

Creek Club, Locust Valley, New York; Hole #: 10; Par: 4; Length: 308; Designer: C. B. Macdonald and Seth Raynor.

Cypress Point Golf Club, Pebble Beach, California; Hole #: 16; Par: 3; Length: 231; Designer: Alister Mackenzie and Robert Hunter.

Cypress Point Golf Club, Pebble Beach, California; Hole #: 17; Par: 4; Length: 375; Designer: Alister Mackenzie and Robert Hunter.

Deepdale Golf Club (NLE), Great Neck, New York; Hole #: 17; Par: 4; Length: 340; Designer: C. B. Macdonald and Seth Raynor.

Dorado Beach Golf Club, Dorado Beach, Puerto Rico; Hole #: 13; Par: 5; Length: 540; Designer: Robert Trent Jones, Sr.

Doral Country Club, Miami, Florida; Hole #: 3; Par: 4; Length: 402; Designer: Dick Wilson.

Doral Country Club, Miami, Florida; Hole #: 9; Par: 3; Length: 181; Designer: Dick Wilson.

Doral Country Club, Miami, Florida; Hole #: 10; Par: 5; Length: 543; Designer: Dick Wilson.

Doral Country Club, Miami, Florida; Hole #: 16; Par: 4; Length: 379; Designer: Dick Wilson.

Doral Country Club, Miami, Florida; Hole #: 18; Par: 4; Length: 437; Designer: Dick Wilson.

Dunes Golf and Beach Club, Myrtle Beach, South Carolina; Hole #: 8; Par: 5; Length: 539; Designer: Robert Trent Jones, Sr.

Dunes Golf and Beach Club, Myrtle Beach, South Carolina; Hole #: 11; Par: 4; Length: 411; Designer: Robert Trent Jones, Sr.

Dunes Golf and Beach Club, Myrtle Beach, South Carolina; Hole #: 13; Par: 5; Length: 560; Designer: Robert Trent Jones, Sr.

Eastbourne, East Sussex, England; Hole #: 17; Par: 3; Length: 210; Designer: Horace Hutchinson.

Fishers Island Golf Club, Fishers Island, New York; Hole #: 14; Par: 4; Length: 425; Designer: Seth Raynor.

Fresh Meadow Country Club (NLE), Port Washington, New York; Hole #: 3; Par: 4; Length: 391; Designer: A. W. Tillinghast.

Ganton Golf Club, Ganton, England; Hole #: 18; Par: 4; Length: 379; Designer: Tom Dunn, Revised by Harry Vardon.

Griffith Park Municipal Golf Course #2, Los Angeles, California; Hole #: 6; Par: 5; Length: 476; Designer: George C. Thomas.

Harbour Town Golf Links, Hilton Head Island, South Carolina; Hole #: 18; Par: 4; Length: 458; Designer: Pete Dye.

Hirona Country Club, Japan; Hole #: 12; Par: 5; Length: 550; Designer: C. H. Alison.

Jupiter Hills Club, Jupiter, Florida; Hole #: 15; Par: 4; Length: 410; Designer: George Fazio.

Kennemer Golf and Country Club, Netherlands; Hole #: 10; Par: 4; Length: 370; Designer: H. S. Colt, C. H. Alison, and J.S.F. Morrison.

Kiawah Golf Course (Ocean), Kiawah Island, South Carolina; Hole #: 9; Par: 4; Length: 464; Designer: Pete Dye.

Killarney Golf and Fishing Club, County Kerry, Ireland; Hole #: 18; Par: 3; Length: 202; Designer: Sir Guy Campbell.

Knoll Country Club, Parsippany, New Jersey; Hole #: 5; Par: 5; Length: 525; Designer: Charles Banks.

La Cumbre Country Club, Santa Barbara, California; Hole #: 2; Par: 4; Length: 418; Designer: Tom Bendelow, revised by George Thomas.

La Cumbre Country Club, Santa Barbara, California; Hole #: 3; Par: 4; Length: 328; Designer: Tom Bendelow, revised by George Thomas.

Laguna Blanca, Santa Barbara, California; Hole #: 4; Par: 4; Length: 422; Designer: George C. Thomas and William P. Bell.

Lido Golf Club (NLE), Lido Beach, New York; Hole #: 5; Par: 4; Length: 378; Designer: C. B. Macdonald and Seth Raynor.

Los Angeles Country Club (North), Los Angeles, California; Hole #: 8; Par: 5; Length: 520; Designer: George C. Thomas.

Magnolia Creek Golf Links South, Ethel, Louisiana; Hole #: 3; Par: 4; Length: 325; Designer: Ault, Clark and Associates.

Mid Ocean Club, Tuckers Town, Bermuda; Hole #: 5; Par: 4; Length: 433; Designer: C. B. Macdonald, Seth Raynor, Charles Banks, and Ralph Barton.

National Golf Links of America, Southampton, New York; Hole #: 14; Par: 4; Length: 355; Designer: C. B. Macdonald.

Navatanee Country Club, Thailand; Hole #: 14; Par: 4; Length: 345; Designer: Robert Trent Jones, Jr.

Navatanee Country Club, Thailand; Hole #: 18; Par: 5; Length: 585; Designer: Robert Trent Jones, Jr.

Old Marsh Golf Club, Palm Beach Gardens, Florida; Hole #: 10; Par: 4; Length: 313; Designer: Pete Dye.

Old Marsh Golf Club, Palm Beach Gardens, Florida; Hole #: 11; Par: 4; Length: 386; Designer: Pete Dye.

Pawleys Plantation Golf and Country Club, Pawleys Island, South Carolina; Hole #: 3; Par: 3; Length: 194; Designer: Jack Nicklaus.

Pebble Beach Golf Links, Pebble Beach, California; Hole #: 8; Par: 4; Length: 425; Designer: Jack Neville, Douglas Grant, and Chandler Egan.

Pebble Beach Golf Links, Pebble Beach, California; Hole #: 18; Par: 5; Length: 540; Designer: Jack Neville, Douglas Grant, and Chandler Egan.

Pine Valley Golf Club, Pine Valley, New Jersey; Hole #: 6; Par: 4; Length: 391; Designer: George Crump and H. S. Colt.

Riviera Country Club, Pacific Palisades, California; Hole #: 13; Par: 4; Length: 421; Designer: George C. Thomas and William P. Bell.

Riviera Country Club, Pacific Palisades, California; Hole #: 7; Par: 4; Length: 408; Designer: George C. Thomas and William P. Bell.

Royal Cinque Ports Golf Club, Deal, England; Hole #: 6; Par: 4; Length: 315; Designer: Tom Dunn, revised by Sir Guy Campbell.

Royal Melbourne Golf Club West, Black Rock, Australia; Hole #: 6; Par: 4; Length: 428; Designer: Alister Mackenzie and Alex Russell.

Royal Melbourne Golf Club West, Black Rock, Australia; Hole #: 8; Par: 4; Length: 305; Designer: Alister Mackenzie and Alex Russell.

Royal Montreal Golf Club, Quebec, Canada; Hole #: 16; Par: 4; Length: 426; Designer: Dick Wilson.

Royal Montreal Golf Club, Quebec, Canada; Hole #: 18; Par: 4; Length: 437; Designer: Dick Wilson.

Royal North Devon Golf Club, Westward Ho!, England; Hole #: 10; Par: 4; Length: 372; Designer: Tom Morris, revised by Herbert Fowler.

Seminole Golf Club, Palm Beach, Florida; Hole #: 15; Par: 4; Length: 496; Designer: Donald Ross.

Seminole Golf Club, Palm Beach, Florida; Hole #: 16; Par: 4; Length: 393; Designer: Donald Ross.

Shinnecock Hills Golf Club (White) (NLE), Southhampton, New York; Hole #: 15; Par: 4; Length: 335; Designer: William Davis, William Dunn, and C. B. Macdonald.

Sotogrande Course, Cadiz, Spain; Hole #: 14; Par: 5; Length: 503; Designer: Robert Trent Jones, Sr.

Sotogrande Course, Cadiz, Spain; Hole #: 17; Par: 3; Length: 174; Designer: Robert Trent Jones, Sr.

The Classic at Madden's, Brainerd, Minnesota; Hole #: 12; Par: 4; Length: 361; Designer: Scott Hoffman.

Tournament Players Club at Sawgrass (Stadium), Ponte Vedra Beach, Florida; Hole #: 18; Par: 4; Length: 440; Designer: Pete Dye.

Tucker's Point Golf Club, Tuckers Town, Bermuda; Hole #: 2; Par: 4; Length: 391; Designer: Charles Banks, remodeled by Roger Rulewich.

Turnberry (Ailsa) Golf Club, Ayrshire, Scotland; Hole #: 9; Par: 4; Length: 475; Designer: Willie Fernie, revised by P. M. Ross.

Wakefield Golf Club, Raleigh, North Carolina; Hole #: 9; Par: 4; Length: 435; Designer: Stan Gentry, Hale Irwin Golf Design.

Wentworth by the Sea Golf Club, Portsmouth, New Hampshire; Hole #: 14; Par: 4; Length: 380; Designer: Geoffrey S. Cornish.

West Sussex Golf Club, Sussex, England; Hole #: 10; Par: 4; Length: 405; Designer: Sir Guy Campbell, C. K. Hutchinson, and S. V. Hotchkin.

Westhampton Country Club (Oneck) (NLE), Westhampton Beach, New York; Hole #: 10; Par: 4; Length: 420; Designer: Charles Banks.

CARDINAL

Avalon Golf Course, Burlington, Washington; Hole #: 8; Par: 5; Length: 550; Designer: Graves and Pascuzzo.

Avalon Golf Course, Burlington, Washington; Hole #: 9; Par: 5; Length: 509; Designer: Graves and Pascuzzo.

Baytowne Golf Club, Destin, Florida; Hole #: 15; Par: 5; Length: 586; Designer: Tom Jackson.

Bellerive, St. Louis, Missouri; Hole #: 8; Par: 5; Length: 581; Designer: Robert Trent Jones, Sr.

Black Butte Ranch Golf Course (Big Meadow), Black Butte Ranch, Oregon; Hole #: 10; Par: 5; Length: 526; Designer: Graves and Pascuzzo.

Black Butte Ranch Golf Course (Big Meadow), Black Butte Ranch, Oregon; Hole #: 16; Par: 5; Length: 508; Designer: Graves and Pascuzzo.

Black Butte Ranch Golf Course, Black Butte Ranch, Oregon; Hole #: 15; Par: 5; Length: 574; Designer: Graves and Pascuzzo.

Black Diamond Ranch (Quarry), Lecanto, Florida; Hole #: 5; Par: 5; Length: 577; Designer: Tom Fazio.

Black Diamond Ranch (Quarry), Lecanto, Florida; Hole #: 9; Par: 5; Length: 544; Designer: Tom Fazio.

Black Diamond Ranch (Quarry), Lecanto, Florida; Hole #: 18; Par: 5; Length: 502; Designer: Tom Fazio.

Black Diamond Ranch (Ranch), Lecanto, Florida; Hole #: 9; Par: 5; Length: 530; Designer: Tom Fazio.

Black Diamond Ranch (Ranch), Lecanto, Florida; Hole #: 16; Par: 5; Length: 594; Designer: Tom Fazio.

Black Lake Golf Club, Nipona, California; Hole #: 6; Par: 5; Length: 515; Designer: Joe Novak.

Cranberry Valley Golf Club, Harwich, Massachusetts; Hole #: 18; Par: 5; Length: 575; Designer: Cornish and Robinson.

Cross Water Golf Course, Sunriver, Oregon; Hole #: 6; Par: 5; Length: 635; Designer: Robert Cupp and John Fought.

Cyprian Keys Golf Club, Boylston, Massachussets; Hole #: 3; Par: 5; Length: 547; Designer: Mark Mungeam.

Daufuskie Island Club and Resort (Melrose), Hilton Head, South Carolina; Hole #: 3; Par: 5; Length: 554; Designer: Jack Nicklaus.

Daufuskie Island Club and Resort (Melrose), Hilton Head, South Carolina; Hole #: 9; Par: 5; Length: 584; Designer: Jack Nicklaus.

Daufuskie Island Club and Resort (Bloody Point), Hilton Head, South Carolina; Hole #: 18; Par: 5; Length: 530; Designer: Weiskopf and Morrish.

Dorado Beach Golf Club (East), Dorado Beach, Puerto Rico; Hole #: 4; Par: 5; Length: 525; Designer: Robert Trent Jones, Sr.

Dunes Golf and Beach Club, Myrtle Beach, South Carolina; Hole #: 13; Par: 5; Length: 590; Designer: Robert Trent Jones, Sr.

Eagle Crest Resort Course, Redmond, Oregon; Hole #: 2; Par: 5; Length: 481; Designer: Bunny Mason.

Furry Creek Golf and Country Club, Lion's Bay, British Columbia, Canada; Hole #: 3; Par: 5; Length: 485; Designer: Graves and Pascuzzo.

Grandover Golf Club (East), Greensboro, North Carolina; Hole #: 13; Par: 5; Length: 565; Designer: Graham and Panks International.

Grandover Golf Club (East), Greensboro, North Carolina; Hole #: 18; Par: 5; Length: 570; Designer: Graham and Panks International.

Grandover Golf Club (West), Greensboro, North Carolina; Hole #: 12; Par: 5; Length: 570; Designer: Graham and Panks International.

Indian Peaks Golf Course, Lafayette, Colorado; Hole #: 4; Par: 5; Length: 532; Designer: Dick Phelps and Hale Irwin.

Indian Peaks Golf Course, Lafayette, Colorado; Hole #: 11; Par: 5; Length: 574; Designer: Dick Phelps and Hale Irwin.

International Golf Club (Pines), Bolton, Massachusetts; Hole #: 11; Par: 5; Length: 590; Designer: Geoffrey Cornish.

Juniper Golf Club, Redmond, Oregon; Hole #: 16; Par: 5; Length: 488; Designer: Fred Sparks.

Kiawah Golf Course (Ocean), Kiawah Island, South Carolina; Hole #: 2; Par: 5; Length: 528; Designer: Pete Dye.

Kiawah Golf Course (Ocean), Kiawah Island, South Carolina; Hole #: 7; Par: 5; Length: 527; Designer: Pete Dye.

Kiawah Golf Course (Ocean), Kiawah Island, South Carolina; Hole #: 11; Par: 5; Length: 562; Designer: Pete Dye.

Kiawah Golf Course (Ocean), Kiawah Island, South Carolina; Hole #: 16; Par: 5; Length: 529; Designer: Pete Dye.

Meadow Lakes, Prineville, Oregon; Hole #: 1; Par: 5; Length: 549; Designer: Bill Robinson.

Osage National Golf Club, Lake of the Ozarks, Missouri; Hole #: 5; Par: 5; Length: 558; Designer: Ed Seay and Arnold Palmer.

Paako Ridge Golf Club, Sandia Park, New Mexico; Hole #: 15; Par: 5; Length: 562; Designer: Ken Dye.

Pelican's West, Bonita Springs, Florida; Hole #: 2; Par: 5; Length: 466; Designer: Tom Fazio.

Pelican's West, Bonita Springs, Florida; Hole #: 5; Par: 5; Length: 573; Designer: Tom Fazio.

Pelican's West, Bonita Springs, Florida; Hole #: 9; Par: 5; Length: 561; Designer: Tom Fazio.

Pelican's West, Bonita Springs, Florida; Hole #: 9; Par: 5; Length: 517; Designer: Tom Fazio.

Pelican's West, Bonita Springs, Florida; Hole #: 4; Par: 5; Length: 525; Designer: Tom Fazio.

Pelican's West, Bonita Springs, Florida; Hole #: 7; Par: 5; Length: 574; Designer: Tom Fazio.

Pinehurst Resort and Country Club (Centennial Course #8), Pinehurst, North Carolina; Hole #: 6; Par: 5; Length: 604; Designer: Tom Fazio.

Port Ludlow Golf Course, Port Ludlow, Washington; Hole #: 4; Par: 5; Length: 512; Designer: Graves and Pascuzzo.

Port Ludlow Golf Course, Port Ludlow, Washington; Hole #: 1; Par: 5; Length: 556; Designer: Graves and Pascuzzo.

Port Ludlow Golf Course, Port Ludlow, Washington; Hole #: 9; Par: 5; Length: 497; Designer: Graves and Pascuzzo.

Prestwick Golf Club, Ayrshire, Scotland; Hole #: 3; Par: 5; Length: 500; Designer: Tom Morris.

Raven Golf Club, Silverthorne, Colorado; Hole #: 11; Par: 5; Length: 599; Designer: Hurdzan/Fry, Tom Lehman.

St. Andrews Golf Club, Hastings-on-Hudson, New York; Hole #: 9; Par: 5; Length: 568; Designer: James Braid.

St. Charles Country Club, Winnipeg, Canada; Hole #: 5; Par: 5; Length: 543; Designer: Donald Ross.

Santa Clara Golf and Tennis Club, Santa Clara, California; Hole #: 14; Par: 5; Length: 517; Designer: Graves and Pascuzzo.

Sea Ranch Golf Links, Sea Ranch, California; Hole #: 1; Par: 5; Length: 525; Designer: Graves and Pascuzzo.

Sea Ranch Golf Links, Sea Ranch, California; Hole #: 6; Par: 5; Length: 545; Designer: Graves and Pascuzzo.

Semi-ah-moo Golf and Country Club, Everett, Washington; Hole #: 9; Par: 5; Length: 509; Designer: Ed Seay and Arnold Palmer.

Semi-ah-moo Golf and Country Club, Everett, Washington; Hole #: 13; Par: 5; Length: 574; Designer: Ed Seay and Arnold Palmer.

Shenendoah Golf Club, Verona, New York; Hole #: 18; Par: 5; Length: 553; Designer: Rick Smith.

Sunriver Golf Course (Meadows), Sunriver, Oregon; Hole #: 2; Par: 5; Length: 578; Designer: Fred Federspiel.

Sunriver Golf Course (Woodlands), Sunriver, Oregon; Hole #: 6; Par: 5; Length: 530; Designer: Robert Trent Jones, Jr.

Thunder Canyon Golf Course, Washoe Valley, Nevada; Hole #: 10; Par: 5; Length: 538; Designer: Graves and Pascuzzo.

Tiger's Eye Golf Links, Sunset Beach, North Carolina; Hole #: 15; Par: 5; Length: 531; Designer: Tim Cate.

Tournament Players Club, Scottsdale, Arizona; Hole #: 13; Par: 5; Length: 576; Designer: Tom Weiskopf and Jay Morrish.

DELL

Burnham and Berrow Golf Course, Somerset, England; Hole #: 3; Par: 4; Length: 384; Designer: Remodeled by C. H. Alison.

Cruden Bay Golf and Country Club, Aberdeen, Scotland; Hole #: 14; Par: 4; Length: 397; Designer: Herbert Fowler and Tom Simpson.

Dorset Field Club, Dorset, Vermont; Hole #: 12; Par: 3; Length: 198; Designer: Steve Durkee.

Hawk Creek Golf Course, Neskowin, Oregon; Hole #: 2; Par: 3; Length: 147; Designer: Harold Schlicting.

Kildonan Golf Course, Winnipeg, Canada; Hole #: 10; Par: 3; Length: 140; Designer: James McDairmid.

Lahinch Golf Club, County Clare, Ireland; Hole #: 6; Par: 3; Length: 156; Designer: Tom Morris.

Old Marsh Golf Club, Palm Beach Garden, Florida; Hole #: 5; Par: 4; Length: 360; Designer: Pete Dye.

Portmarnock Golf Club, Dublin, Ireland; Hole #: 7; Par: 3; Length: 184; Designer: George Ross and W. C. Pickemon.

Southport and Ainsdale Golf Club, Southport, England; Hole #: 1; Par: 3; Length: 200; Designer: J. A. Steer.

Tenby Golf Club, Dyfed, Wales; Hole #: 4; Par: 4; Length: 439; Designer: C. K. Cotton.

The Links, Seascale, England; Hole #: 6; Par: 4; Length: 473; Designer: Willie Campbell.

The Whins, Cruden Bay, Scotland; Hole #: 14; Par: 4; Length: 372; Designer: Herbert Fowler and Tom Simpson.

Wallasey Golf Club, Cheshire, England; Hole #: 17; Par: 4; Length: 464; Designer: Tom Morris.

Waterville Golf Links, County Kerry, Ireland; Hole #: 12; Par: 3; Length: 200; Designer: Eddie Hackett.

West Lancashire Golf Club, Lancashire, England; Hole #: 16; Par: 5; Length: 531; Designer: Remodeled by Fred W. Hawtree.

EDEN

Augusta National Golf Club, Augusta, Georgia; Hole #: 4; Par: 3; Length: 220; Designer: Alister Mackenzie with Robert Tyre Jones.

Augusta National Golf Club, Augusta, Georgia; Hole #: 5; Par: 4; Length: 450; Designer: Alister Mackenzie with Robert Tyre Jones.

Fishers Island Golf Club, Fishers Island, New York; Hole #: 11; Par: 3; Length: 136; Designer: Seth Raynor.

Garden City Golf Club, Garden City, New York; Hole #: 18; Par: 3; Length: 190; Designer: Devereux Emmet, revised by Walter Travis.

Lido Golf Club (NLE), Lido Beach, New York; Hole #: 3; Par: 3; Length: 175; Designer: C. B. Macdonald and Seth Raynor.

Maidstone Club (East) (NLE), East Hampton, New York; Hole #: 2; Par: 3; Length: 150; Designer: Willie Park, revised by Seth Raynor.

Makena Golf Club, Maui, Hawaii; Hole #: 15; Par: 3; Length: 188; Designer: Robert Trent Jones, Jr.

Meadow Club, Fairfax, California; Hole #: 5; Par: 3; Length: 146; Designer: Alister Mackenzie and Robert Hunter.

National Golf Links, Southampton, New York; Hole #: 13; Par: 3; Length: 170; Designer: C. B. Macdonald.

Rye Golf Club, Deal, England; Hole #: 14; Par: 3; Length: 184; Designer: H. S. Colt and Douglas Rolland.

St. Andrews (Old Course), Fife, Scotland; Hole #: 11; Par: 3; Length: 172; Designer: Nature.

Saucon Valley Country Club, Bethlehem, Pennsylvania; Hole #: 5; Par: 3; Length: 168; Designer: William and David Gordon.

Shinnecock Hills Golf Club (NLE), Southhampton, New York; Hole #: 11; Par: 3; Length: 160; Designer: C. B. Macdonald and Seth Raynor.

Sunningdale Golf Club (Old), Berkshire, England; Hole #: 13; Par: 3; Length: 185; Designer: Willie Park, Jr., and H. S. Colt.

Tamarack Country Club, Greenwich, Connecticut; Hole #: 3; Par: 3; Length: 160; Designer: Charles Banks.

The Links (NLE), Roslyn, New York; Hole #: 16; Par: 3; Length: 154; Designer: C. B. Macdonald and Seth Raynor.

Westhampton Country Club (Oneck) (NLE), Westhampton, New York; Hole #: 17; Par: 3; Length: 160; Designer: Charles Banks.

ISLAND GREEN

Aberdeen Golf and Country Club, Boynton Beach, Florida; Hole #: 8; Par: 5; Length: 581; Designer: Desmond Muirhead.

Brooklake Country Club, Florham Park, New Jersey; Hole #: 10; Par: 4; Length: 402; Designer: Cornish, Silva, and Mungeam.

Carnoustie Golf Links, Barry Angus, Scotland; Hole #: 18; Par: 4; Length: 440; Designer: Allan Robertson.

Cherry Hills Country Club, Denver, Colorado; Hole #: 17; Par: 5; Length: 529; Designer: William Flynn.

Cobbs Creek Golf Club, Philadelphia, Pennsylvania; Hole #: 12; Par: 3; Length: 110; Designer: Hugh Wilson.

Coeur d'Alene Resort Golf Club, Coeur d'Alene, Idaho; Hole #: 14; Par: 3; Length: 150; Designer: Scott Miller.

Fair Oaks Golf Park, Fairfax, Virginia; Hole #: 9; Par: 3; Length: 116; Designer: Ault Clark and Associates.

Golden Horseshoe Golf Club (Gold), Williamsburg, Virginia; Hole #: 16; Par: 3; Length: 169; Designer: Robert Trent Jones, Sr.

Golf Club at Desert Mountain (Cochise), Scottsdale, Arizona; Hole #: 7; Par: 3; Length: 215; Designer: Jack Nicklaus.

Golf Club at Desert Mountain (Cochise), Scottsdale, Arizona; Hole #: 15; Par: 5; Length: 548; Designer: Jack Nicklaus.

Homestead Golf and Country Club, Lynden, Washington; Hole #: 18; Par: 5; Length: 525; Designer: William Overdorf.

Key West Golf Club (NLE), Key West, Florida; Hole #: 10; Par: 4; Length: 340; Designer: William B. Langford and Theodore J. Moreau.

Meadowbrook Hunt Club, Westbury, New York; Hole #: 10; Par: 3; Length: 110; Designer: Devereux Emmet.

Mission Hills Country Club (Old), Rancho Mirage, California; Hole #: 18; Par: 5; Length: 646; Designer: Desmond Muirhead.

PGA West (Stadium), La Quinta, California; Hole #: 17; Par: 3; Length: 166; Designer: Pete Dye.

Pine Valley Golf Club, Pine Valley, New Jersey; Hole #: 14; Par: 3; Length: 168; Designer: George Crump and H. S. Colt.

Ponte Vedra Golf Club (Ocean Course), Ponte Vedra Beach, Florida; Hole #: 9; Par: 3; Length: 150; Designer: Herbert Strong.

Secession Golf Club, Beaufort, South Carolina; Hole #: 17; Par: 3; Length: 134; Designer: Bruce Devlin.

Shackamaxon Golf and Country Club, Scotch Plains, New Jersey; Hole #: 9; Par: 4; Length: 376; Designer: A. W. Tillinghast.

Stone Harbor Golf Club, Stone Harbor, New Jersey; Hole #: 7; Par: 3; Length: 120; Designer: Desmond Muirhead.

Teeth of the Dog Golf Course, La Romana, Dominican Republic;
Hole #: 13; Par: 3; Length: 179; Designer: Pete Dye.

The Pit Golf Links, Aberdeen, North Carolina; Hole #: 12; Par: 3;
Length: 167; Designer: Dan Maples.

Tournament Players Club at Sawgrass (Stadium), Ponte Vedra
Beach, Florida; Hole #: 17; Par: 3; Length: 132; Designer: Pete
Dye.

Tournament Players Club at The Woodlands, Houston, Texas;
Hole #: 13; Par: 5; Length: 533; Designer: Bernard von Hagge
and Bruce Devlin.

LONG

Aspen Lakes Golf Course, Sisters, Oregon; Hole #: 3; Par: 5; Length:
606; Designer: William Overdorf.

Baltimore Country Club, Timonium, Maryland; Hole #: 14; Par: 5;
Length: 600; Designer: A. W. Tillinghast.

Baltusrol Golf Club, Springfield, New Jersey; Hole #: 17; Par: 5;
Length: 623; Designer: A. W. Tillinghast.

Black Mountain Country Club, Black Mountain, North Carolina;
Hole #: 17; Par: 5; Length: 745; Designer: Ross Taylor.

Boca Raton Resort Golf Club (NLE), Boca Raton, Florida; Hole #:
17; Par: 5; Length: 570; Designer: William Flynn and Howard
Toomey.

Broken Top, Bend, Oregon; Hole #: 4; Par: 5; Length: 611; Designer:
Tom Weiskopf and Jay Morrish.

Canterwood Golf and Country Club, Gig Harbor, Washington;
Hole #: 14; Par: 5; Length: 602; Designer: Graves and
Pascuzzo.

Carnoustie Golf Links, Barry Angus, Scotland; Hole #: 6; Par: 5;
Length: 578; Designer: Allan Robertson.

Center Valley Club, Allentown, Pennsylvania; Hole #: 6; Par: 5;
Length: 514; Designer: Cornish, Silva, and Mungeam.

Cross Water Golf Course, Sunriver, Oregon; Hole #: 6; Par: 5;
Length: 635; Designer: Robert Cupp and John Fought.

Cross Water Golf Course, Sunriver, Oregon; Hole #: 12; Par: 5;
Length: 687; Designer: Robert Cupp and John Fought.

Emerald Bay Golf Club, Destin, Florida; Hole #: 13; Par: 5; Length: 611; Designer: Robert Cupp.

Estancia Club, Scottsdale, Arizona; Hole #: 14; Par: 5; Length: 608; Designer: Tom Fazio.

International Golf Club, Bolton, Massachusetts; Hole #: 5; Par: 5; Length: 695; Designer: Geoffrey Cornish.

Lido Golf Club (NLE), Lido Beach, New York; Hole #: 17; Par: 5; Length: 563; Designer: C. B. Macdonald and Seth Raynor.

Maderas Country Club, Poway, California; Hole #: 18; Par: 5; Length: 600; Designer: Graves and Pascuzzo.

Nairn Golf Course, Nairn, Scotland; Hole #: 7; Par: 5; Length: 551; Designer: Archie Simpson.

National Golf Links of America, Southampton, New York; Hole #: 9; Par: 5; Length: 545; Designer: C. B. Macdonald.

Pinehurst Resort and Country Club (Centennial Course #8), Pinehurst, North Carolina; Hole #: 6; Par: 5; Length: 604; Designer: Tom Fazio.

Prescott Lakes Golf Club, Prescott, Arkansas; Hole #: 6; Par: 5; Length: 838; Designer: Hale Irwin.

Raven Golf Club, Silverthorne, Colorado; Hole #: 16; Par: 5; Length: 601; Designer: Hurdzan/Fry, Tom Lehman.

St. Andrews (Old Course), Fife, Scotland; Hole #: 14; Par: 5; Length: 581; Designer: Nature.

Secession Golf Club, Beaufort, South Carolina; Hole #: 9; Par: 5; Length: 631; Designer: Bruce Devlin.

Sonoma Golf Club, Sonoma, California; Hole #: 8; Par: 5; Length: 610; Designer: Sam Whiting, revised by Graves and Pascuzzo.

Thunder Canyon Golf Course, Washoe Valley, Nevada; Hole #: 9; Par: 5; Length: 606; Designer: Graves and Pascuzzo.

Troon North Golf Club, Scottsdale, Arizona; Hole #: 14; Par: 5; Length: 604; Designer: Tom Weiskopf and Jay Morrish.

Twelve Bridges Golf Club, Lincoln, California; Hole #: 8; Par: 5; Length: 604; Designer: Dick Phelps.

Widgi Creek Golf Club, Bend, Oregon; Hole #: 3; Par: 5; Length: 653; Designer: Graves and Pascuzzo.

Widgi Creek Golf Club, Bend, Oregon; Hole #: 17; Par: 5; Length: 600; Designer: Graves and Pascuzzo.

CLASSIC GOLF HOLE DESIGN

PUNCH BOWL

Aberdovey Golf Club, Aberdovey, Wales; Hole #: 1; Par: 4; Length: 441; Designer: R. M. Ruck, remodeled by H. S. Colt.

Aberdovey Golf Club, Aberdovey, Wales; Hole #: 3; Par: 3; Length: 173; Designer: R. M. Ruck, remodeled by H. S. Colt.

Black Creek Country Club, Chattanooga, Tennessee; Hole #: 6; Par: 5; Length: 562; Designer: Brian Silva.

Cottonwoods/Grand Casino Golf Course, Tunica, Mississippi; Hole #: 14; Par: 4; Length: 480; Designer: Hale Irwin Golf Design.

Cruden Bay Golf and Country Club, Aberdeen, Scotland; Hole #: 3; Par: 4; Length: 286; Designer: Herbert Fowler and Tom Simpson.

Deepdale Golf Club (NLE), Great Neck, New York; Hole #: 10; Par: 4; Length: 390; Designer: C. B. Macdonald and Seth Raynor.

Fishers Island Golf Club, Fishers Island, New York; Hole #: 4; Par: 4; Length: 397; Designer: Seth Raynor.

Medinah Country Club, Medinah, Illinois; Hole #: 12; Par: 4; Length: 384; Designer: Tom Bendelow.

Ojai Valley Inn and Country Club, Ojai, California; Hole #: 16; Par: 4; Length: 392; Designer: George C. Thomas and William P. Bell.

Olympic Country Club (Ocean), San Francisco, California; Hole #: 12; Par: 4; Length: 380; Designer: Willy Watson.

Plum Lake Golf Club, Sayner, Wisconsin; Hole #: 4; Par: 3; Length: 145; Designer: C. B. Macdonald.

Royal Cinque Ports Golf Club, Deal, England; Hole #: 3; Par: 5; Length: 494; Designer: Tom Dunn.

Royal Liverpool Golf Club, Hoylake, England; Hole #: 9; Par: 4; Length: 393; Designer: Robert Chambers, Jr., and George Morris.

Royal Porthcawl, Mid-Glamorgan, Wales; Hole #: 9; Par: 4; Length: 384; Designer: Charles Gibson.

St. Enodoc Golf Club, Cornwall, England; Hole #: 6; Par: 4; Length: 378; Designer: James Braid.

St. Petersburg Country Club (NLE), St. Petersburg, Florida; Hole #: 12; Par: 3; Length: 110; Designer: A. W. Tillinghast.

Seascale Golf Club, Cumbria, England; Hole #: 15; Par: 4; Length: 312; Designer: Willie Campbell.

Shawnee Country Club, Milford, Delaware; Hole #: 12; Par: 4; Length: 337; Designer: Ed Ault and Al Jamison.

Sodus Point Heights Golf Club, Sodus Point, New York; Hole #: 15; Par: 4; Length: 456; Designer: Geoffrey Cornish and William G. Robinson.

Tamarack Country Club, Greenwich, Connecticut; Hole #: 11; Par: 4; Length: 432; Designer: Charles Banks.

Wyantenuck Country Club, Great Barrington, Massachusetts; Hole #: 15; Par: 4; Length: 339; Designer: Charles Banks.

REDAN

Augusta National Golf Club, Augusta, Georgia; Hole #: 15; Par: 5; Length: 520; Designer: Alister Mackenzie with Robert Tyre Jones.

Baytowne Golf Club, Destin, Florida; Hole #: 1; Par: 4; Length: 371; Designer: Tom Jackson.

Baytowne Golf Club, Destin, Florida; Hole #: 5; Par: 5; Length: 491; Designer: Tom Jackson.

Baytowne Golf Club, Destin, Florida; Hole #: 7; Par: 3; Length: 172; Designer: Tom Jackson.

Baytowne Golf Club, Destin, Florida; Hole #: 17; Par: 3; Length: 186; Designer: Tom Jackson.

Black Creek Country Club, Chattanooga, Tennessee; Hole #: 11; Par: 3; Length: 181; Designer: Brian Silva.

Black Diamond Ranch (Quarry), Lecanto, Florida; Hole #: 15; Par: 4; Length: 371; Designer: Tom Fazio.

Black Diamond Ranch (Ranch), Lecanto, Florida; Hole #: 4; Par: 4; Length: 435; Designer: Tom Fazio.

Black Diamond Ranch (Ranch), Lecanto, Florida; Hole #: 10; Par: 5; Length: 505; Designer: Tom Fazio.

Blind Brook Club, Purchase, New York; Hole #: 10; Par: 3; Length: 168; Designer: Seth Raynor with George Low.

Blue Heron Pines, Atlantic City, New Jersey; Hole #: 16; Par: 3; Length: 218; Designer: Stephen Kay.

Brickyard Crossing Golf Course, Indianapolis, Indiana; Hole #: 7; Par: 3; Length: 190; Designer: Pete Dye.

Camargo Golf Club, Cincinnati, Ohio; Hole #: 15; Par: 3; Length: 192; Designer: Seth Raynor.

Chicago Golf Club, Chicago, Illinois; Hole #: 7; Par: 3; Length: 200; Designer: C. B. Macdonald, revised by Seth Raynor.

Crooked Stick Golf Club, Carmel, Indiana; Hole #: 13; Par: 3; Length: 182; Designer: Pete Dye.

Cyprian Keys Golf Club, Boylston, Massachusetts; Hole #: 6; Par: 3; Length: 224; Designer: Cornish, Silva, and Mungeam.

Cyprian Keys Golf Club, Boylston, Massachusetts; Hole #: 16; Par: 3; Length: 190; Designer: Cornish, Silva, and Mungeam.

Dedham Country and Polo Club, Dedham, Massachusetts; Hole #: 15; Par: 4; Length: 372; Designer: Seth Raynor.

Deepdale Golf Club (NLE), Great Neck, New York; Hole #: 15; Par: 3; Length: 190; Designer: C. B. Macdonald and Seth Raynor.

Doral Golf Club (Blue Monster II), Rye Brook, New York; Hole #: 6; Par: 4; Length: 345; Designer: Robert Von Hagge.

Dunes Golf and Tennis Club, Sanibel Island, Florida; Hole #: 6; Par: 3; Length: 151; Designer: Mark McCumber.

Fishers Island Golf Club, Fishers Island, New York; Hole #: 2; Par: 3; Length: 172; Designer: Seth Raynor.

Garden City Golf Club, Garden City, New York; Hole #: 2; Par: 3; Length: 137; Designer: Walter Travis.

Gibson Island Country Club (NLE), Gibson Island, Maryland; Hole #: 3; Par: 3; Length: 181; Designer: C. B. Macdonald and Seth Raynor.

Grandover Golf Club, Greensboro, North Carolina; Hole #: 11; Par: 3; Length: 190; Designer: Graham and Panks International.

Kiawah (Ocean) Golf Club, Kiawah Island, South Carolina; Hole #: 14; Par: 3; Length: 194, Designer: Pete Dye.

La Cumbre Country Club, Santa Barbara, California; Hole #: 3; Par: 3; Length: 240; Designer: Tom Bendelow.

Legends Golf and Country Club, Fort Myers, Florida; Hole #: 2; Par: 5; Length: 531; Designer: Joe Lee.

Legends Golf and Country Club, Fort Myers, Florida; Hole #: 7; Par: 4; Length: 370; Designer: Joe Lee.

Mid Ocean Club, Tucker's Town, Bermuda; Hole #: 17; Par: 3; Length: 220; Designer: C. B. Macdonald and Seth Raynor.

Montclair Golf Club, Montclair, New Jersey; Hole #: 3; Par: 3; Length: 217; Designer: Charles Banks.

Muirfield Village Golf Club, Dublin, Ohio; Hole #: 16; Par: 3; Length: 215; Designer: Jack Nicklaus.

National Golf Links of America, Southampton, New York; Hole #: 4; Par: 3; Length: 185; Designer: C. B. Macdonald.

North Berwick Golf Club, North Berwick, Scotland; Hole #: 15; Par: 3; Length: 192; Designer: David Strath.

Oakland Golf Club (NLE), Bayside, New York; Hole #: 13; Par: 3; Length: 190; Designer: Tom Bendelow.

Ocean Links (NLE), Newport, Rhode Island; Hole #: 3; Par: 3; Length: 191; Designer: Seth Raynor.

Osage National Golf Club, Lake of the Ozarks, Missouri; Hole #: 5; Par: 5; Length: 525; Designer: Ed Seay and Arnold Palmer.

Paako Ridge Golf Club, Sandia Park, New Mexico; Hole #: 6; Par: 4; Length: 327; Designer: Keith Foster.

Pebble Beach Golf Links, Pebble Beach, California; Hole #: 17; Par: 3; Length: 218; Designer: Jack Neville, Douglas Grant, and Chandler Egan.

Pine Valley Golf Club, Pine Valley, New Jersey; Hole #: 3; Par: 3; Length: 180; Designer: George C. Crump and H. S. Colt.

Pine Valley Golf Club, Pine Valley, New Jersey; Hole #: 13; Par: 4; Length: 445; Designer: George Crump and H. S. Colt.

Piping Rock Club, Locust Valley, New York; Hole #: 3; Par: 3; Length: 175; Designer: C. B. Macdonald and Seth Raynor.

Riviera Country Club, Pacific Palisades, California; Hole #: 4; Par: 3; Length: 235; Designer: George C. Thomas and William P. Bell.

Royal Sydney Golf Club, Sydney, Australia; Hole #: 14; Par: 3; Length: 190; Designer: S. R. Robbie.

St. Andrews Golf Club, Hastings-on-Hudson, New York; Hole #: 10; Par: 3; Length: 219, Designer: James Braid.

Shenendoah Golf Club, Verona, New York; Hole #: 6; Par: 3; Length: 186; Designer: Rick Smith.

Shenendoah Golf Club, Verona, New York; Hole #: 7; Par: 4; Length: 398; Designer: Rick Smith.

Shenendoah Golf Club, Verona, New York; Hole #: 9; Par: 3; Length: 182; Designer: Rick Smith.

Shinnecock Hills Golf Club (White) (NLE), Southampton, New York; Hole #: 14; Par: 3; Length: 160; Designer: William Davis, William Dunn, and C. B. Macdonald.

Shinnecock Hills Golf Club (White) (NLE), Southampton, New York; Hole #: 7; Par: 3; Length: 184; Designer: William Flynn and Howard Toomey.

Somerset Country Club, St. Paul, Minnesota; Hole #: 4; Par: 3; Length: 185; Designer: Seth Raynor.

Somerset Hills Country Club (NLE), Bernardsville, New Jersey; Hole #: 2 and/or 11; Par: 3; Length: 180; Designer: A. W. Tillinghast.

Stratton Mountain Country Club (Forest Course), Stratton, Vermont; Hole #: 7; Par: 3; Length: 174; Designer: Cornish and Silva.

Swinley Forest Golf Club, England; Hole #: 4; Par: 3; Length: 165; Designer: H. S. Colt.

Tamarack Country Club, Greenwich, Connecticut; Hole #: 7; Par: 3; Length: 183; Designer: Charles Banks.

The Links (NLE), Roslyn, New York; Hole #: 13; Par: 3; Length: 221; Designer: C. B. Macdonald and Seth Raynor.

The Pit Golf Links, Aberdeen, North Carolina; Hole #: 6; Par: 4; Length: 371; Designer: Dan Maples.

The Pit Golf Links, Aberdeen, North Carolina; Hole #: 1; Par: 4; Length: 411; Designer: Dan Maples.

Thunder Canyon Golf Course, Washoe Valley, Nevada; Hole #: 1; Par: 5; Length: 577; Designer: Graves and Pascuzzo.

Tiger's Eye Golf Links, Sunset Beach, North Carolina; Hole #: 14; Par: 4; Length: 381; Designer: Tim Cate.

Tiger's Eye Golf Links, Sunset Beach, North Carolina; Hole #: 15; Par: 5; Length: 531; Designer: Tim Cate.

Tournament Players Club at Sawgrass, Ponte Vedra Beach, Florida; Hole #: 3; Par: 3; Length: 162; Designer: Pete Dye.

Tower Ridge Country Club, Simsbury, Connecticut; Hole #: 5; Par: 4; Length: 392; Designer: Geoffrey Cornish.

Tower Ridge Country Club, Simsbury, Connecticut; Hole #: 9; Par: 4; Length: 354; Designer: Geoffrey Cornish.

Westhampton Country Club (Oneck) (NLE), Westhampton, New York; Hole #: 7; Par: 3; Length: 187; Designer: Seth Raynor.

Westhampton Country Club (Oneck) (NLE), Westhampton, New York; Hole #: 9; Par: 3; Length: 190; Designer: Charles Banks.

Whippoorwill Club, Armonk, New York; Hole #: 17; Par: 3; Length: 158; Designer: Charles Banks.

Widgi Creek Golf Club, Bend, Oregon; Hole #: 11; Par: 4; Length: 325; Designer: Robert Muir Graves.

Yale University Golf Course, New Haven, Connecticut; Hole #: 13; Par: 3; Length: 212; Designer: C. B. Macdonald, Seth Raynor, Charles Banks, and Ralph Barton.

Yeamans Hall Club, Hanahan, South Carolina; Hole #: 5; Par: 4; Length: 418; Designer: Seth Raynor.

Yeamans Hall Club, Hanrahan, South Carolina; Hole #: 6; Par: 3; Length: 175; Designer: Seth Raynor.

REVERSE REDAN

Augusta National Golf Club, Augusta, Georgia; Hole #: 6; Par: 3; Length: 190; Designer: Alister Mackenzie with Robert Tyre Jones.

Bay Point Yacht and Country Club (Lagoon Legend), Panama City, Florida; Hole #: 18; Par: 4; Length: 392; Designer: Von Hagge and Devlin.

Bayside Golf Links (NLE), Bayside, New York; Hole #: 11; Par: 3; Length: 180; Designer: Alister Mackenzie.

Baytowne Golf Club, Destin, Florida; Hole #: 2; Par: 4; Length: 414; Designer: Tom Jackson.

Bellerive Country Club, St. Louis, Missouri; Hole #: 13; Par: 3; Length:179; Designer: Robert Trent Jones, Senior.

Black Creek Country Club, Chattanooga, Tennessee; Hole #: 7; Par: 3; Length: 247; Designer: Brian Silva.

Black Diamond Ranch (Highlands), Lecanto, Florida; Hole #: 4; Par: 5; Length: 537; Designer: Tom Fazio.

Black Diamond Ranch (Ranch), Lecanto, Florida; Hole #: 13; Par: 4; Length: 307; Designer: Tom Fazio.

Castlewood Golf Club (Hill), Pleasanton, California; Hole #: 12; Par: 3; Length: 136; Designer: William P. Bell.

Cyprian Keys Golf Club, Boylston, Massachusetts; Hole #: 9; Par: 3; Length: 190; Designer: Cornish, Silva, and Mungeam.

Daufuskie Island Club and Resort (Bloody Point), Hilton Head, South Carolina; Hole #: 18; Par: 5; Length: 530; Designer: Weiskopf and Morrish.

Daufuskie Island Club and Resort (Melrose), Hilton Head, South Carolina; Hole #: 4; Par: 4; Length: 411; Designer: Jack Nicklaus.

Daufuskie Island Club and Resort (Melrose), Hilton Head, South Carolina; Hole #: 10; Par: 4; Length: 419; Designer: Jack Nicklaus.

Daufuskie Island Club and Resort (Melrose), Hilton Head, South Carolina; Hole #: 12; Par: 5; Length: 525; Designer: Jack Nicklaus.

Dedham Country and Polo Club, Dedham, Massachusetts; Hole #: 17; Par: 3; Length: 177; Designer: Seth Raynor.

Dunes Golf and Tennis Club, Sanibel Island, Florida; Hole #: 9; Par: 3; Length: 131; Designer: Mark McCumber.

Dunes Golf and Tennis Club, Sanibel Island, Florida; Hole #: 13; Par: 4; Length: 381; Designer: Mark McCumber.

Edina Country Club, Edina, Minnesota; Hole #: 2; Par: 3; Length: 160; Designer: Tom Bendelow, revised in-house.

Emerald Bay Golf Club, Destin, Florida; Hole #: 6; Par: 4; Length: 425; Designer: Robert Cupp.

Emerald Bay Golf Club, Destin, Florida; Hole #: 18; Par: 5; Length: 512; Designer: Robert Cupp.

Estancia Club, Scottsdale, Arizona; Hole #: 17; Par: 4; Length: 408; Designer: Tom Fazio.

Fox Chapel Country Club, Pittsburgh, Pennsylvania; Hole #: 6; Par: 3; Length: 195; Designer: Seth Raynor and Charles Banks.

Gibson Island Country Club (NLE), Gibson Island, Maryland; Hole #: 3; Par: 3; Length: 181; Designer: C. B. Macdonald and Seth Raynor.

Grandover Golf Club (East), Greensboro, North Carolina; Hole #: 12; Par: 3; Length: 125; Designer: Graham and Panks International.

Grandover Golf Club (West), Greensboro, North Carolina; Hole #: 9; Par: 4; Length: 430; Designer: Graham and Panks International.

Grandover Golf Club (West), Greensboro, North Carolina; Hole #: 16; Par: 5; Length: 550; Designer: Graham and Panks International.

Kayak Point Golf Club, Stanwood, Washington; Hole #: 3; Par: 3; Length: 181; Designer: Peter Thomson, Michael Wolveridge, and Ronald Fream.

Los Angeles Country Club (North), Los Angeles, California; Hole #: 11; Par: 3; Length: 220; Designer: George C. Thomas and William P. Bell.

Magnolia Creek Golf Links, League City, Texas; Hole #: 8E; Par: 3; Length: 201; Designer: Ault, Clark & Associates.

Muirfield Village Golf Club, Dublin, Ohio; Hole #: 2; Par: 4; Length: 455; Designer: Jack Nicklaus and Desmond Muirhead.

Osage National Golf Club (Mountain Nine), Lake of the Ozarks, Missouri; Hole #: 2; Par: 3; Length: 175; Designer: Ed Seay and Arnold Palmer.

Osage National Golf Club (Mountain Nine), Lake of the Ozarks, Missouri; Hole #: 4; Par: 3; Length: 166; Designer: Ed Seay and Arnold Palmer.

Osage National Golf Club (River Nine), Lake of the Ozarks, Missouri; Hole #: 4; Par: 3; Length: 216; Designer: Ed Seay and Arnold Palmer.

St. Andrews Golf Club (Fox Hill), Hastings-on-Hudson, New York; Hole #: 13; Par: 3; Length: 209; Designer: Wm. H. Tucker, revised by Morris Poucher, J. Braid, J. R. Stutt, Jack Nicklaus.

Secession Golf Club, Beaufort, South Carolina; Hole #: 16; Par: 5; Length: 493; Designer: Bruce Devlin.

Stratton Mountain Country Club (Mountain), Stratton, Vermont; Hole #: 2; Par: 3; Length: 205; Designer: Cornish and Robinson.

The Dunes Golf and Tennis Club, Sanibel Island, Florida; Hole #: 4; Par: 4; Length: 297; Designer: Mark McCumber.

The Links (NLE), Roslyn, New York; Hole #: 13; Par: 3; Length: 221; Designer: C. B. Macdonald and Seth Raynor.

The Pit Golf Links, Aberdeen, North Carolina; Hole #: 2; Par: 5; Length: 579; Designer: Dan Maples.

The Pit Golf Links, Aberdeen, North Carolina; Hole #: 10; Par: 4;
Length: 390; Designer: Dan Maples.

The Pit Golf Links, Aberdeen, North Carolina; Hole #: 11; Par: 4;
Length: 390; Designer: Dan Maples.

The Pit Golf Links, Aberdeen, North Carolina; Hole #: 14; Par: 3;
Length: 144; Designer: Dan Maples.

Thunder Canyon Golf Course, Washoe Valley, Nevada; Hole #: 2;
Par: 3; Length: 159; Designer: Graves and Pascuzzo.

Thunder Canyon Golf Course, Washoe Valley, Nevada; Hole #: 8;
Par: 3; Length: 177; Designer: Graves and Pascuzzo.

Tiger's Eye Golf Links, Sunset Beach, North Carolina; Hole #: 1;
Par: 4; Length: 377; Designer: Tim Cate.

Tiger's Eye Golf Links, Sunset Beach, North Carolina; Hole #: 7;
Par: 5; Length: 562; Designer: Tim Cate.

Tiger's Eye Golf Links, Sunset Beach, North Carolina; Hole #: 9;
Par: 4; Length: 415; Designer: Tim Cate.

Tiger's Eye Golf Links, Sunset Beach, North Carolina; Hole #: 12;
Par: 4; Length: 452; Designer: Tim Cate.

Tiger's Eye Golf Links, Sunset Beach, North Carolina; Hole #: 18;
Par: 5; Length: 592; Designer: Tim Cate.

Winged Foot Golf Club (East), Mamaroneck, New York; Hole #: 13;
Par: 3; Length: 146; Designer: A. W. Tillinghast.

ROAD

Augusta National Golf Club, Augusta, Georgia; Hole #: 14; Par: 4;
Length: 420; Designer: Alister Mackenzie with Robert Tyre
Jones.

Blind Brook Club, Purchase, New York; Hole #: 11; Par: 4; Length:
330; Designer: Seth Raynor with George Low.

Deepdale Golf Club (NLE), Great Neck, New York; Hole #: 14; Par:
4; Length: 440; Designer: C. B. Macdonald and Seth Raynor.

Golden Ocala Golf and Country Club, Ocala, Florida; Hole #: 13;
Par: 4; Length: 460; Designer: Ron Garl.

Grand Cypress Resort, Orlando, Florida; Hole #: 17; Par: 5; Length:
485; Designer: Jack Nicklaus.

Lido Golf Club (NLE), Lido Beach, New York; Hole #: 6; Par: 5;
Length: 493; Designer: C. B. Macdonald and Seth Raynor.

National Golf Links of America, Southampton, New York; Hole #: 7; Par: 5; Length: 480; Designer: C. B. Macdonald.

Ocean Links (NLE), Newport, Rhode Island; Hole #: 8; Par: 5; Length: 510; Designer: Seth Raynor.

Prince's Golf Club, Sandwich, England; Hole #: 3(Shore); Par: 3; Length: 176; Designer: C. Hutchings and P. M. Lucas.

Royal Liverpool Golf Club, Hoylake, England; Hole #: 2; Par: 4; Length: 369; Designer: Robert Chambers, Jr., and George Morris.

Royal Liverpool Golf Club, Hoylake, England; Hole #: 16; Par: 5; Length: 533; Designer: Robert Chambers, Jr., and George Morris.

Royal Liverpool Golf Club, Hoylake, England; Hole #: 17; Par: 4; Length: 429; Designer: Robert Chambers, Jr., and George Morris.

Royal Troon Golf Club (Portland Course), Ayrshire, Scotland; Hole #: 15; Par: 5; Length: 494; Designer: Charles Hunter, revised by Alister Mackenzie.

St. Andrews (Old Course), Fife, Scotland; Hole #: 17; Par: 4; Length: 461; Designer: Nature.

Shinnecock Hills Golf Club (NLE), Southampton, New York; Hole #: 17; Par: 4; Length: 383; Designer: C. B. Macdonald and Seth Raynor.

Somerset Country Club, St. Paul, Minnesota; Hole #: 9; Par: 5; Length: 539; Designer: Seth Raynor.

The Links (NLE), Roslyn, New York; Hole #: 18; Par: 4; Length: 357; Designer: C. B. Macdonald and Seth Raynor.

Westhampton Country Club (Oneck) (NLE), Westhampton, New York; Hole #: 18; Par: 4; Length: 430; Designer: Charles Banks.

SHORT

Aspen Lakes Golf Course, Sisters, Oregon; Hole #: 12; Par: 3; Length: 116; Designer: William Overdorf.

Bayside Golf Links (NLE), Bayside, New York; Hole #: 14; Par: 3; Length: 150; Designer: Alister Mackenzie.

Black Creek Country Club, Chattanooga, Tennessee; Hole #: 3; Par: 3; Length: 168; Designer: Brian Silva.

Blind Brook Club, Purchase, New York; Hole #: 15; Par: 3; Length: 152; Designer: Seth Raynor with George Low.

Blue Rocky Springs (East), Vallejo, California; Hole #: 2; Par: 3; Length: 136; Designer: Jack Fleming.

Boca Raton Resort Golf Club (NLE), Boca Raton, Florida; Hole #: 14; Par: 3; Length: 135; Designer: William Flynn.

Carnoustie Golf Links, Barry Angus, Scotland; Hole #: 8; Par: 3; Length: 183; Designer: Allan Robertson.

Carnoustie Golf Links (Championship), Barry Angus, Scotland; Hole #: 3; Par: 3; Length: 130; Designer: Allan Robertson.

Chicago Golf Club, Wheaton, Illinois; Hole #: 10; Par: 3; Length: 139; Designer: C. B. Macdonald and Charles Banks.

Crooked River Ranch and Golf Course, Crooked River Ranch, Oregon; Hole #: 16; Par: 3; Length: 125; Designer: Bunny Mason.

Cypress Point Golf Club, Pebble Beach, California; Hole #: 15; Par: 3; Length: 140; Designer: Alister Mackenzie.

Daufuskie Island Club and Resort (Melrose), Hilton Head, South Carolina; Hole #: 8; Par: 3; Length: 136; Designer: Jack Nicklaus.

Deepdale Golf Club (NLE), Great Neck, New York; Hole #: 8; Par: 3; Length: 130; Designer: C. B. Macdonald and Seth Raynor.

Dunes Golf and Tennis Club, Sanibel Island, Florida; Hole #: 2; Par: 3; Length: 96; Designer: Mark McCumber.

Dunes Golf and Tennis Club, Sanibel Island, Florida; Hole #: 9; Par: 3; Length: 131; Designer: Mark McCumber.

El Caballero Country Club, Tarzana, California; Hole #: 17; Par: 3; Length: 115; Designer: W. P. Bell and George Thomas.

Estancia Club, Scottsdale, Arizona; Hole #: 11; Par: 3; Length: 137; Designer: Tom Fazio.

Furry Creek Golf and Country Club, Lion's Bay, British Columbia, Canada; Hole #: 6; Par: 3; Length: 107; Designer: Graves and Pascuzzo.

Gibson Island Country Club (NLE), Gibson Island, Maryland; Hole #: 8; Par: 3; Length: 157; Designer: C. B. Macdonald and Seth Raynor.

Gleneagles (Kings) Golf Course, Perthshire, Scotland; Hole #: 16; Par: 3; Length: 135; Designer: J. Braid with C. K. Hutchinson.

Grandover Golf Club (East), Greensboro, North Carolina; Hole #: 12; Par: 3; Length: 125; Designer: Graham and Panks International.

Grandover Golf Club (West), Greensboro, North Carolina; Hole #: 15; Par: 3; Length: 140; Designer: Graham and Panks International.

Highland Municipal Golf Course, Pocatello, Idaho; Hole #: 13; Par: 3; Length: 140; Designer: Percey A. Hill.

International (World Tour), Orlando, Florida; Hole #: 4; Par: 3; Length: 120; Designer: Joe Lee.

Inverness Club, Toledo, Ohio; Hole #: 3; Par: 3; Length: 135; Designer: Donald Ross.

Juniper Golf Club, Redmond, Oregon; Hole #: 17; Par: 3; Length: 127; Designer: Fred Sparks.

Las Sendas, Mesa, Arizona; Hole #: 2; Par: 3; Length: 135; Designer: Robert Trent Jones, Jr.

Las Sendas, Mesa, Arizona; Hole #: 16; Par: 3; Length: 120; Designer: Robert Trent Jones, Jr.

Lido Golf Club (NLE), Lido Beach, New York; Hole #: 14; Par: 3; Length: 148; Designer: C. B. Macdonald and Seth Raynor.

Longmeadow Country Club, Longmeadow, Massachusetts; Hole #: 16; Par: 3; Length: 120; Designer: Donald Ross.

Meadowbrook Hunt Club, Westbury, New York; Hole #: 10; Par: 3; Length: 140; Designer: Devereux Emmet.

Midland Pacific Country Club, Honolulu, Hawaii; Hole #: 6; Par: 3; Length: 130; Designer: Seth Raynor and Charles Banks.

National Golf Links, Southampton. New York; Hole #: 6; Par: 3; Length: 135; Designer: C. B. Macdonald.

Oakland Golf Club (NLE), Bayside, New York; Hole #: 2; Par: 3; Length: 150; Designer: Tom Bendelow, revised by Seth Raynor.

Osage National Golf Club, Lake of the Ozarks, Missouri; Hole #: 4; Par: 3; Length: 158; Designer: Ed Seay and Arnold Palmer.

Pine Needles Golf Course, Southern Pines, North Carolina; Hole #: 3; Par: 3; Length: 134; Designer: Donald Ross.

Pine Valley Golf Club, Pine Valley, New Jersey; Hole #: 10; Par: 3; Length: 143; Designer: George Crump and H. S. Colt.

Raven Golf Club, Phoenix, Arizona; Hole #: 2; Par: 3; Length: 137; Designer: Graham and Panks International.

Riviera Country Club, Pacific Palisades, California; Hole #: 6; Par: 3; Length: 130; Designer: George C. Thomas.

Riviera Country Club, Pacific Palisades, California; Hole #: 16; Par: 3; Length: 125; Designer: George C. Thomas.

Royal Dornoch Golf Club (Struie), Dornoch, Scotland; Hole #: 2; Par: 3; Length: 125; Designer: Old Tom Morris.

Royal Dornoch Golf Club (Struie), Dornoch, Scotland; Hole #: 18; Par: 3; Length: 129; Designer: Old Tom Morris.

St. Andrews (Old Course), Fife, Scotland; Hole #: 8; Par: 3; Length: 178; Designer: Nature.

Santa Clara Golf and Tennis Club, Santa Clara, California; Hole #: 8; Par: 3; Length: 140; Designer: Graves and Pascuzzo.

Secession Golf Club, Beaufort, South Carolina; Hole #: 17; Par: 3; Length: 134; Designer: Bruce Devlin and P. B. Dye.

Seminole Golf Club, Palm Beach, Florida; Hole #: 13; Par: 3; Length: 142; Designer: Donald Ross.

Sharp Creek Golf Club, Pacifica, California; Hole #: 4; Par: 3; Length: 150; Designer: Alister Mackenzie.

Shinnecock Hills Golf Club (NLE), Southampton, New York; Hole #: 3; Par: 3; Length: 120; Designer: C. B. Macdonald and Seth Raynor.

Sitwell Park Golf Club, Yorkshire, England; Hole #: 18; Par: 3; Length: 135; Designer: Alister Mackenzie.

Sonoma Golf Club, Sonoma, California; Hole #: 17; Par: 3; Length: 140; Designer: Sam Whiting, revised by Graves and Pascuzzo.

Tailer's Ocean Links (NLE), Newport, Rhode Island; Hole #: 6; Par: 3; Length: 140; Designer: Seth Raynor.

Tamarack Country Club, Greenwich, Connecticut; Hole #: 15; Par: 3; Length: 135; Designer: Charles Banks.

The Links (NLE), Roslyn, New York; Hole #: 8; Par: 3; Length: 150; Designer: C. B. Macdonald and Seth Raynor.

Timber Point Golf Club, Great River, New York; Hole #: 12; Par: 3; Length: 140; Designer: Charles Alison.

Wannamoisett Country Club, Rumford, Rhode Island; Hole #: 3; Par: 3; Length: 131; Designer: Donald Ross.

Westhampton Country Club (Oneck) (NLE), Westhampton, New York; Hole #: 3; Par: 3; Length: 150; Designer: Charles Banks.

Whippoorwill Club, Armonk, New York; Hole #: 4; Par: 3; Length: 159; Designer: Charles Banks.

Widgi Creek Golf Club, Bend, Oregon; Hole #: 5; Par: 3; Length: 138; Designer: Graves and Pascuzzo.

Winged Foot Golf Club, Mamaroneck, New York; Hole #: 10; Par: 3; Length: 190; Designer: A. W. Tillinghast.

Yale University Golf Course, New Haven, Connecticut; Hole #: 5; Par: 3; Length: 135; Designer: C. B. Macdonald and Seth Raynor.

BIBLIOGRAPHY

Bahto, George, with Dane Bath. *The Legend of the Knoll*. New Jersey: The Knoll Golf Utility, 1993.

Barclay, James A. *Golf in Canada: A History*. Toronto, Canada: McLelland and Stewart, 1992.

Barclay, James A. *The Toronto Terror: The Life and Works of Stanley Thompson, Golf Course Architect*. Chelsea, MI: Sleeping Bear Press, 2000.

Bauer, Aleck. *Hazards: Those Essential Elements in a Golf Course Without Which the Game Would be Tame and Uninteresting*. Chicago: Tony Rubovitis, 1913; Droitwich, Worcestershire, England: Grant Books, 1993.

Browning, Robert. *A History of Golf*. New York: E. P. Dutton, 1955; Stamford, CT: Classics of Golf, 1985.

Clark, Robert. *Golf, a Royal and Ancient Game*. London: Macmillan, 1899.

Clarke, Amber. "Wooden Sticks Golf Club." *GreenMaster,* August/September, 2000.

Colt, H. S., and C. H. Alison. *Some Essays on Golf Course Architecture*. New York: Charles Scribners Sons, 1920; Droitwich, Worcestershire, England: Grant Books, 1993.

Colville, George M. *Five Open Champions and the Musselburgh Golf Story*. Musselburgh, Scotland: Colville Books, 1980.

Cornish, Geoffrey S., and Ronald E. Whitten. Foreword by Robert Trent Jones. *The Golf Course*. New York: Rutledge Press, 1987; Stamford, CT: Classics of Golf, 1989.

Cornish, Geoffrey S., and Ronald E. Whitten. *The Architects of Golf*. New York: HarperCollins, 1993.

Darwin, Bernard. *The Golf Courses of the British Isles*. London: Duckworth and Co.; Pownal, VT: Storey Communications, Alisa, 1988.

Darwin, Bernard, Sir Guy Campbell, et al. *A History of Golf in Britain*. London: Cassel and Co., 1952.

Davis, William H. *The World's Best Golf.* Trumbull, CT: Golf Digest, 1991.

Doak, Thomas. *The Anatomy of a Golf Course.* New York: Lyons and Burford, 1992.

Doak, Thomas. *The Confidential Guide to Golf Courses.* Chelsea, MI: Sleeping Bear Press, 1996.

Doak, Thomas, James S. Scott, and Raymond M. Haddock. *Dr. Alister Mackenzie.* Chelsea, MI: Sleeping Bear Press, 2001.

Dye, Pete, with Mark Shaw. *Bury Me in a Pot Bunker.* New York: Addison-Wesley, 1995.

Fazio, Tom, with Cal Brown. *Golf Course Designs.* New York: Harry N. Abrams, 2000.

Finegan, James W. *Pine Valley Golf Club, A Unique Haven of the Game.* Pine Valley, NJ: Pine Valley Golf Club, 2000.

Finegan, James W. *The House of Max.* USGA. U.S. Open Championship, 2001.

Goldstein, Harriet, and Vetta Goldstein. *Art in Everyday Life,* 4th ed. New York: Macmillan, 1967.

Gordon, John. *The Great Golf Courses of America.* With photography by Michael French. Willowdale, Ontario, Canada: Firefly Books, 1999.

Gordon, John. *The Great Golf Courses of Canada.* With photography by Michael French. Willowdale, Ontario, Canada: Firefly Books, 1993.

Graves, Robert Muir and Geoffrey S. Cornish. *Golf Course Design.* New York: John Wiley & Sons, 1998.

Hackett, J. Alan. *Manitoba Links, a Kaleidoscopic History of Golf.* Winnipeg, Manitoba, Canada: Gold Quill Publishing, 1998.

Haultain, Arnold. *The Mystery of Golf.* Copyright 1908 by Theodore Arnold Haultain; reprinted by Classics of Golf, Stamford, CT, 1986, with a Foreword by H. W. Wind and Afterword by John Updike.

Hawtree, Fred W. *Aspects of Golf Course Architecture I 1889–1924.* Droitwich, Worcestershire, England: Grant Books, 1998.

Hawtree, Fred W. *Colt & Co. Golf Course Architects.* Woodstock, Oxford, England: Cambuc Archive, 1991.

Hawtree, Fred W. *The Golf Course: Planning, Design, Construction and Maintenance.* London: E. and F. S. Spon, 1983; revised in 1996 in collaboration with golf architect Dr. Martin Hawtree.

Hawtree, Fred W. *Triple Baugé.* Woodstock, Oxford, England: Cambuc Archive, 1996.

Helphand, Kenneth W. "Learning from Linksland." *Landscape Journal* (Spring 1995): 74–84.

Henderson, J. T., and D. I. Stirk. *Golf in the Making.* London: Henderson and Stirk, 1979.

Hotelling, Neal. *Pebble Beach Golf Links*. Chelsea, MI: Sleeping Bear Press, 1999.

Hunter, Robert. *The Links*. New York: Charles Scribners Sons, 1926; Far Hills, NJ: USGA Rare Book Collection.

Hurdzan, Michael J., Ph.D. "Evolution of the Modern Green." *PGA Magazine* (January/February/March/April 1985). Reprinted in pamphlet form by the American Society of Golf Course Architects, n.d.

Hurdzan, Michael J., Ph.D. *Golf Course Architecture: Design, Construction, and Restoration*. Chelsea, MI: Sleeping Bear Press, 1996.

Jenkins, Dan. *The Best 18 Holes in America*. New York: Delacorte Press, 1966.

Jones, Robert Trent, with Larry Dennis. *Golf's Magnificent Challenge*. New York: McGraw-Hill, 1989.

Jones, Robert Trent, Jr. *Golf by Design*. Boston: Little, Brown, 1993.

Jones, Robert Tyre. *Golf Is My Game*. Garden City, NY: Doubleday, 1960.

Kains, Robert. *Golf Course Design and Construction*. Guelph, Ontario, Canada: University of Guelph, 1993.

Klein, Bradley S. *Discovering Donald Ross, the Architect and His Courses*. Chelsea, MI: Sleeping Bear Press, 2001.

Klein, Bradley S. *Rough Meditations*. Chelsea, MI: Sleeping Bear Press, 1997.

Klemme, Mike A. *A View from the Rough*. Chelsea, MI: Sleeping Bear Press, 1995.

Labbance, Bob, and Gordon Wittaveen. *Keepers of the Green, a History of Golf Course Management*. Chelsea, MI: Ann Arbor Press; Golf Course Superintendents of America, 2001.

Labbance, Robert. *The Old Man: The Biography of Walter J. Travis*. Chelsea, MI: Sleeping Bear Press, 2000.

Langford, William. *Placing Hazards*. Chicago: privately printed, 1995.

Leslie, Mark. "Settle the Bet." *Golf Magazine* (October 2001).

Love, William R. *An Environmental Approach to Golf Course Development*. Chicago: The American Society of Golf Course Architects, 1992; updated 1999.

Low, John. *Concerning Golf*. London: Hodder and Stoughton, 1903; Far Hills, NJ: USGA Rare Book Collection, 1987.

Lyle, Sandy, with Bob Ferrier. *The Championship Courses of Scotland*. Surrey, England: Kingswood Tadworth; Surrey, England: World's Work, Ltd., The Windmill Press, 1982.

Macdonald, Charles Blair. "The Ideal Golf Course, a Standard of Comparison." *The Outing Magazine,* 1907.

Macdonald, Charles Blair. *Scotland's Gift GOLF*. New York: Charles Scribners Sons, 1928; Stamford, CT: Classics of Golf, 1985.

Mackenzie, Alister. *Golf Architecture*. London: Simpkin, Marshall, Hamilton, Kent & Co., 1920; Stamford, CT: Classics of Golf, 1988; Droitwich, Worcestershire, England: Grant Books, 1982.

Mackenzie, Alister. *The Spirit of St. Andrews*. Chelsea, MI: Sleeping Bear Press, 1995.

Mead, Daniel W., and Joseph Reid Akerman. *Contract Specifications and Engineering Relations*. New York: McGraw-Hill, 1956.

Muirhead, Desmond, with Tip Anderson. *St. Andrews, How to Play the Old Course*. Newport Beach, CA: Newport Press, 2000.

Muirhead, Desmond, and Guy L. Rando. *Golf Course Development and Real Estate*. Washington, DC: Urban Land Institute, 1994.

Orians, G. H., and J. H. Heerwagen. "Evolved Responses to Landscapes," in *The Adapted Mind*, J. Barkow, L. Cosmides, and J. Tooby (eds.). New York: Oxford University Press, 1992, pp. 555–579.

Park, Willie, Jr. *The Game of Golf*. London: Longmans Green and Co., 1896.

Peper, George, and the Editors of *Golf Magazine*. *The 500 World's Greatest Golf Holes*. New York: Artisan, 2000.

Price, Robert. *Scotland's Golf Courses*. Aberdeen, Scotland: Aberdeen University Press, 1989.

Richardson, Forrest L. *Routing the Golf Course: The Art and Science That Forms the Golf Journey*. New York: John Wiley & Sons, 2002.

Rosenberg, Fred. "Charles Henry 'Steam Shovel' Banks." *The Jersey Golfer Magazine* (Spring 1997).

Ross, Donald J. *Golf Has Never Failed Me*. Chelsea, MI: Sleeping Bear Press, 1996.

Ryde, Peter, D.M.A. Steele, and H. W. Wind. *Encyclopedia of Golf*. New York: Viking Press, 1975.

Sasaki, Hideo. *Landscape Architect Quarterly* (July 1950).

Shackelford, Geoff. *The Captain: George C. Thomas, Jr., and His Golf Architecture*. Santa Monica, CA: Captain Fantastic Publishing, 1996; Chelsea, MI: Sleeping Bear Press, 1997.

Shackelford, Geoff. *The Golden Age of Golf Design*. Chelsea, MI: Sleeping Bear Press, 1999.

Shackelford, Geoff. *Masters of the Links*. Chelsea, MI: Sleeping Bear Press, 1997.

Sheehan, Lawrence. *A Passion for Golf*. New York: Clarkson Potter, 1994.

Skyzinski, Richard. "Going to Extremes." *Golf Journal* (March/April 2001): 38–41.

Smith, Douglas LaRue. *Winged Foot Story: The Golf, the People, the Friendly Trees*. With sketches by Rachel M. Therrien. Racine, WI: Western Publishing, 1984.

Steel, Donald. *Classic Golf Links of England, Wales, and Ireland.* Gretna, LA: Pelican Publishing, 1993.

Stimpson, Edward S. III. *Forty-One Years from Invention to Convention.* West Falmouth, MA: Lighthouse Press, 1995.

Strawn, John. *Driving the Green.* New York: HarperCollins, 1991; New York: Burford Books, 1997.

Thomas, George C. *Golf Architecture in America: Its Strategy and Construction.* Los Angeles: Times-Mirror Press, 1927; Far Hills, NJ: USGA Rare Book Collection, 1990; Chelsea, MI: Sleeping Bear Press, 1997.

Tillinghast, A. W. *Gleanings from the Wayside.* Researched, compiled, designed, and edited by Richard C. Wolffe, Jr., Robert S. Trebus, and Stuart F. Wolffe. Warren, NJ: Treewolf Productions, 2001.

Tillinghast, A. W. *Reminiscences of the Links.* Researched, compiled, designed, and edited by Richard C. Wolffe, Jr., Robert S. Trebus, and Stuart F. Wolffe. Warren, NJ: Treewolf Productions, 1998.

Tillinghast, A. W. *The Course Beautiful.* Researched, compiled, designed, and edited by Richard C. Wolffe, Jr., Robert S. Trebus, and Stuart F. Wolffe. Warren, NJ: Treewolf Productions, 1995.

Travis, Walter J. *Practical Golf.* New York and London: Harper & Brothers, 1901.

United States Golf Association. *Golf: The Greatest Game.* New York: HarperCollins, 1994.

Ward-Thomas, Pat, Herbert Warren Wind, Charles Price, and Peter Thompson. Foreword by Alistair Cooke. *The World Atlas of Golf.* New York: Random House, 1976.

Wethered, H. N., and T. Simpson. *The Architectural Side of Golf.* London: Longmans Green & Co., 1929; Droitwich, Worcestershire, England: Grant Books, 1995.

Wexler, Daniel. *The Missing Links. America's Greatest Lost Golf Courses and Holes.* Chelsea, MI: Sleeping Bear Press, 2000.

Whitten, Ron. "Black Creek Demands Good Shot-Making." GolfDigest.com, July 31, 2001.

Whitten, Ron. "Worth the 'Pilgrim'age to Plymouth." GolfDigest.com, July 31, 2001.

Whitten, Ron. "You Go Your Way, I'll Go Mine: Reversible Courses—Layouts That Can Be Played Coming or Going." *Golf Digest* (June 1987).

Wind, Herbert Warren. "Royal Worlington and Newmarket." *New Yorker* (June 22, 1981).

Wind, Herbert Warren (ed.). *The Complete Golfer.* New York: Simon & Schuster, 1954.

INDEX

Numbers in *italics* indicate pages on which figures appear.

Foster Golf Links, Washington, 175
Foulis, Robert, 12–13, 26
Foulis brothers, 158
Fowler, Herbert, 23, 114, 245
Fowler and Simpson, 224
Foxburg Country Club, Pennsylvania, 21
Fox Chapel Golf Club, Pennsylvania, 62, 78
Franklin Hills Country Club, Michigan, 160–161
Fringe swale, 54
Fullmer, Paul, xi

G
Gamer, Don, xii
Garden City Golf Club, New York, 23, 24, 26, 226
Gardiner's Bay Country Club, New York, 78
Garl, Ron, 62
Gathering bunkers, 185
Gentry, Stan, 220
George, Lester, 14
Gerrish, Timothy, xi
Gibralter hole, 196, 198–199, 201
Gibson Island Country Club, Maryland, 78, 79, 257, 267
Ginger Beer hole, 150–151, 178, *179*
Gizaza Sporting Club, Egypt, 20
Gleneagles, Scotland, 272
Glenview Country Club, Illinois, 100–101, *102*
Golden Bear International, 62
Golden Horseshoe Golf Club, Virginia, 233
Golden Valley, Minnesota, 170
Goldstein, Harriet and Vetta, 4–9
Golf:
    forebear games to, 15–17, *26*, 34–35
    global spread of, 20–21, *31–33*
    Golden Age of, 24
Golf: A Royal and Ancient Game (Clark), 16
Golf Club at Desert Mountain, Arizona, 235
Golf Club at Quail Lodge, California, *183*
Golf course architects, 14, 44, 51–52
Golf course design:
    art principles in, 4–10
    basic considerations in, 2–3
    biological appeal and, 10
    Frank Lloyd Wright's vision and, 1, 2, 3
    as landscape architecture, 2
    three Ps of, 3
    See also Adaptations of classic holes; Classic holes; Composition; Routing systems; *specific holes*
Golf course design, history of:
    balls, clubs, and rules, *29*
    budgets/costs, 24
    bunkers, 48–50
    early courses, 17–22
    18-stakes method, 22–23
    eras of, *27*
    evolution from pall-mall (mail), 34–44
    styles, *30*
    turfgrass management, *28*
    in United States, 23–24, 51–53
    work-in-progress courses, 24–25
Golf Course Designs (Fazio and Brown), 24
Golf Courses of the British Isles (Darwin), 65, 125, 185, 188
Golf Course Superintendents Association (GCSAA), viii, 28
Golf de Biarritz, France, 196, *206*
Golf girdles the globe, 20–21

Golfklubber Islands Golf Course, Iceland, 20
Goosedubs, *144*
Gordon, David, 229, 231
Gordon, William F., 228–229
Grand Cypress Resort, Florida, 165, 261
Grandover Golf Club, North Carolina, 254, 255
Grant, Douglas, 217, 248
Grau, 28
Grave bunker, 179
Graves, Robert Muir, 2, 154, 163, 255
Greenbrier Golf Club, West Virginia, 78
Green Park—Norwood Golf Club, North Carolina, 78
Greens:
    bunkers in, 186–187
    contouring, 158
    double, 164–167
    elevation, 48, 142, 156, *157*, 158
    falling away, 168–171
    geometric shapes, 158–159
    hogback (hogsback), 84, 142, *143*, 144
    Island, 232–239, 290–291
    maintenance, 28, 155
    Plateau, 87, *88*, 156, *157*, 198, *265*
    Postage Stamp, 160, *162*, 196, 199–200
    Punch Bowl, 74, 85, 156, *157*, 176, 243–247, 293–294
    shapes, *171*
    size, 160–163
    steeply contoured, 168
    styles, *172*
    terraced, 90, *91*
Griffith Park Municipal Golf Course, California, 212
Gullane Links, 11, 100, 189, 191
Gutta-percha ball, 18, 26, 29

H
Haagsche Golf Club, Netherlands, 21
Hackensack Country Club, New Jersey, 78
Hackett, J. Alan, 223
Hagge, Bernard von, 235
Hamm, Gene, 121
Harmony, aspects of, 5
Harris, Robert Bruce, 185
Hatch, Walter B., 101
Hawk Creek, Oregon, 223
Hawtree, Fred W., ix, 17, 34
Hayden Lake Country Club, Idaho, *75*, 159, *160*, 175–176, *176*
Hayling, England, 108
Hazards (Bauer), 172
Heathland courses, 27, 30, 51
Heerwargen, J. H., 10
Hell bunker, 49, 99, 179
Hell's Half Acre hole, 185, *186*, 196, 201
Helphand, Kenneth L., 3, 55
Helsingfors Golf Course, Finland, 20
Henderson, J. T., 17
Hickory Ridge Country Club, Massachusetts, 161, *163*, 200
Highland Country Club, Indiana, 75
Highland Links, Canada, 123
Hilton, Harold, 260
History of Golf: The Royal and Ancient Game (Browning), 16
Hoffman, Scott, 213
Hogan, Ben, 55
Hogback (hogsback) holes, 84, 141–142, *143*, 144
Hole arrangement. *See* Routing systems

THE OLD COURSE AT ST. ANDREWS

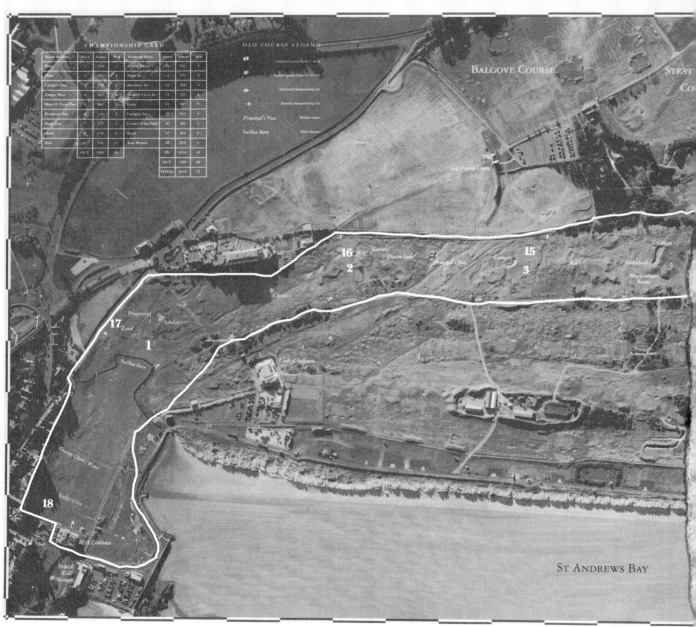

CLASSIC GOLF HOLE DESIGN

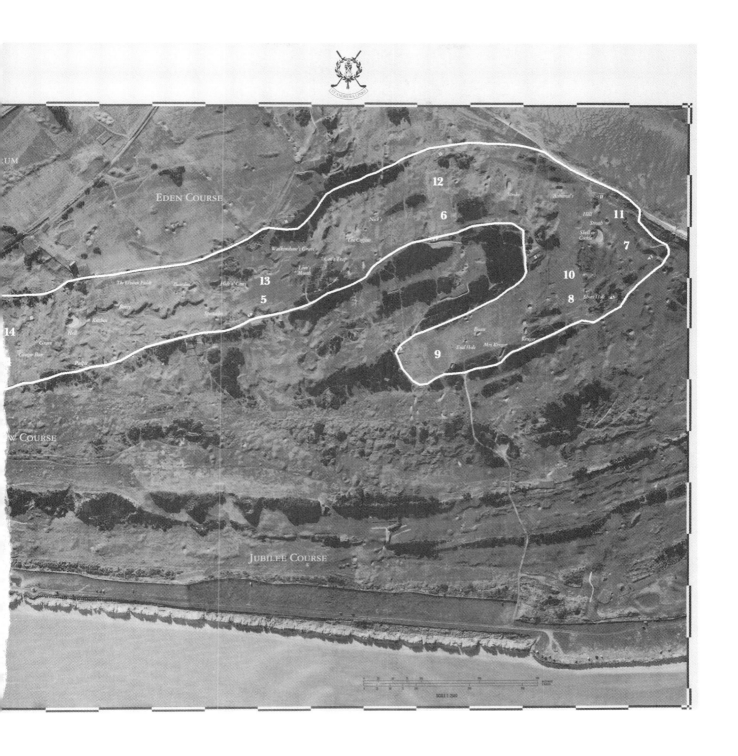